Oh My Goddess!

ああっ女神さまっ

42

STORY AND ART BY
Kosuke Fujishima

TRANSLATION BY
Dana Lewis AND Christopher Lewis

LETTERING AND TOUCHUP BY
Susie Lee AND Betty Dong
WITH Tom2K

DARK HORSE MANGA™

CHAPTER 262
State of Emergency?!..............3

CHAPTER 263
Sense of Beauty...................27

CHAPTER 264
Spell Canceling...................51

CHAPTER 265
Strongest and Most Beloved
Machine, Charge! 76

CHAPTER 266
Counterattack
Cut 'n' Grind....................101

CHAPTER 267
Burst Free,
Machine Heart!.................117

CHAPTER 268
A Test of Resolve...............141

Letters to the Enchantress....166

CHAPTER 262

State of Emergency?!

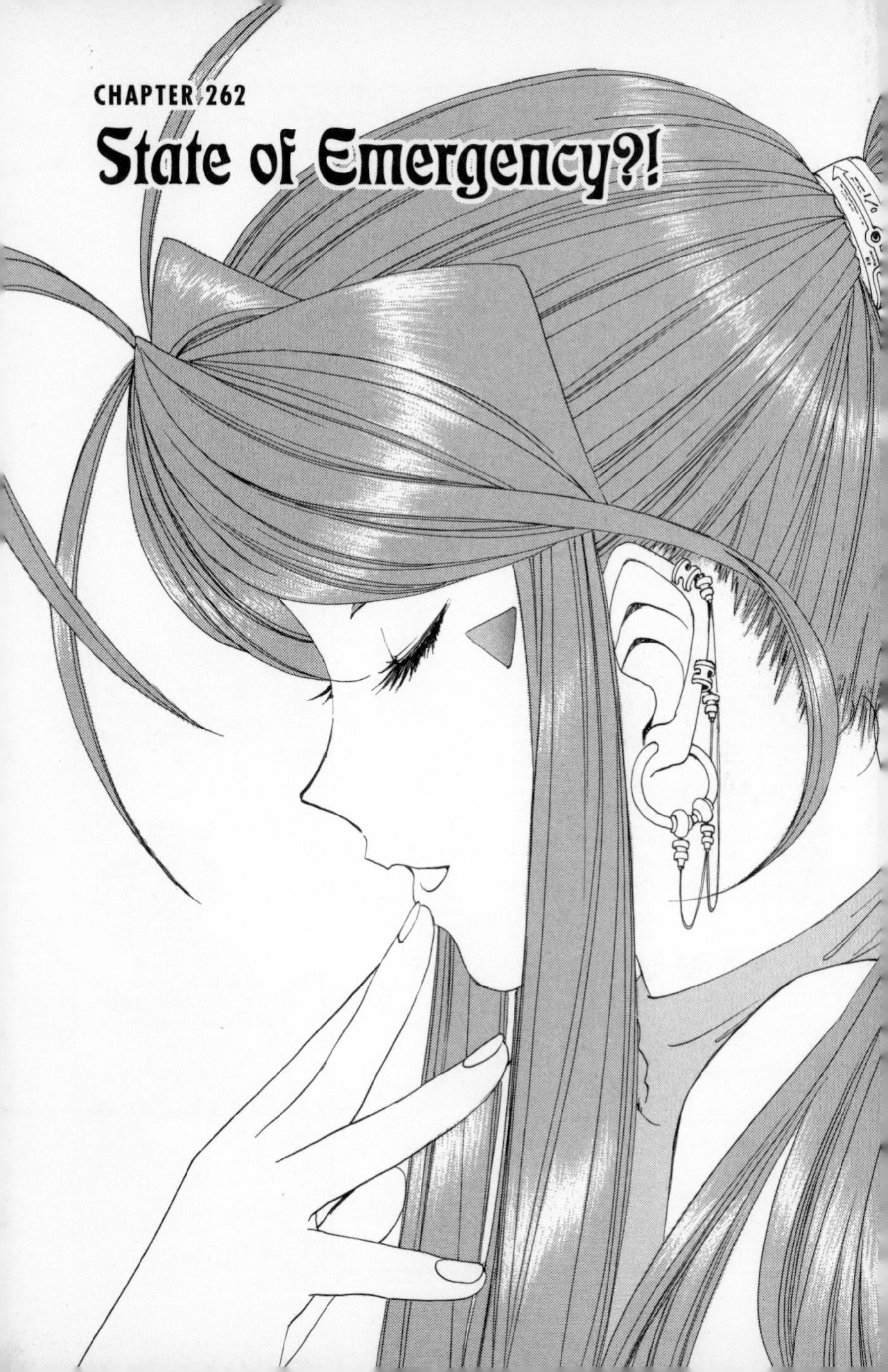

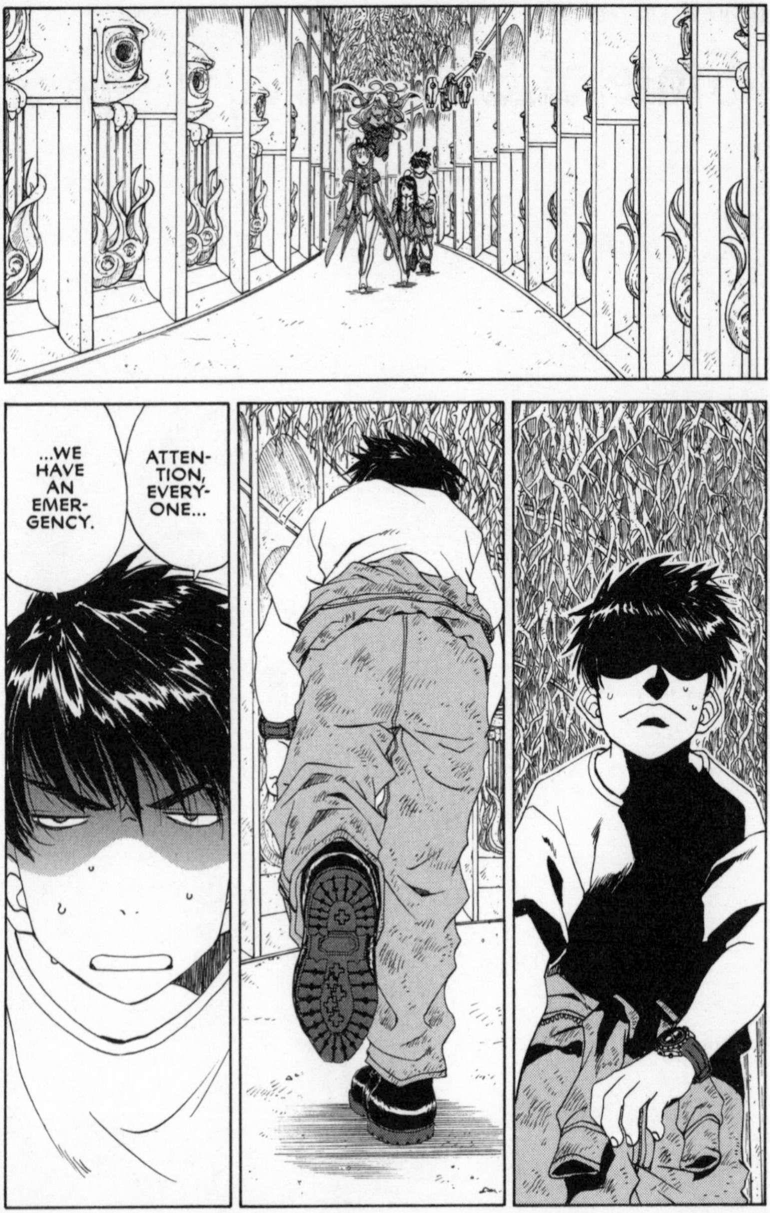
ATTENTION, EVERYONE...
...WE HAVE AN EMERGENCY.

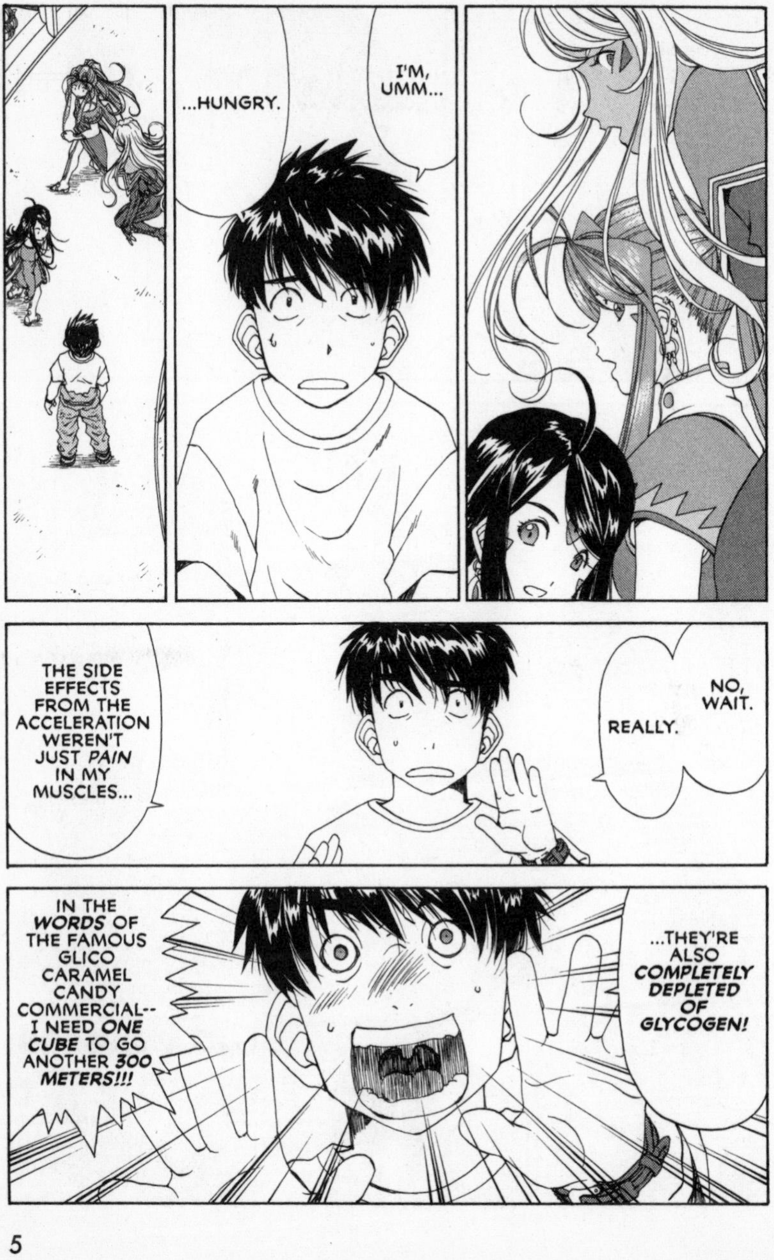
I'M, UMM...
...HUNGRY.
NO, WAIT. REALLY.
THE SIDE EFFECTS FROM THE ACCELERATION WEREN'T JUST *PAIN* IN MY MUSCLES...
...THEY'RE ALSO ***COMPLETELY DEPLETED*** OF GLYCOGEN!
IN THE ***WORDS*** OF THE FAMOUS GLICO CARAMEL CANDY COMMERCIAL-- I NEED ***ONE CUBE*** TO GO ANOTHER ***300 METERS!!!***

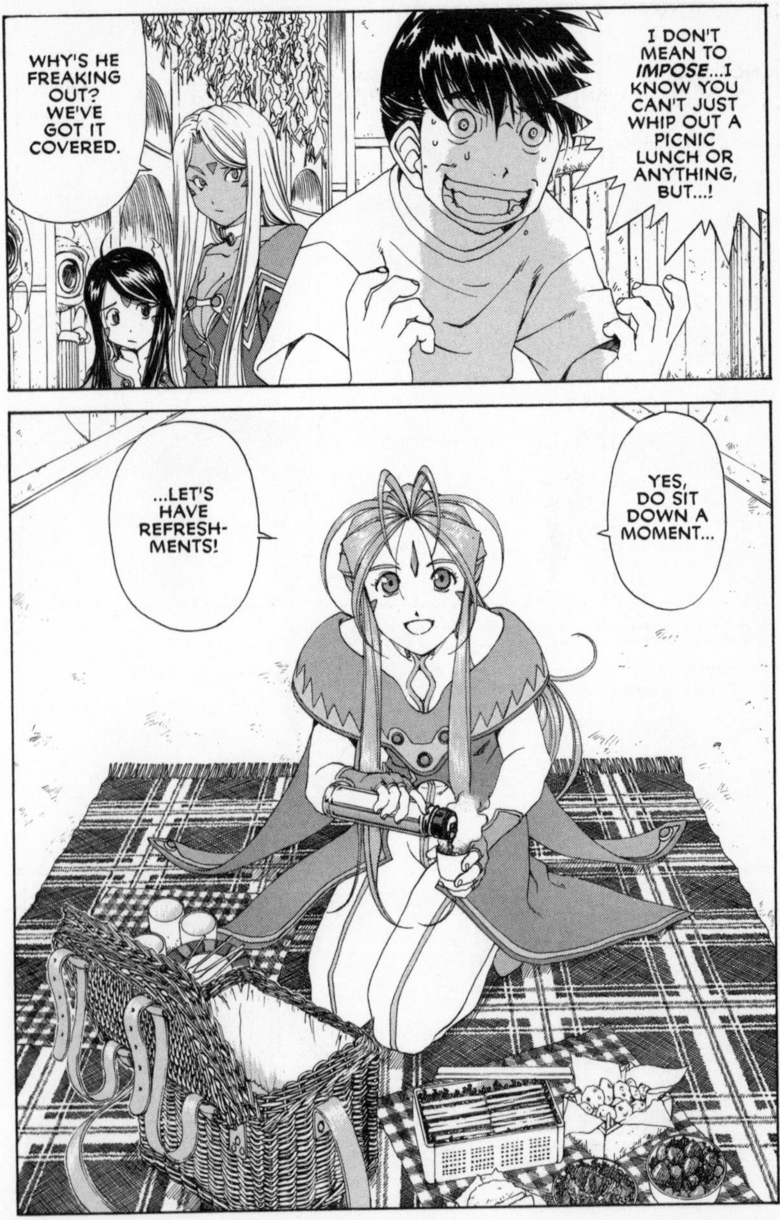
I DON'T MEAN TO *IMPOSE*...I KNOW YOU CAN'T JUST WHIP OUT A PICNIC LUNCH OR ANYTHING, BUT...!
WHY'S HE FREAKING OUT? WE'VE GOT IT COVERED.
YES, DO SIT DOWN A MOMENT...
...LET'S HAVE REFRESH-MENTS!

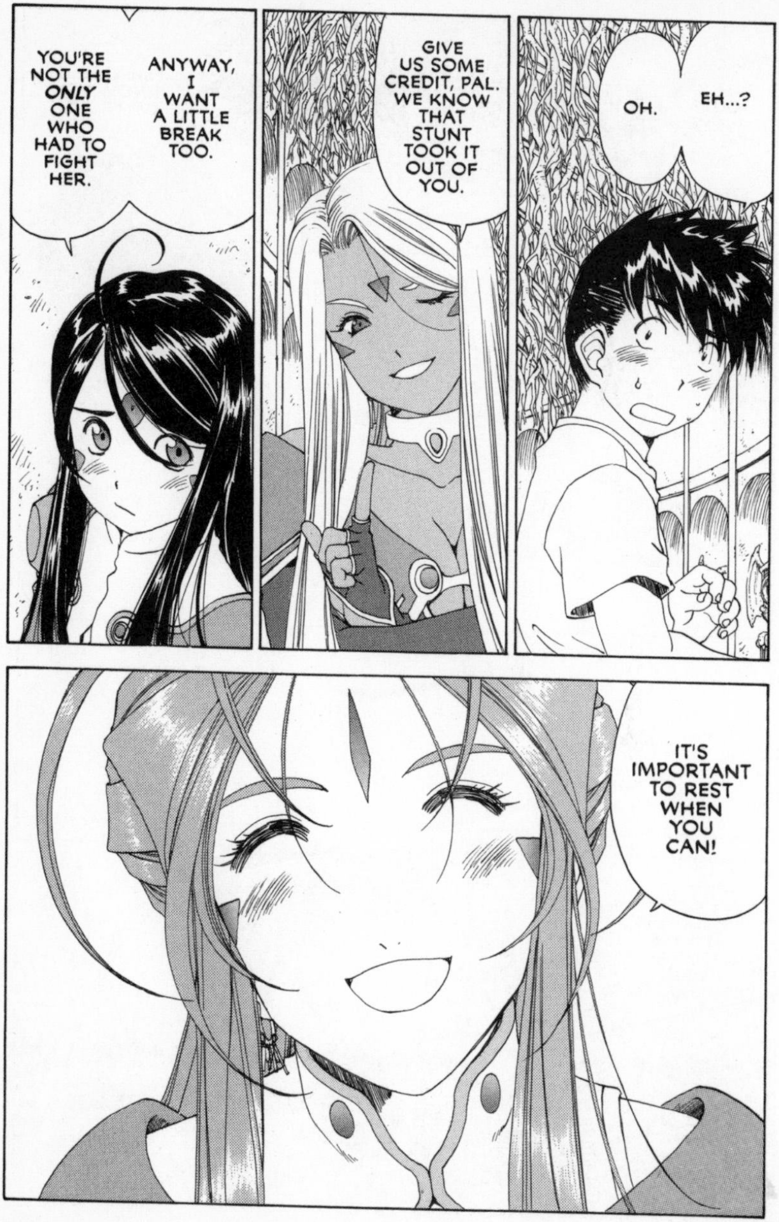
EH...?
OH.
GIVE US SOME CREDIT, PAL. WE KNOW THAT STUNT TOOK IT OUT OF YOU.
ANYWAY, I WANT A LITTLE BREAK TOO.
YOU'RE NOT THE *ONLY* ONE WHO HAD TO FIGHT HER.
IT'S IMPORTANT TO REST WHEN YOU CAN!

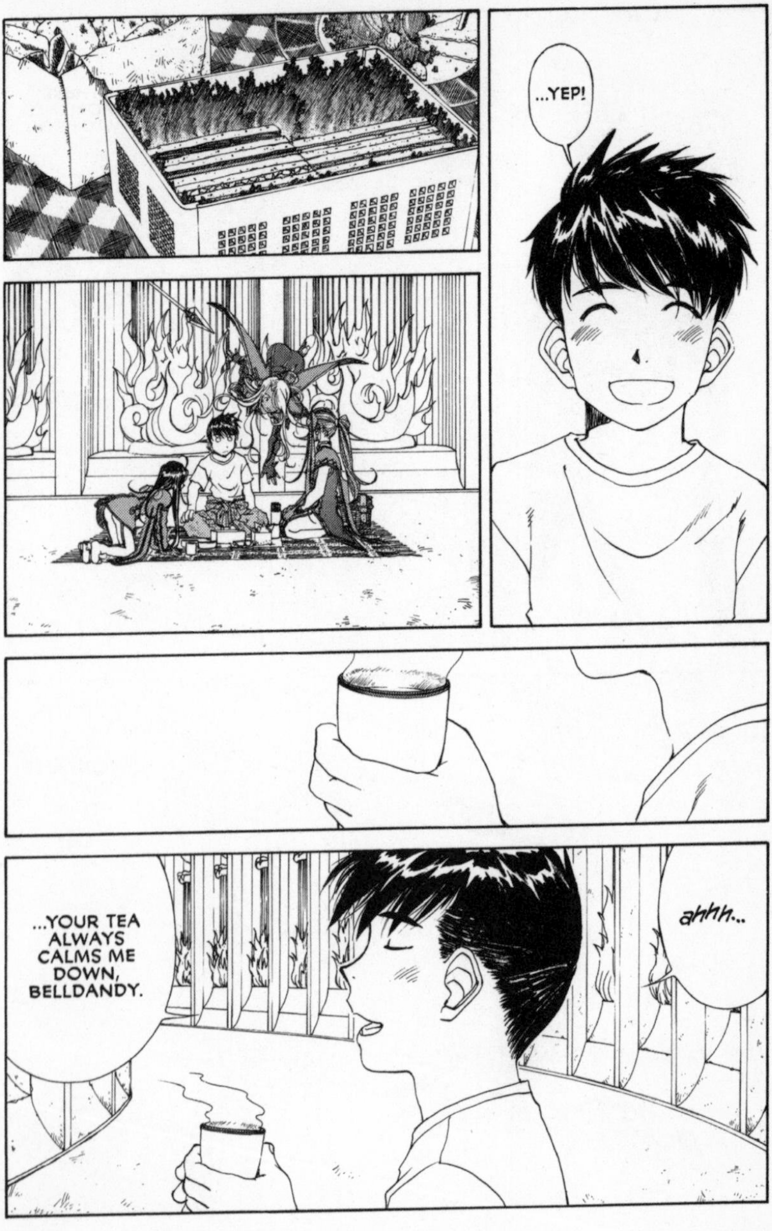
...YEP!
ahhh...
...YOUR TEA ALWAYS CALMS ME DOWN, BELLDANDY.

...KEIICHI.

I LOVE THESE MOMENTS WITH YOU, TOO...

A-AND, SAY, THESE COOKIES ARE *GREAT!!*

...YEAH!

AH...?

...THIS ONE'S YUMMY, TOO.

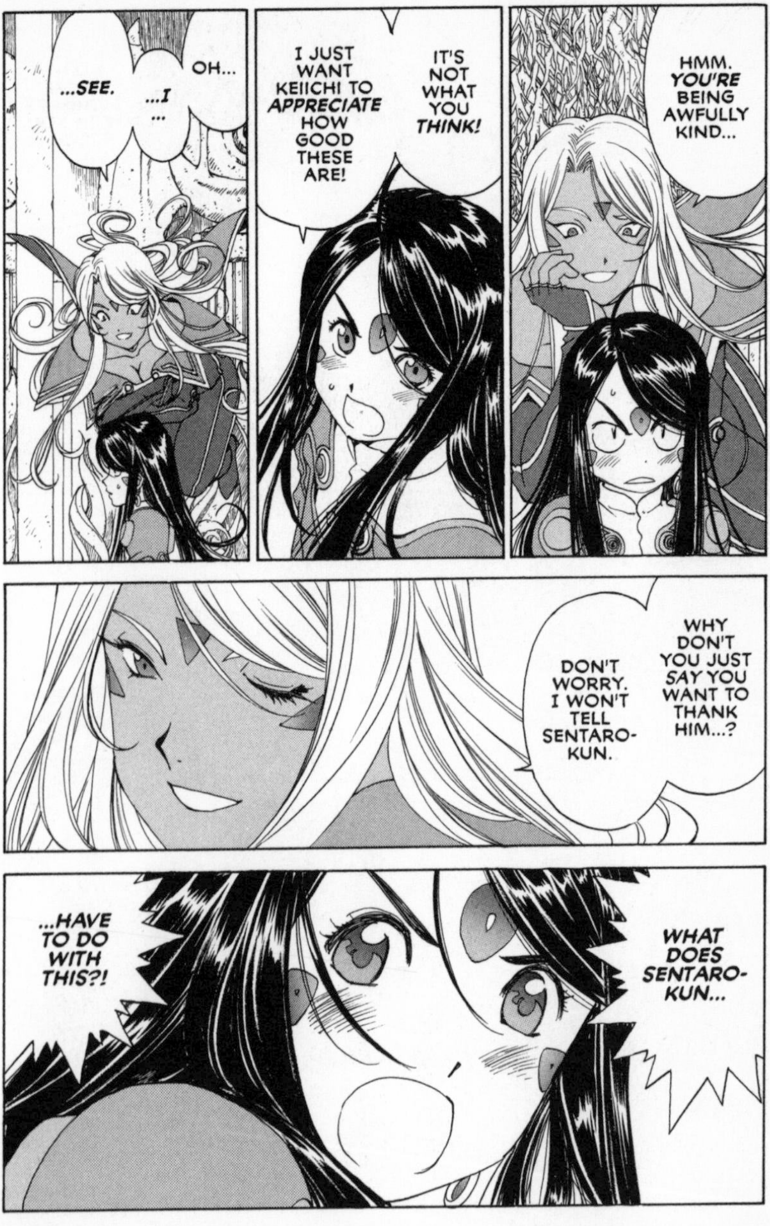
HMM. *YOU'RE* BEING AWFULLY KIND...
IT'S NOT WHAT YOU *THINK!*
I JUST WANT KEIICHI TO *APPRECIATE* HOW GOOD THESE ARE!
OH...
...I ...
...SEE.
WHY DON'T YOU JUST *SAY* YOU WANT TO THANK HIM...?
DON'T WORRY. I WON'T TELL SENTARO-KUN.
WHAT DOES SENTARO-KUN...
...HAVE TO DO WITH THIS?!

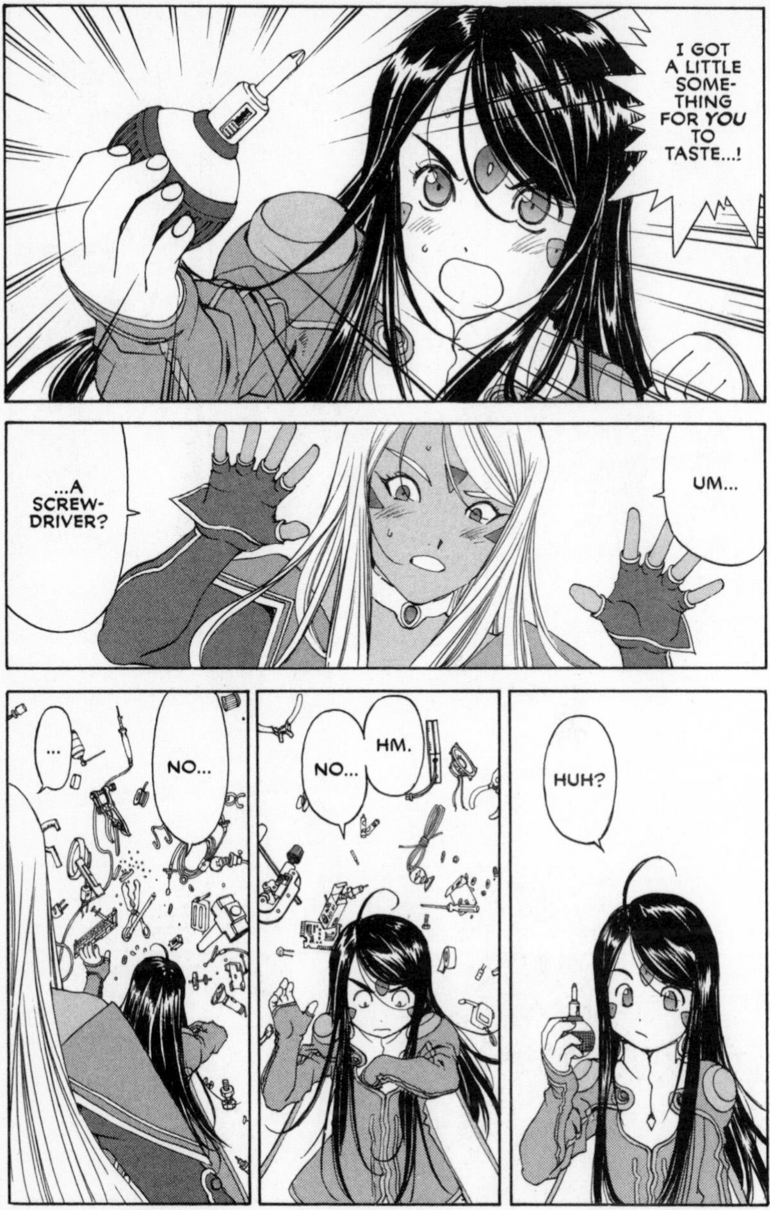
I GOT A LITTLE SOME-THING FOR *YOU* TO TASTE...!
UM...
...A SCREW-DRIVER?
HUH?
HM.
NO...
NO...
...

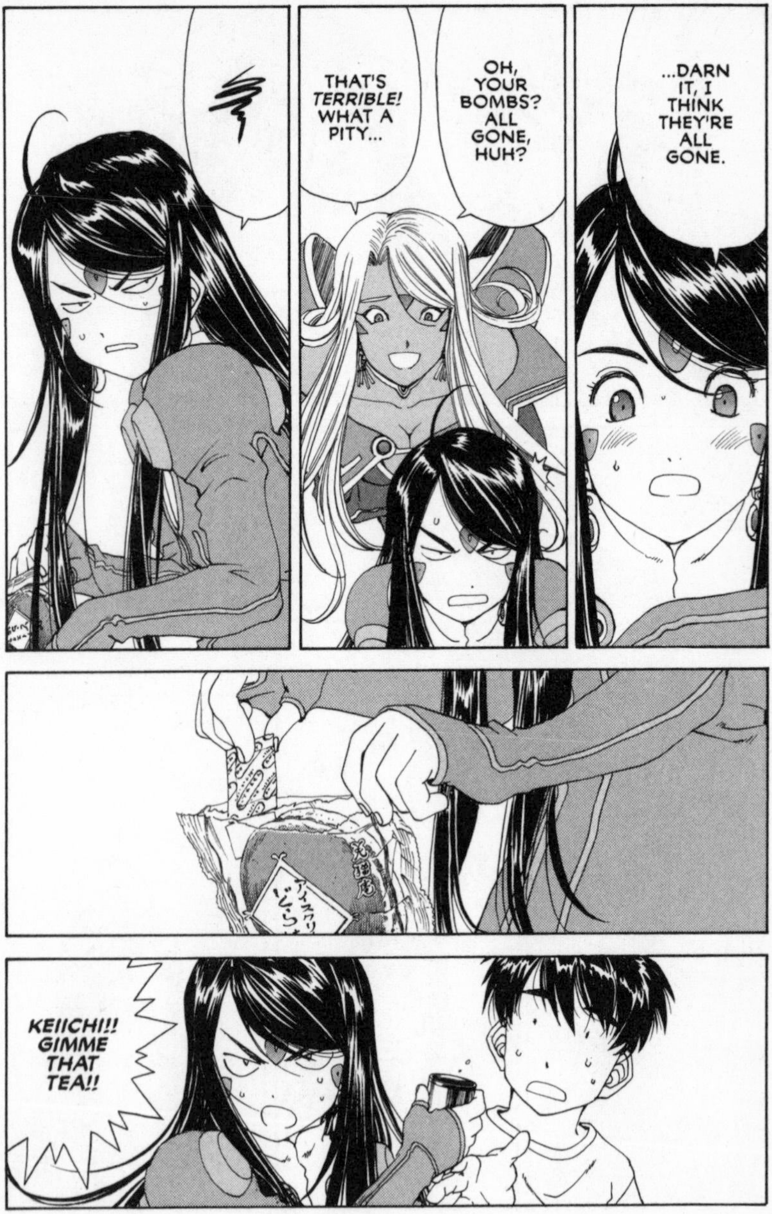
...DARN IT, I THINK THEY'RE ALL GONE.
OH, YOUR BOMBS? ALL GONE, HUH?
THAT'S *TERRIBLE!* WHAT A PITY...
KEIICHI!! GIMME THAT TEA!!

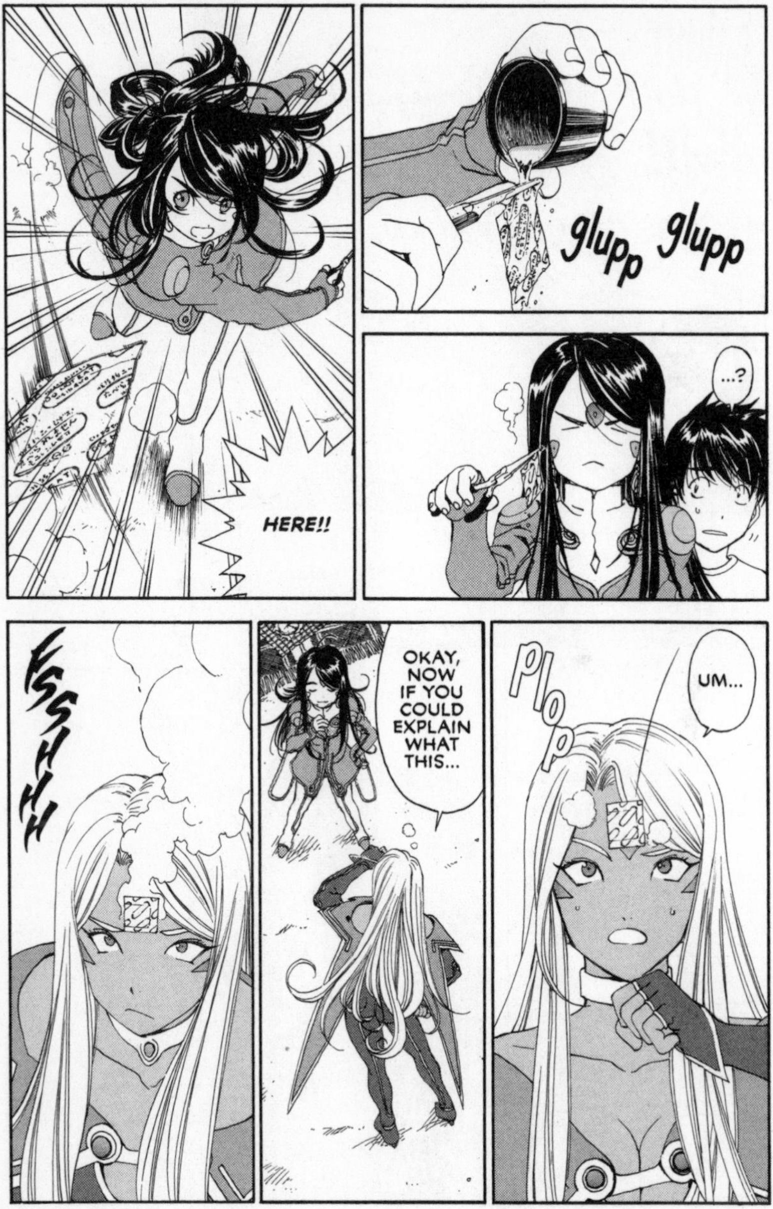
glupp glupp
...?
HERE!!
Plop
UM...
OKAY, NOW IF YOU COULD EXPLAIN WHAT THIS...
FSSHHH

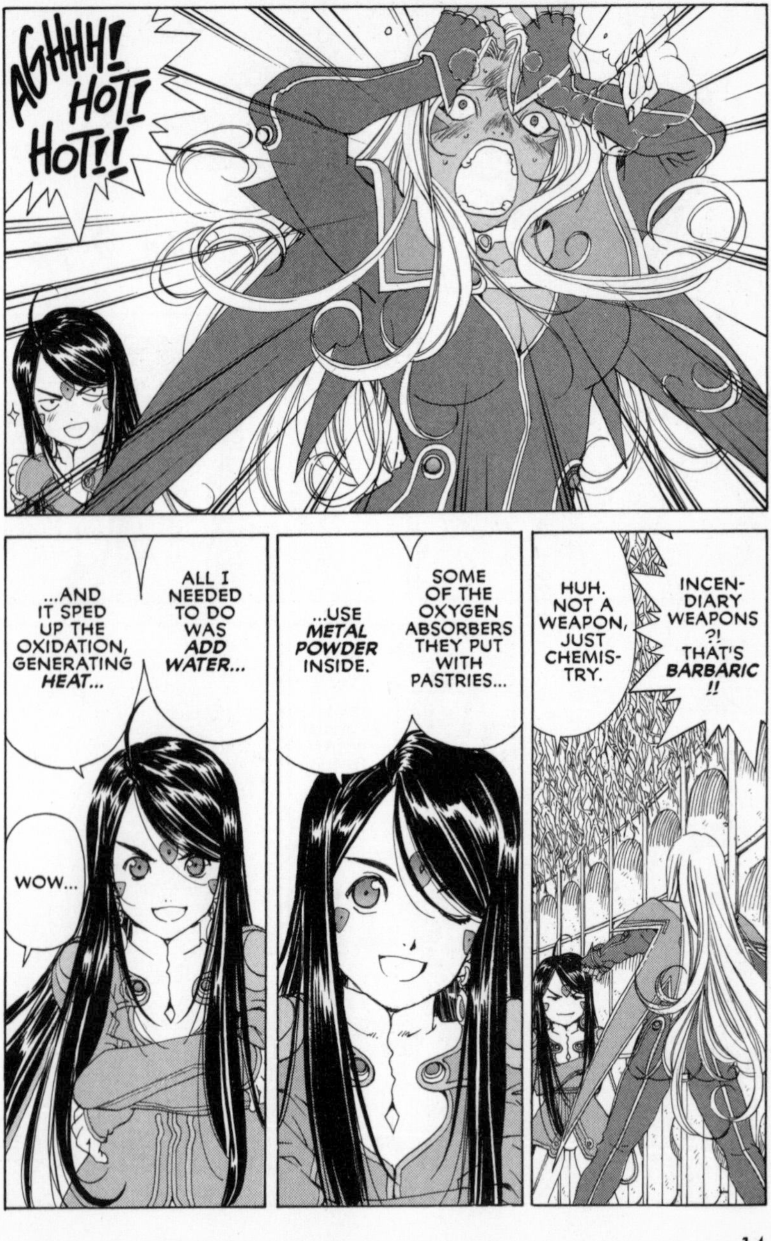
AGHHH! HOT! HOT!!
INCEN-DIARY WEAPONS?! THAT'S BARBARIC!!
HUH. NOT A WEAPON, JUST CHEMIS-TRY.
SOME OF THE OXYGEN ABSORBERS THEY PUT WITH PASTRIES...
...USE METAL POWDER INSIDE.
ALL I NEEDED TO DO WAS ADD WATER...
...AND IT SPED UP THE OXIDATION, GENERATING HEAT...
WOW...

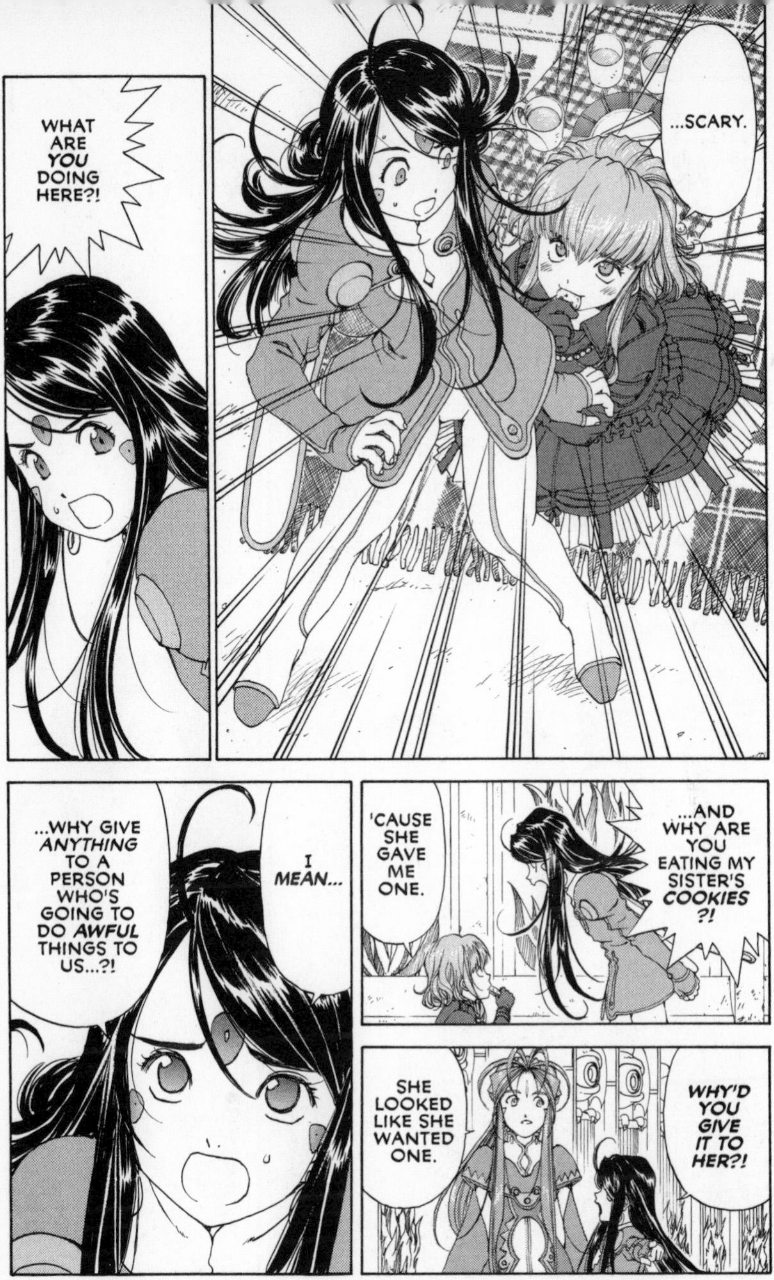
...SCARY.
WHAT ARE *YOU* DOING HERE?!
...AND WHY ARE YOU EATING MY SISTER'S *COOKIES* ?!
'CAUSE SHE GAVE ME ONE.
WHY'D YOU GIVE IT TO HER?!
SHE LOOKED LIKE SHE WANTED ONE.
I *MEAN...*
...WHY GIVE *ANYTHING* TO A PERSON WHO'S GOING TO DO *AWFUL* THINGS TO US...?!

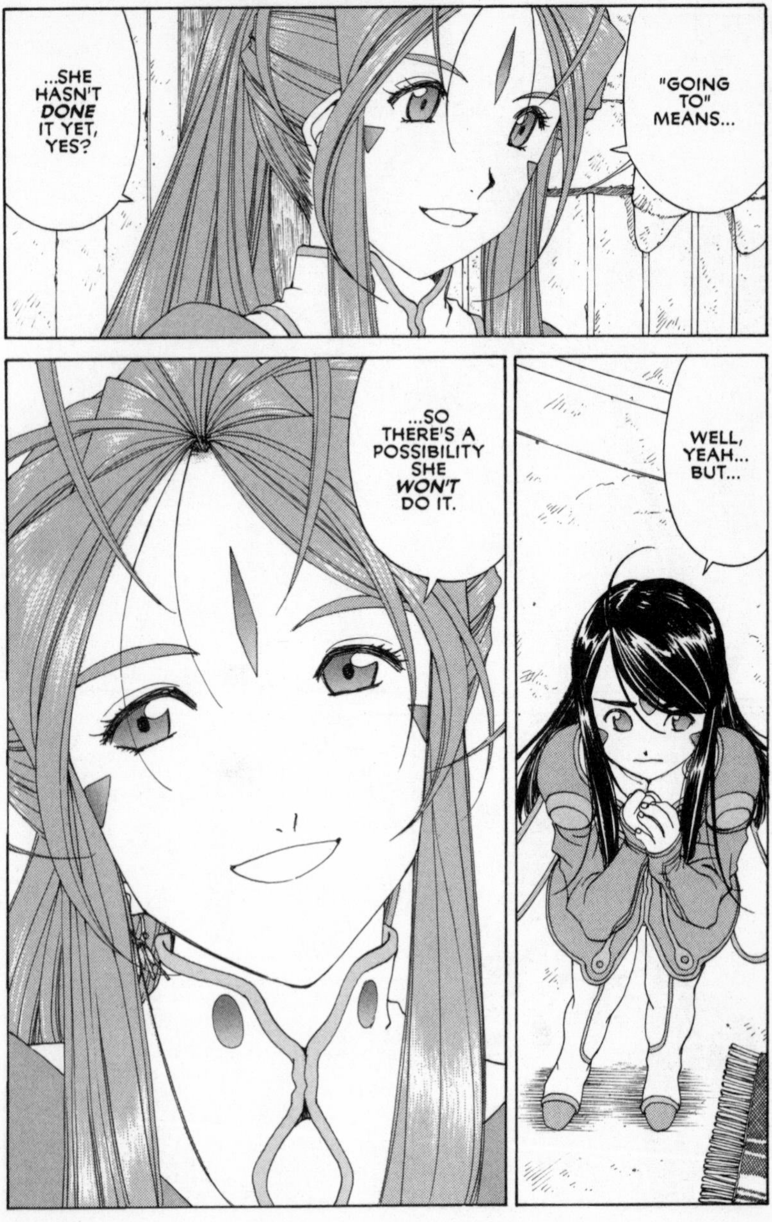
"GOING TO" MEANS...
...SHE HASN'T *DONE* IT YET, YES?
WELL, YEAH... BUT...
...SO THERE'S A POSSIBILITY SHE *WON'T* DO IT.

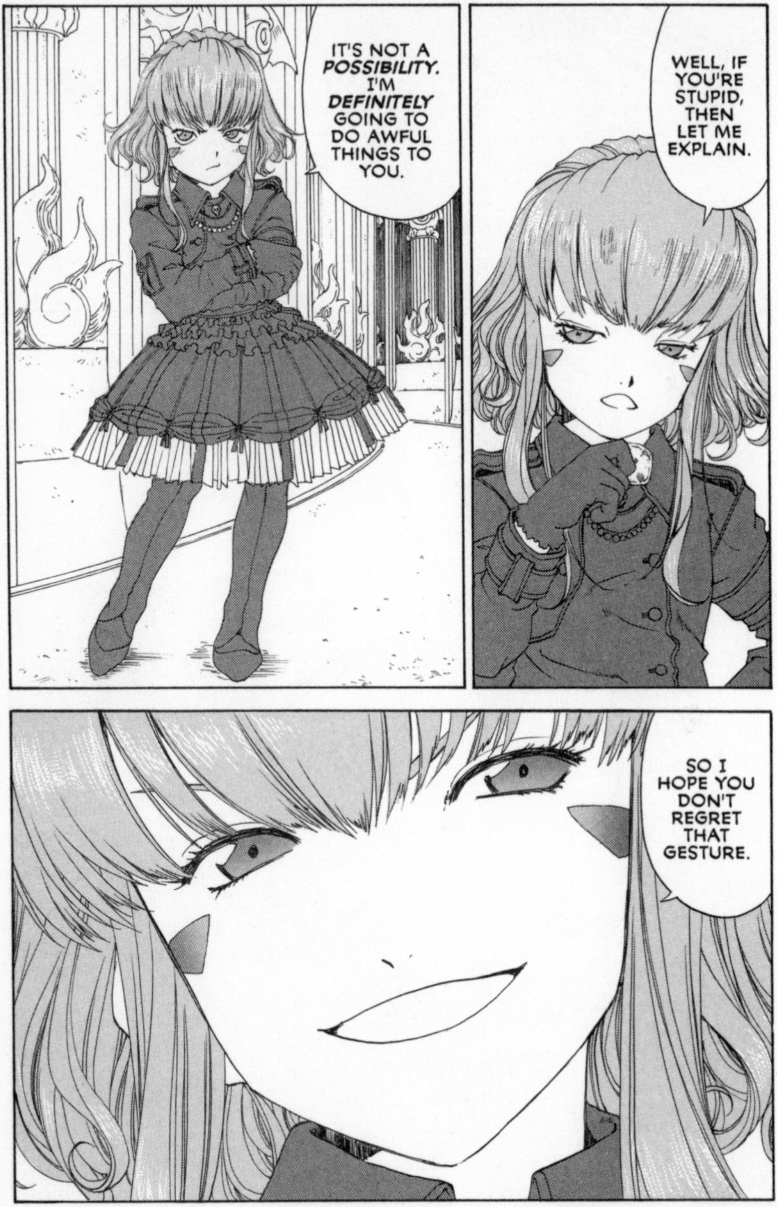
WELL, IF YOU'RE STUPID, THEN LET ME EXPLAIN.
IT'S NOT A *POSSIBILITY.* I'M *DEFINITELY* GOING TO DO AWFUL THINGS TO YOU.
SO I HOPE YOU DON'T REGRET THAT GESTURE.

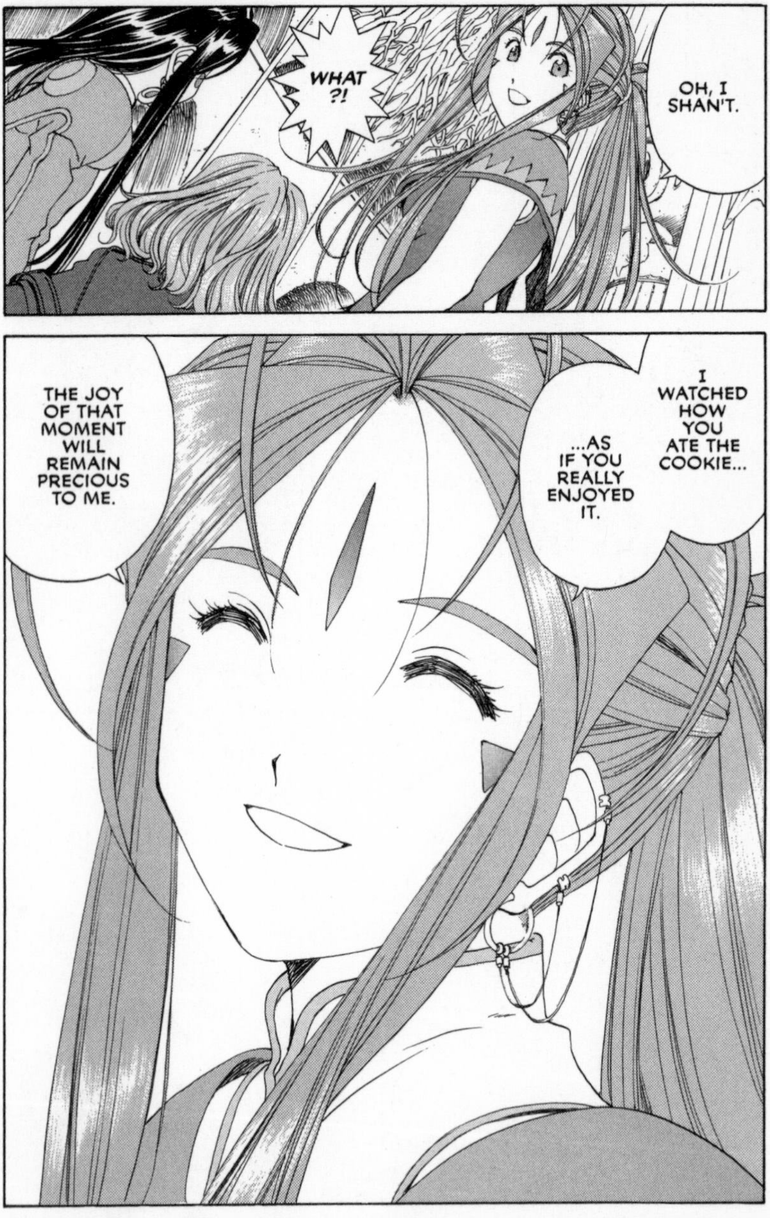
OH, I SHAN'T.
WHAT ?!
I WATCHED HOW YOU ATE THE COOKIE...
...AS IF YOU REALLY ENJOYED IT.
THE JOY OF THAT MOMENT WILL REMAIN PRECIOUS TO ME.

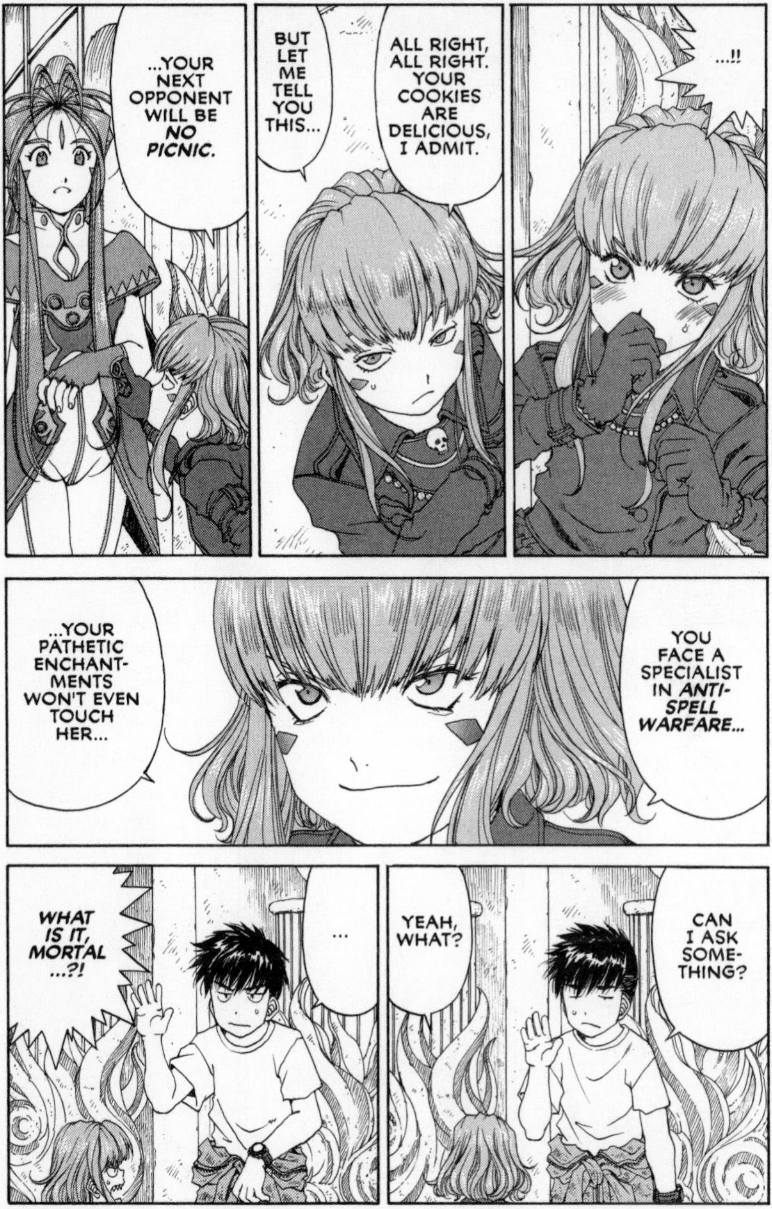
...!!
ALL RIGHT, ALL RIGHT. YOUR COOKIES ARE DELICIOUS, I ADMIT.
BUT LET ME TELL YOU THIS...
...YOUR NEXT OPPONENT WILL BE *NO PICNIC.*
YOU FACE A SPECIALIST IN *ANTI-SPELL WARFARE...*
...YOUR PATHETIC ENCHANT-MENTS WON'T EVEN TOUCH HER...
CAN I ASK SOME-THING?
YEAH, WHAT?
...
WHAT IS IT, MORTAL ...?!

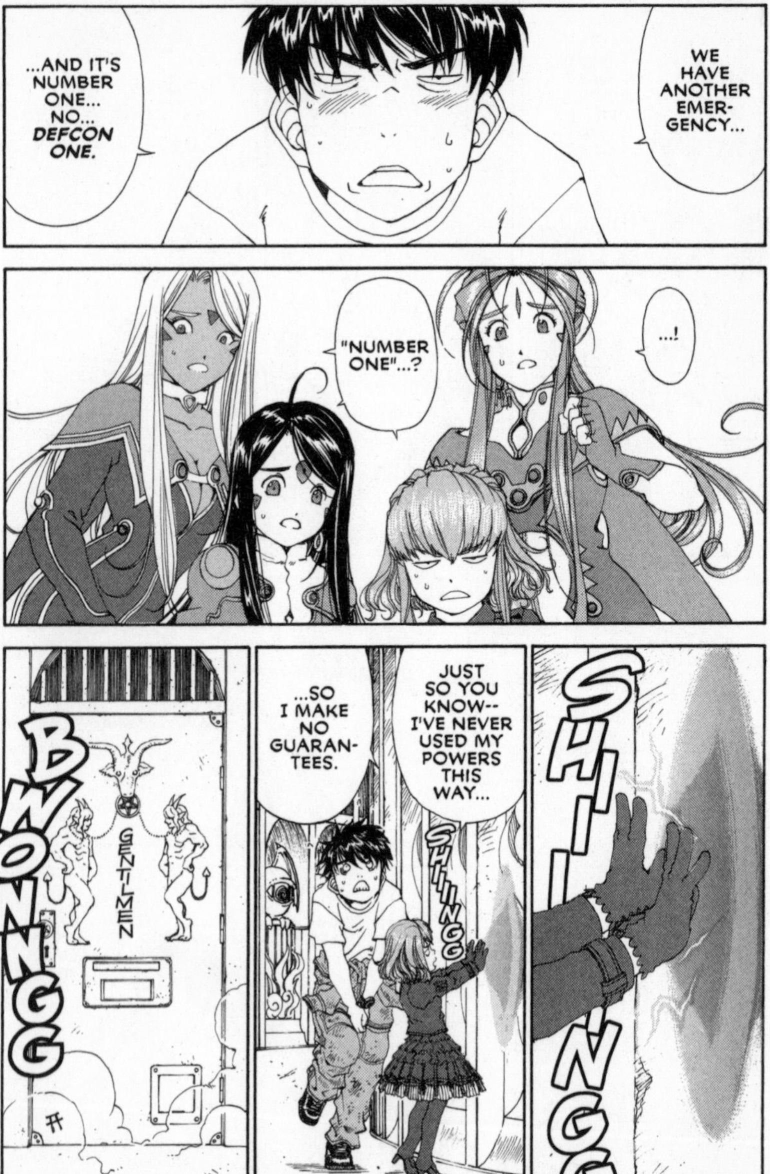

WE HAVE ANOTHER EMERGENCY...
...AND IT'S NUMBER ONE... NO... ***DEFCON ONE.***
...!
"NUMBER ONE"...?
SHIIINGG
JUST SO YOU KNOW-- I'VE NEVER USED MY POWERS THIS WAY...
...SO I MAKE NO GUARANTEES.
SHIIINGG
BWONNGG
GENTLMEN

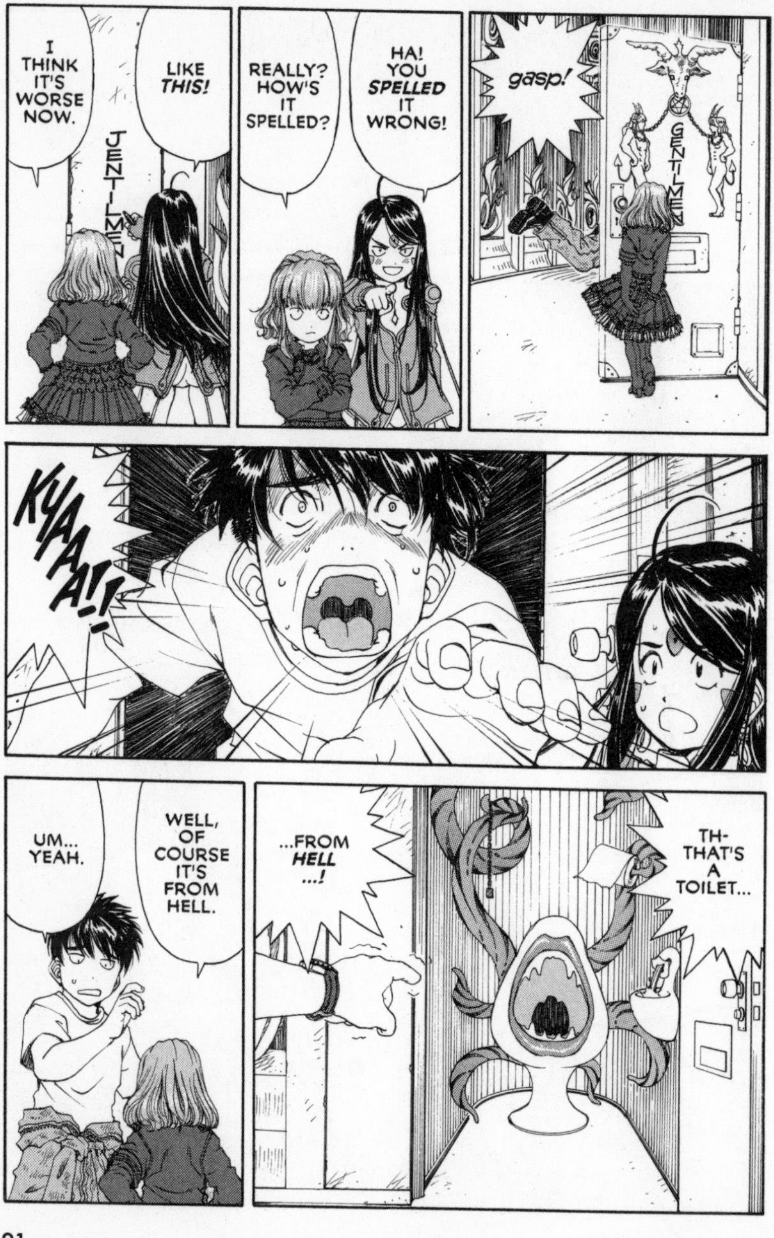
gasp!
GENTLMEN
HA! YOU *SPELLED* IT WRONG!
REALLY? HOW'S IT SPELLED?
LIKE *THIS!*
I THINK IT'S WORSE NOW.
JENTILMEN
KYAAAA-!!
TH-THAT'S A TOILET...
...FROM *HELL* ...!
WELL, OF COURSE IT'S FROM HELL.
UM... YEAH.

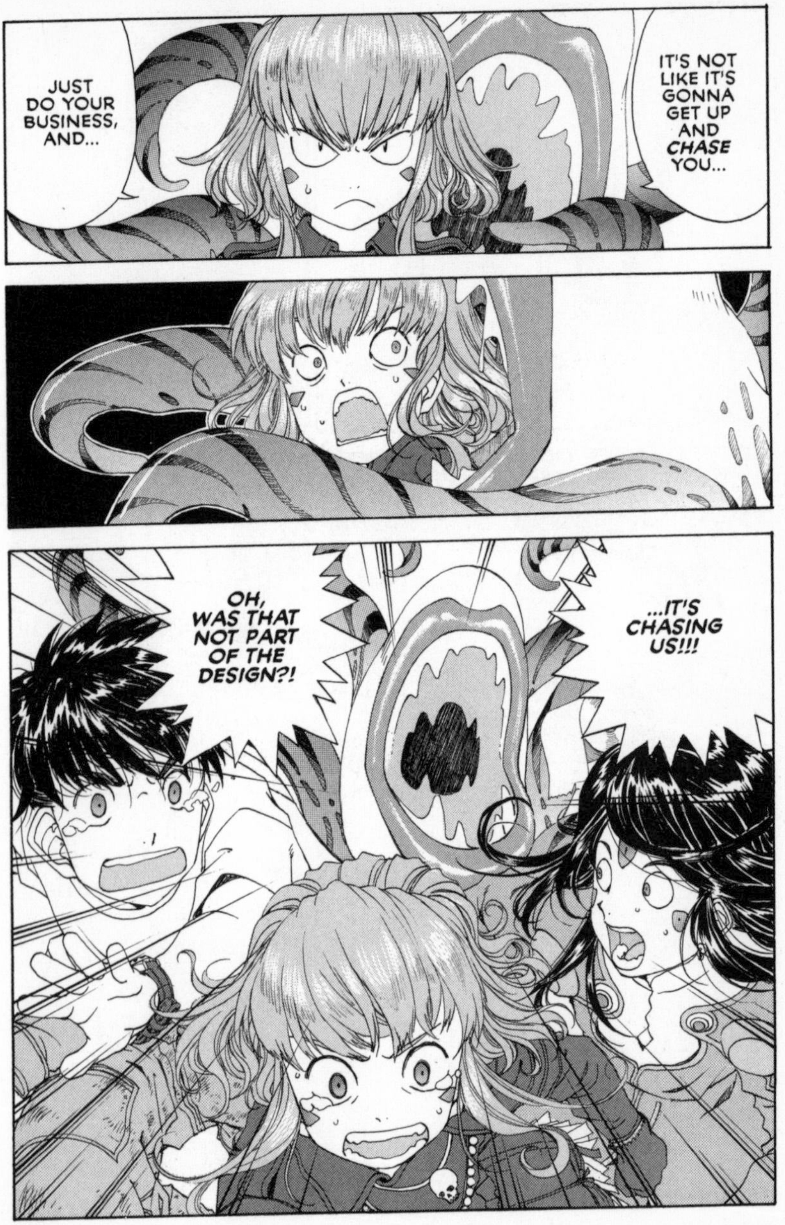
IT'S NOT LIKE IT'S GONNA GET UP AND *CHASE* YOU...
JUST DO YOUR BUSINESS, AND...
...IT'S CHASING US!!!
OH, WAS THAT NOT PART OF THE DESIGN?!

NO! THIS CAN'T BE THE END! PLEASE! *NOT LIKE THIS!!*

WE'RE TRAPPED !!

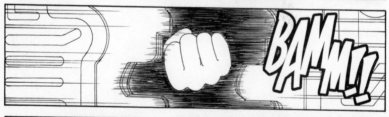

BAMM!!

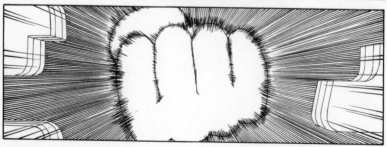

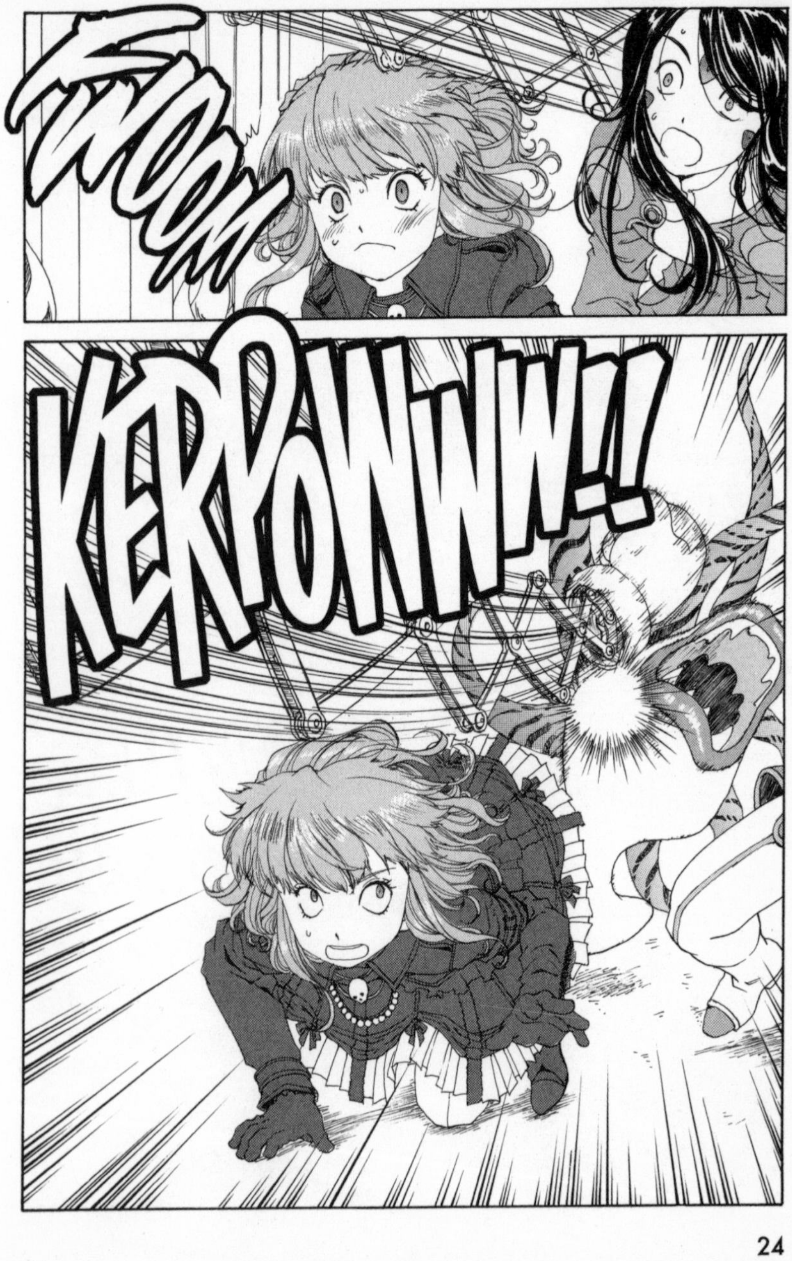
FWOOM
KERPOWWW!!

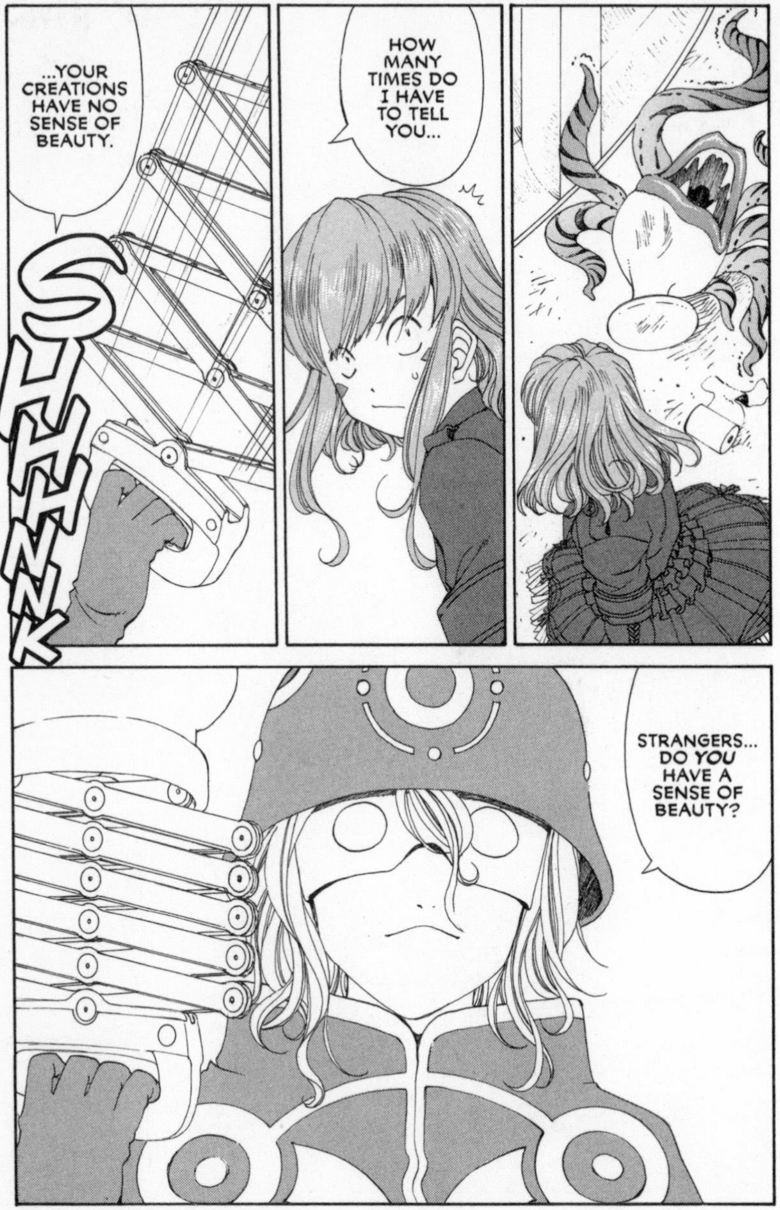
HOW MANY TIMES DO I HAVE TO TELL YOU...
...YOUR CREATIONS HAVE NO SENSE OF BEAUTY.
SHHHNNK
STRANGERS... DO *YOU* HAVE A SENSE OF BEAUTY?

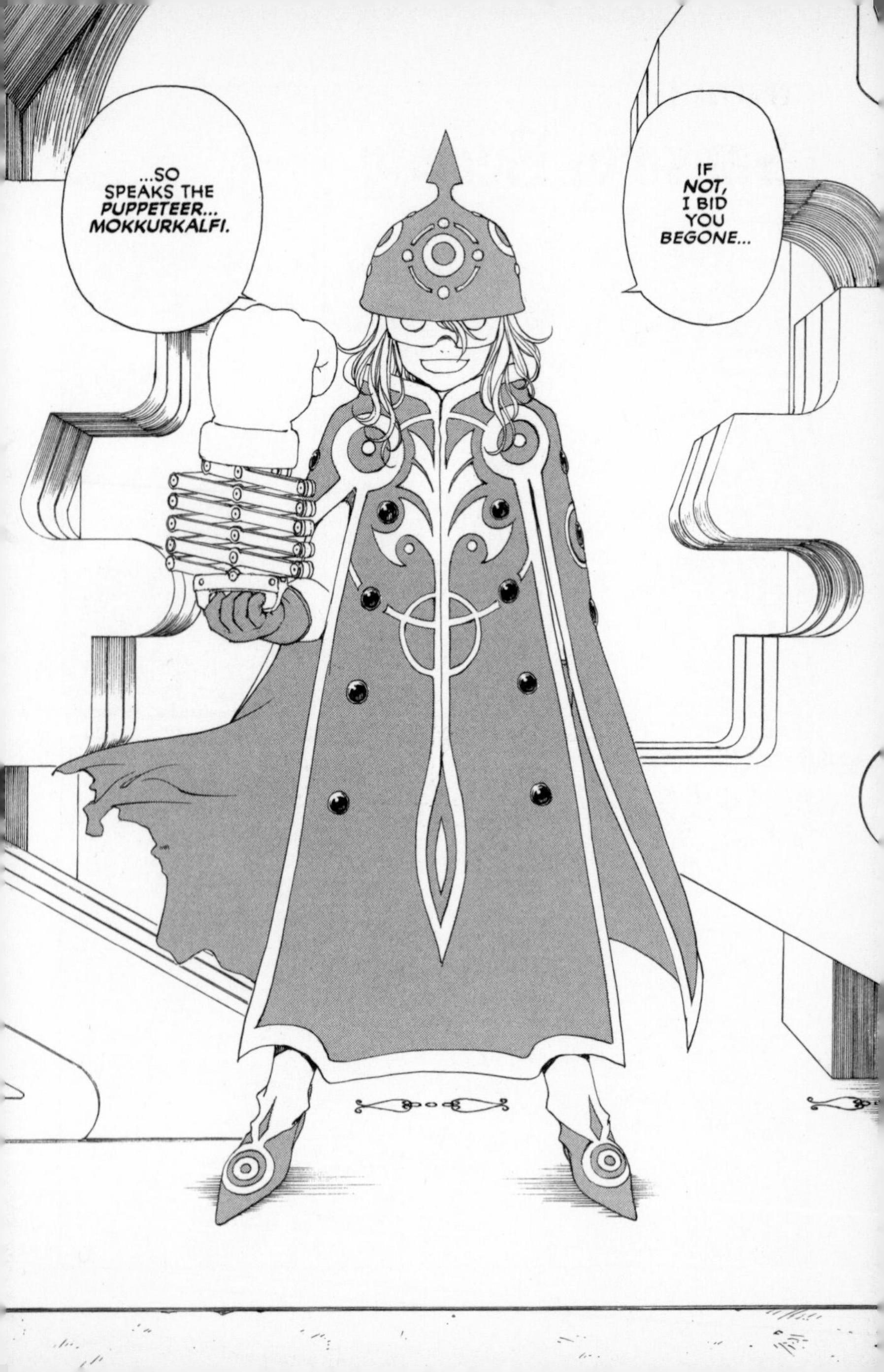
IF NOT, I BID YOU BEGONE...
...SO SPEAKS THE PUPPETEER... MOKKURKALFI.

CHAPTER 263

Sense of Beauty

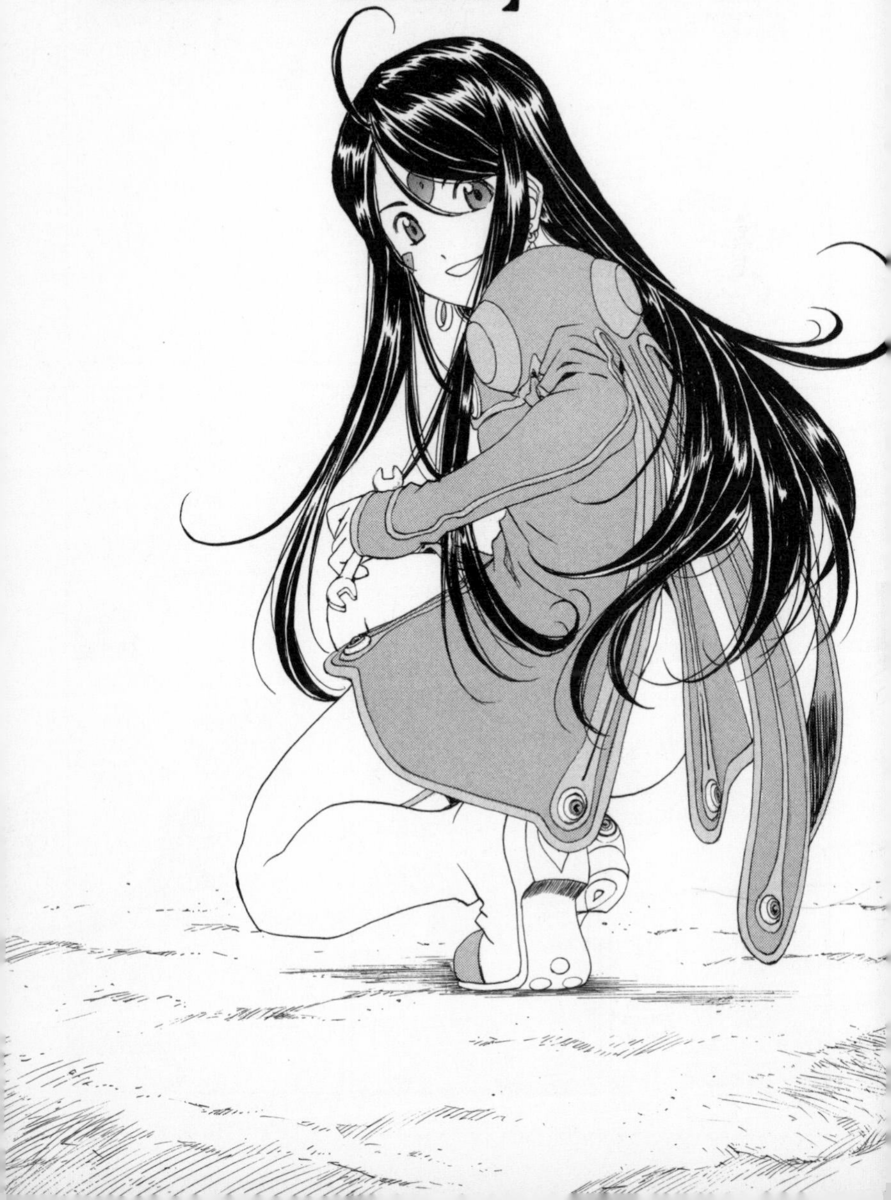

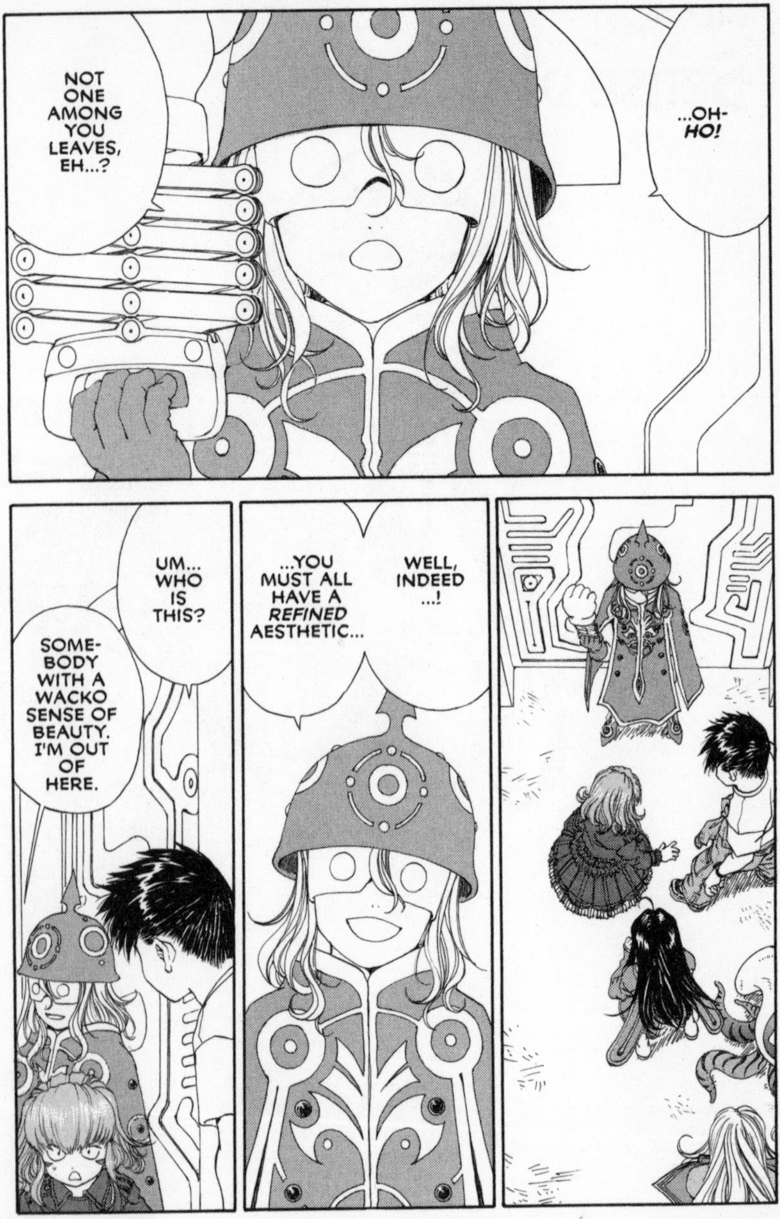
...OH-HO!
NOT ONE AMONG YOU LEAVES, EH...?
WELL, INDEED...!
...YOU MUST ALL HAVE A *REFINED* AESTHETIC...
UM... WHO IS THIS?
SOME-BODY WITH A WACKO SENSE OF BEAUTY. I'M OUT OF HERE.

HMMM...
...YOU'RE GOOD.
I GUESS YOU'LL DO, TOO.
YOU "GUESS" ...?
AND YOU SHOULD BE OKAY.
EVERY-ONE, LET'S FIRST TIDY UP THE MESS FROM--
...
YOU'RE *HOPE-LESS.*
!!
HEY! EVEN I DON'T THINK I'M SOME KIND OF *HUNK!!*
BUT I *KNOW* I'VE GOT A SENSE OF BEAUTY!!
YOU'RE UNQUALI-FIED TO EVEN VOICE AN OPINION--

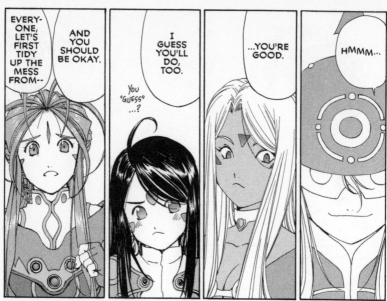

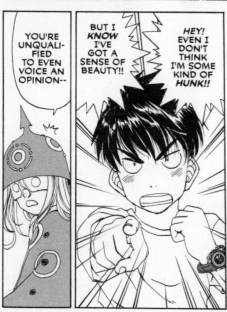

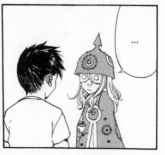

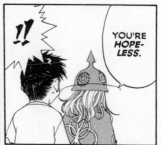

GRUNT!

HAHHHH!

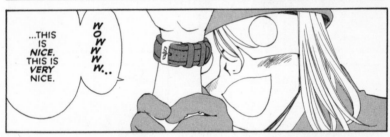

...THIS IS *NICE*. THIS IS *VERY* NICE.

WOWWWW...

I GRANT YOU PERMISSION TO ENTER, TOO...

UNDER-STOOD.

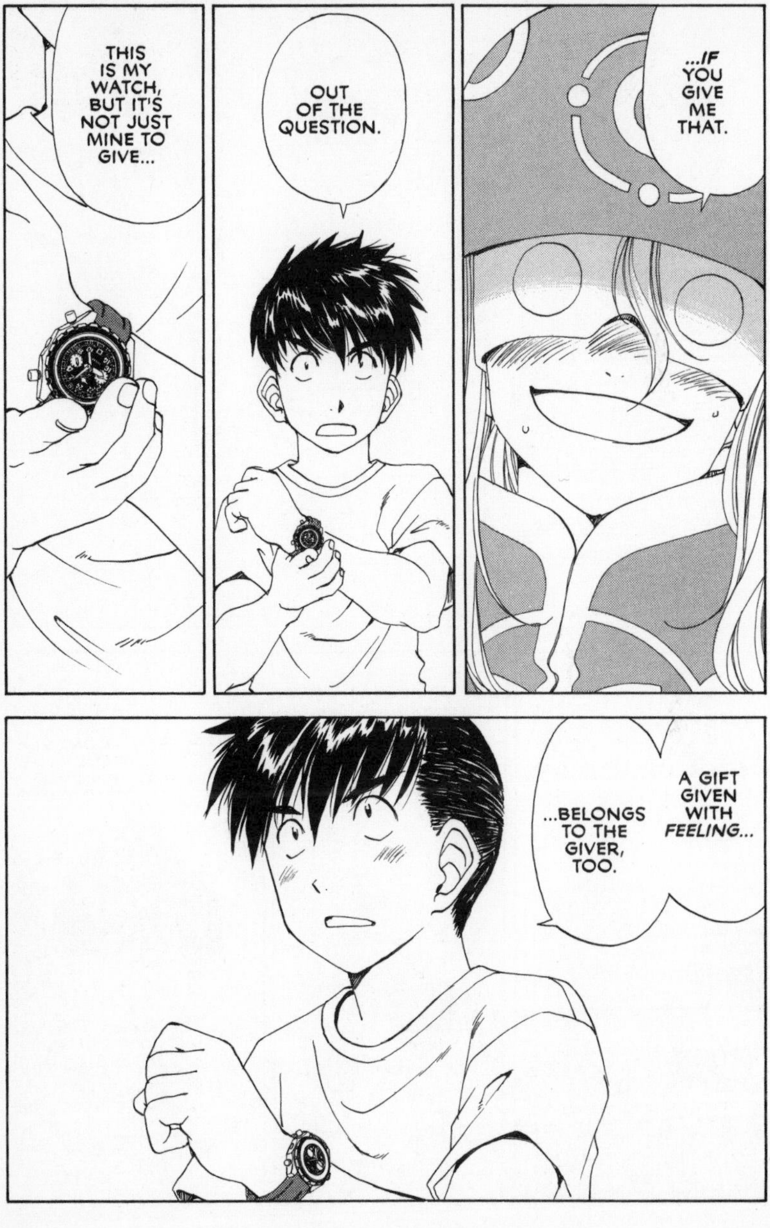
...*IF* YOU GIVE ME THAT.
OUT OF THE QUESTION.
THIS IS MY WATCH, BUT IT'S NOT JUST MINE TO GIVE...
A GIFT GIVEN WITH *FEELING*...
...BELONGS TO THE GIVER, TOO.

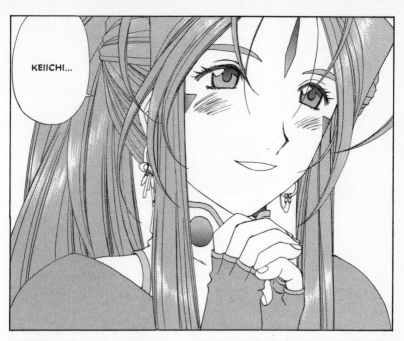

KEIICHI...
...ALL THE MORE SO WHEN IT COMES FROM YOUR BELOVED BELLDANDY?
YES, EXACTLY...
...HEY! WHAT ARE YOU--
HMPH! WELL, SO BE IT.
MOKKURKALFI IS MAGNANIMOUS...

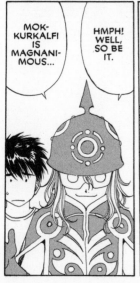

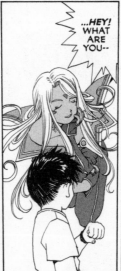

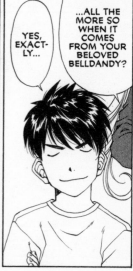

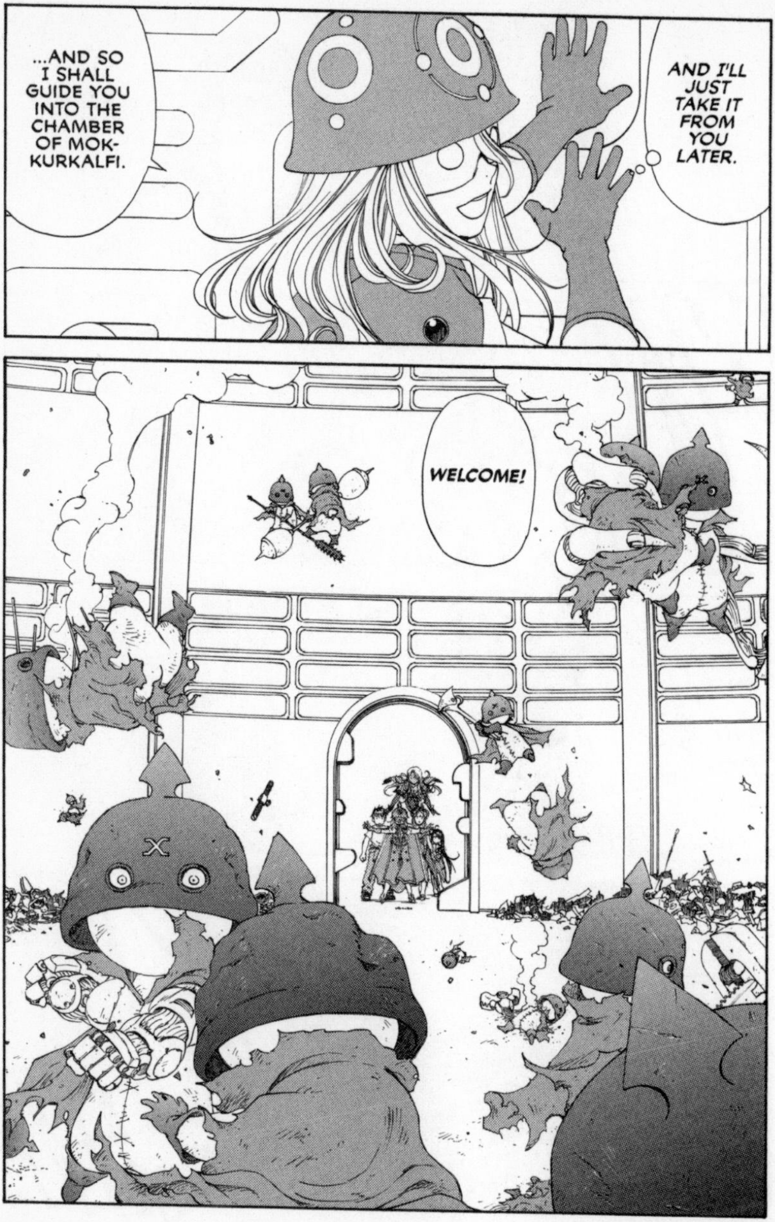

...AND SO I SHALL GUIDE YOU INTO THE CHAMBER OF MOK-KURKALFI.
AND I'LL JUST TAKE IT FROM YOU LATER.
WELCOME!

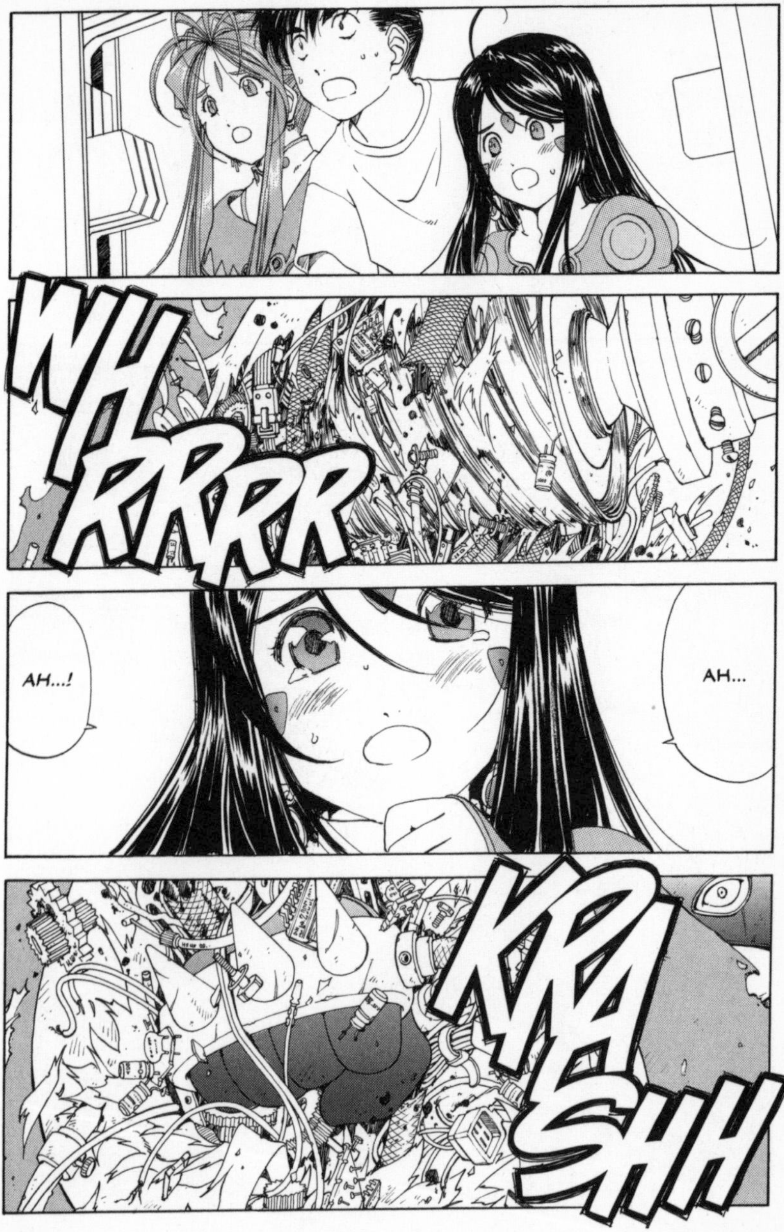
WHRRRR
AH...
AH...!
KRASHH

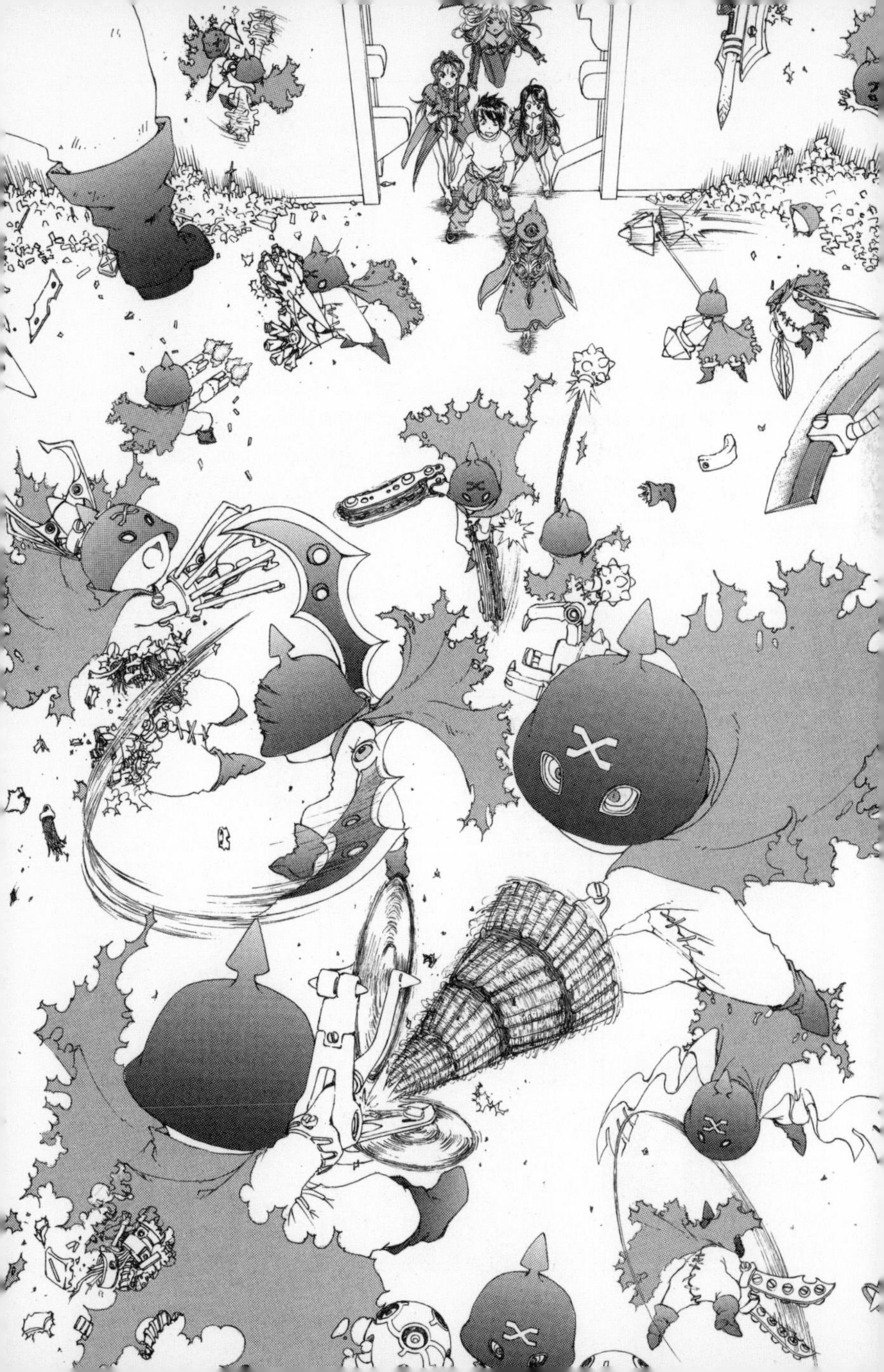

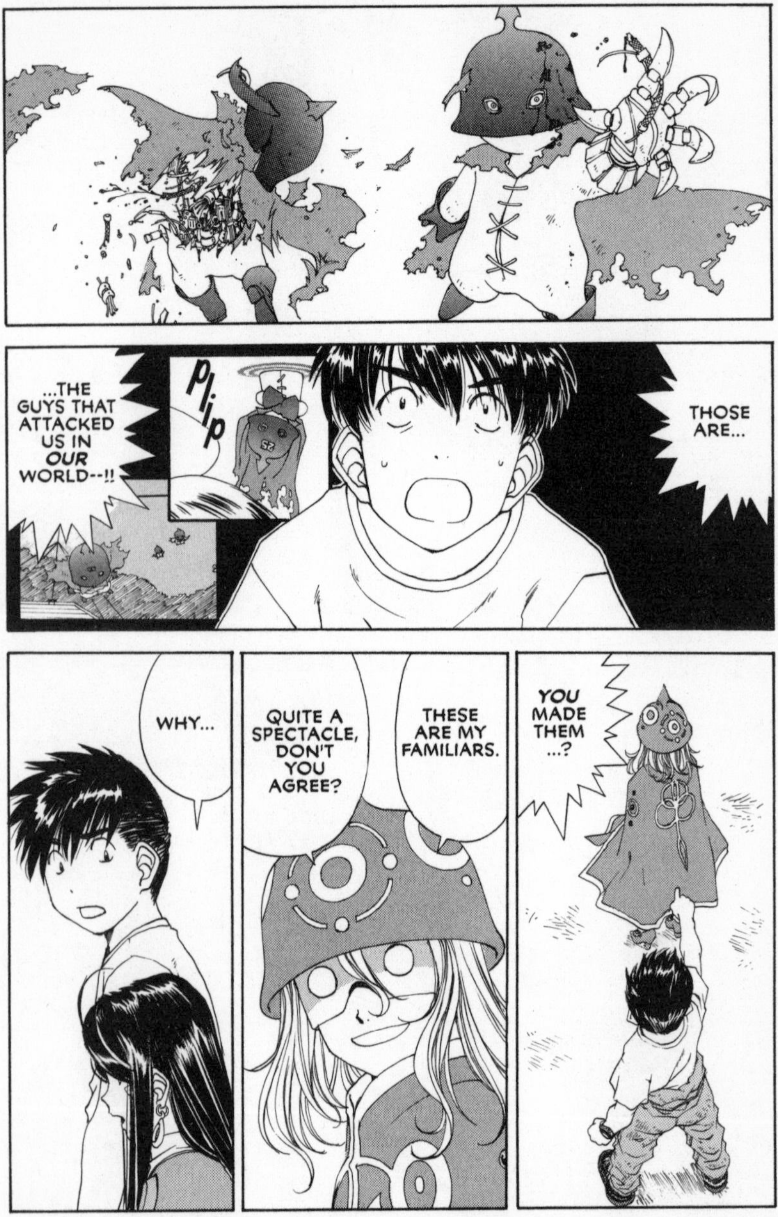
THOSE ARE...
plip
...THE GUYS THAT ATTACKED US IN *OUR* WORLD--!!
YOU MADE THEM ...?
THESE ARE MY FAMILIARS.
QUITE A SPECTACLE, DON'T YOU AGREE?
WHY...

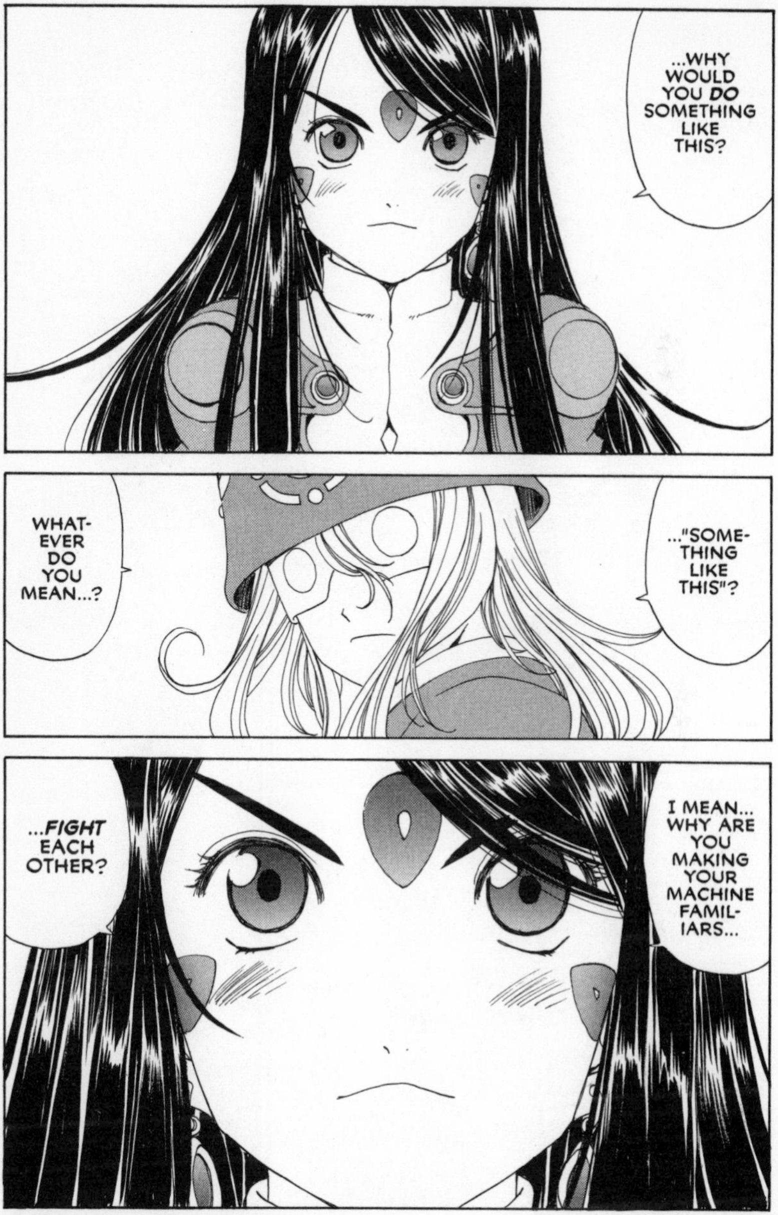
...WHY WOULD YOU *DO* SOMETHING LIKE THIS?
..."SOMETHING LIKE THIS"?
WHATEVER DO YOU MEAN...?
I MEAN... WHY ARE YOU MAKING YOUR MACHINE FAMILIARS...
...*FIGHT* EACH OTHER?

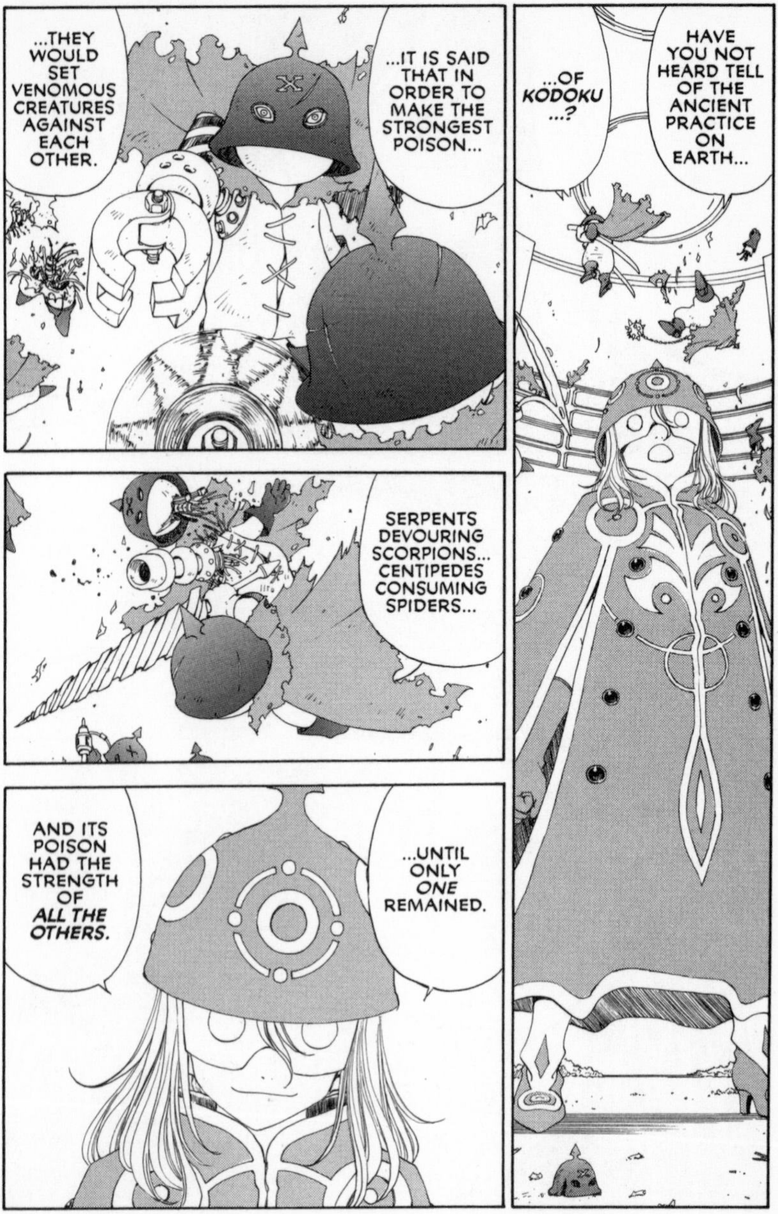
HAVE YOU NOT HEARD TELL OF THE ANCIENT PRACTICE ON EARTH...
...OF *KODOKU* ...?
...IT IS SAID THAT IN ORDER TO MAKE THE STRONGEST POISON...
...THEY WOULD SET VENOMOUS CREATURES AGAINST EACH OTHER.
SERPENTS DEVOURING SCORPIONS... CENTIPEDES CONSUMING SPIDERS...
...UNTIL ONLY *ONE* REMAINED.
AND ITS POISON HAD THE STRENGTH OF ***ALL THE OTHERS.***

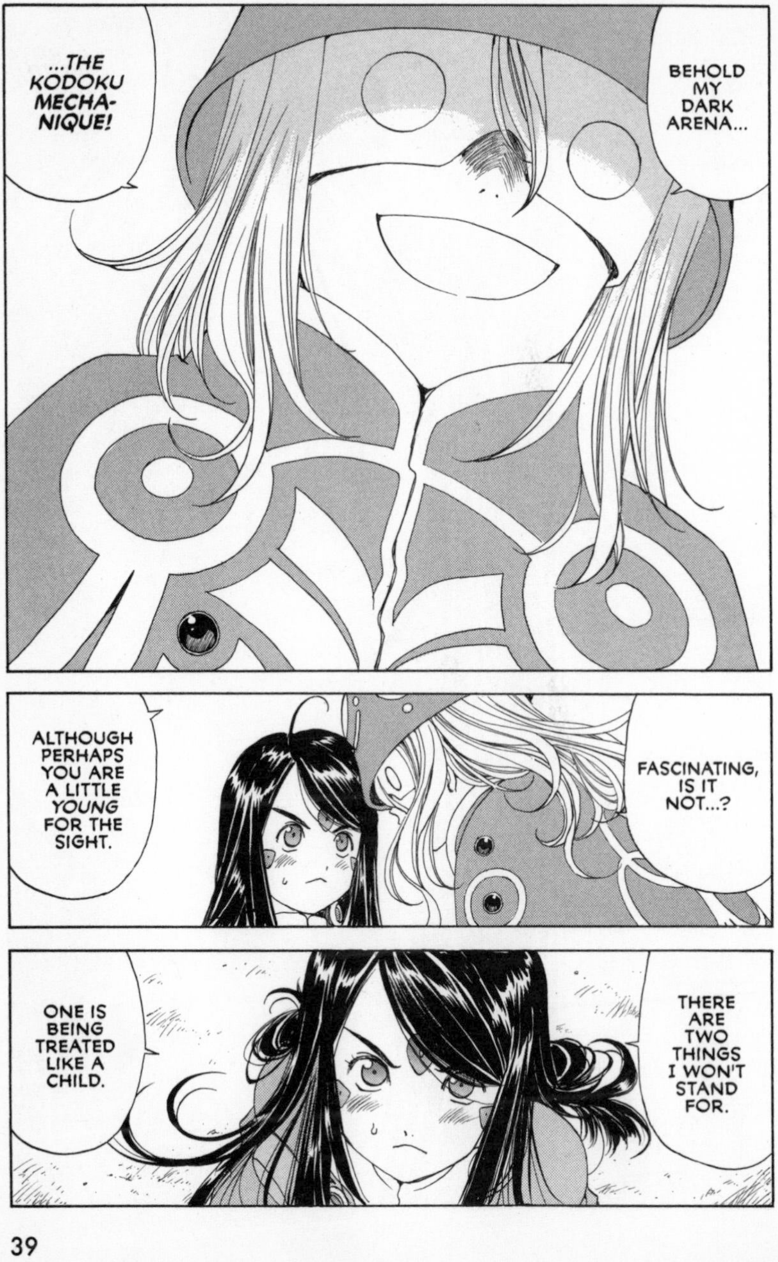
BEHOLD MY DARK ARENA...
...THE KODOKU MECHANIQUE!
FASCINATING, IS IT NOT...?
ALTHOUGH PERHAPS YOU ARE A LITTLE *YOUNG* FOR THE SIGHT.
THERE ARE TWO THINGS I WON'T STAND FOR.
ONE IS BEING TREATED LIKE A CHILD.

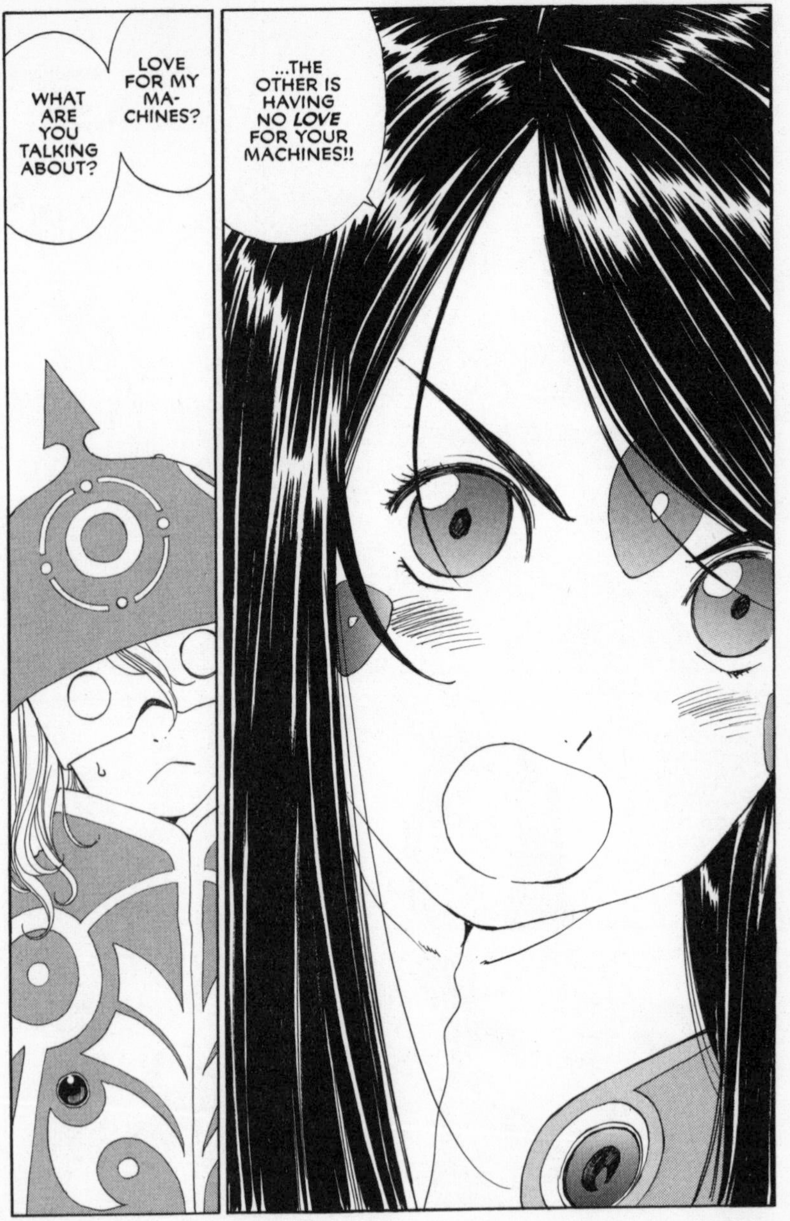
...THE OTHER IS HAVING NO *LOVE* FOR YOUR MACHINES!!
LOVE FOR MY MA-CHINES?
WHAT ARE YOU TALKING ABOUT?

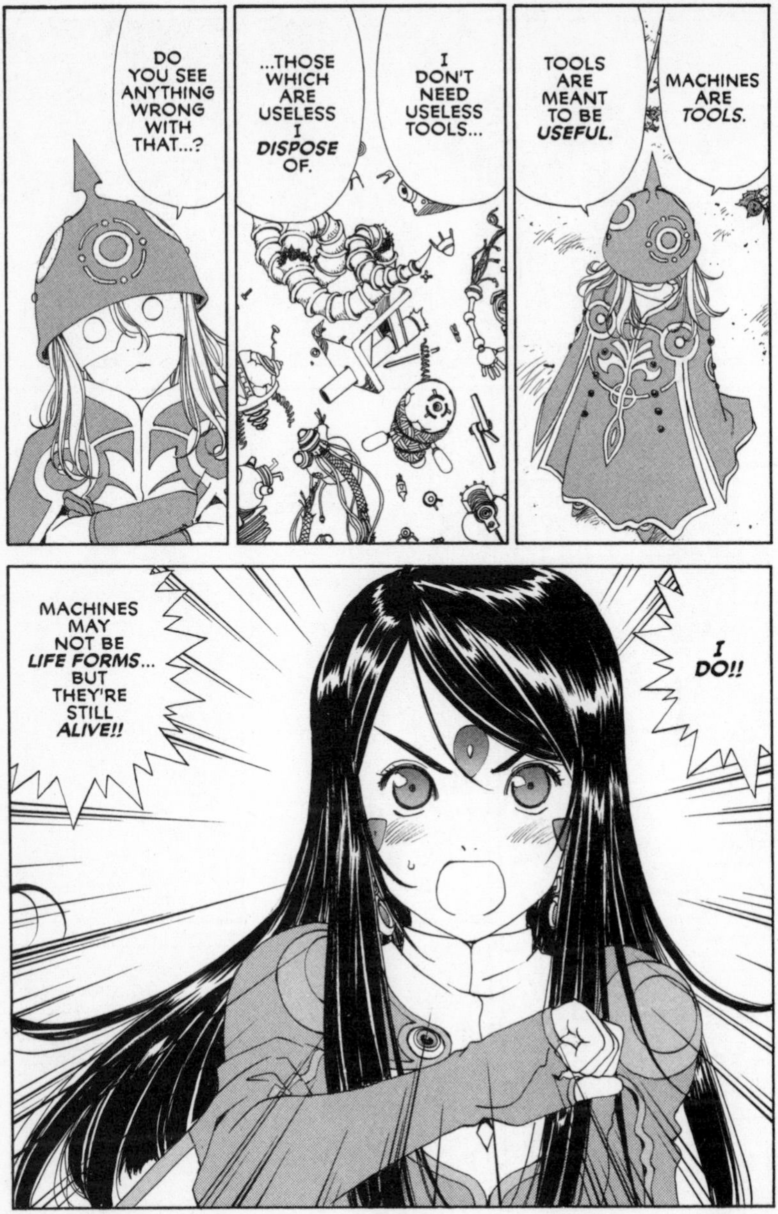
MACHINES ARE TOOLS.
TOOLS ARE MEANT TO BE USEFUL.
I DON'T NEED USELESS TOOLS...
...THOSE WHICH ARE USELESS I DISPOSE OF.
DO YOU SEE ANYTHING WRONG WITH THAT...?
I DO!!
MACHINES MAY NOT BE LIFE FORMS... BUT THEY'RE STILL ALIVE!!

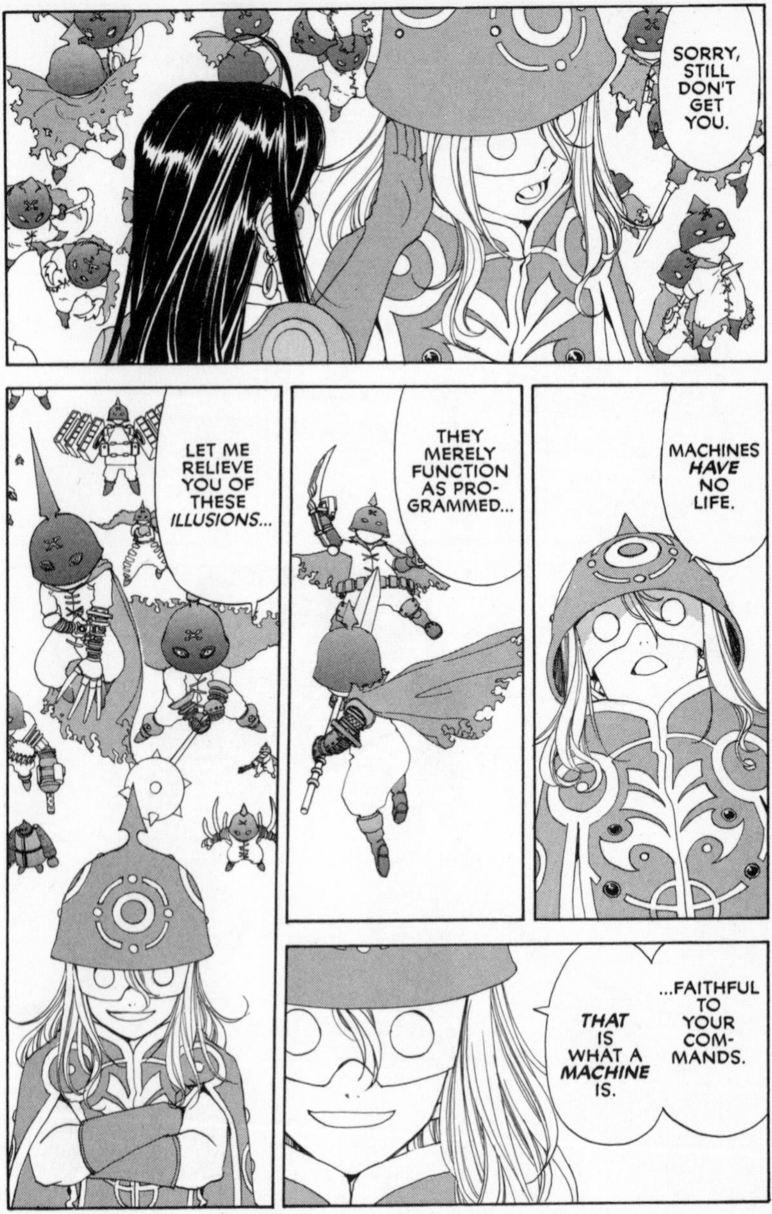
SORRY, STILL DON'T GET YOU.
MACHINES *HAVE* NO LIFE.
THEY MERELY FUNCTION AS PRO-GRAMMED...
...FAITHFUL TO YOUR COM-MANDS.
THAT IS WHAT A *MACHINE* IS.
LET ME RELIEVE YOU OF THESE *ILLUSIONS*...

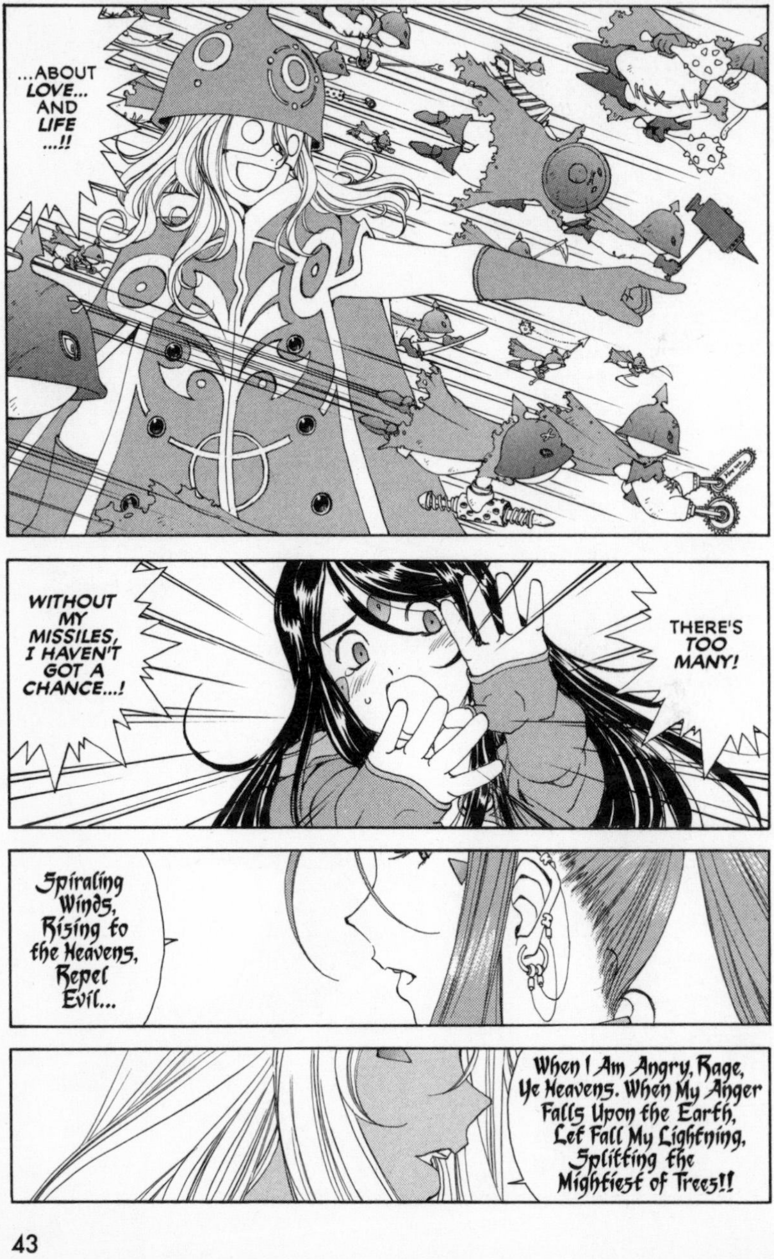

...ABOUT LOVE... AND LIFE ...!!
THERE'S TOO MANY!
WITHOUT MY MISSILES, I HAVEN'T GOT A CHANCE...!
Spiraling Winds, Rising to the Heavens, Repel Evil...
When I Am Angry, Rage, Ye Heavens. When My Anger Falls Upon the Earth, Let Fall My Lightning, Splitting the Mightiest of Trees!!

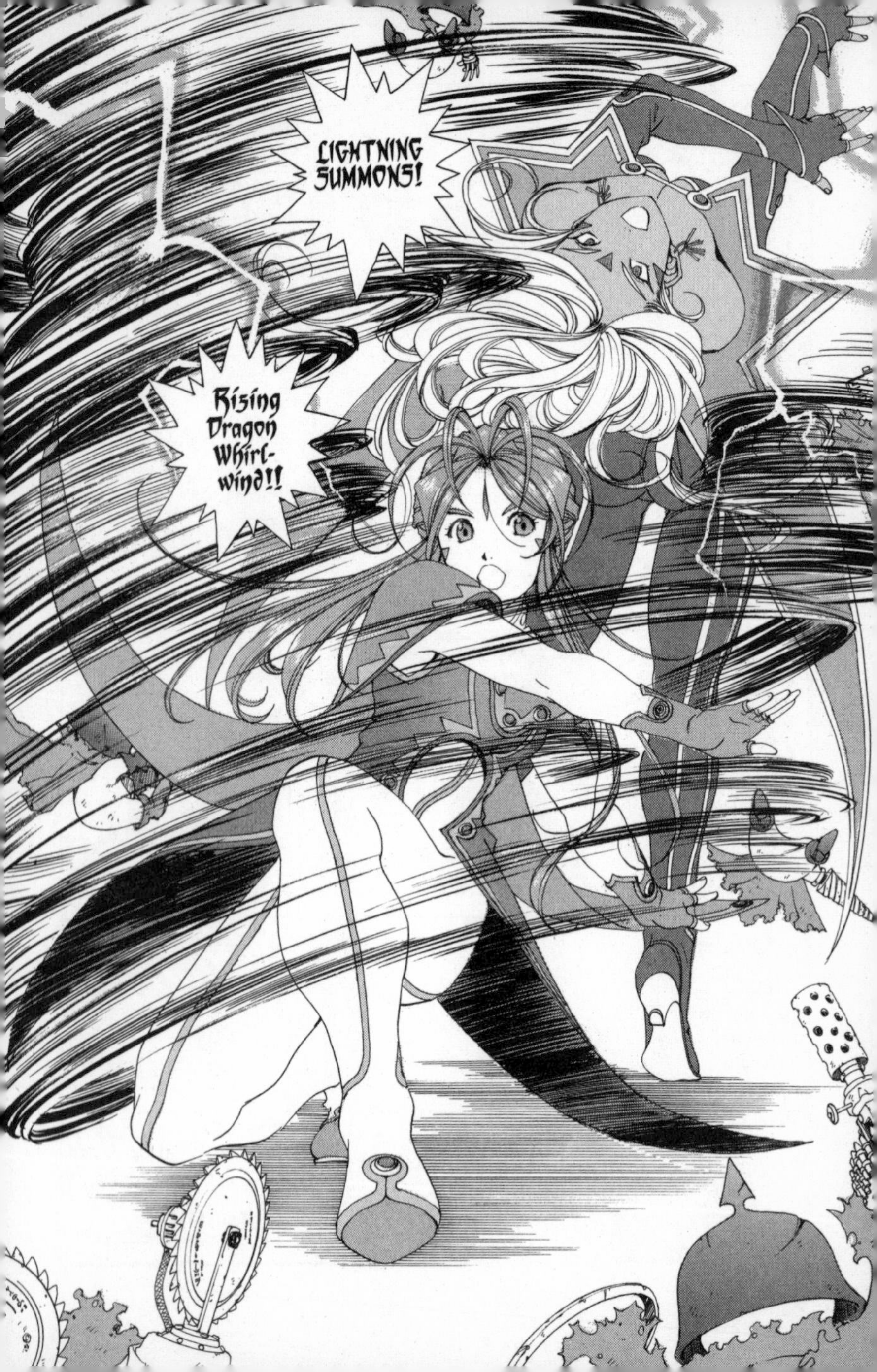
LIGHTNING SUMMONS!
Rising Dragon Whirl-wind!!

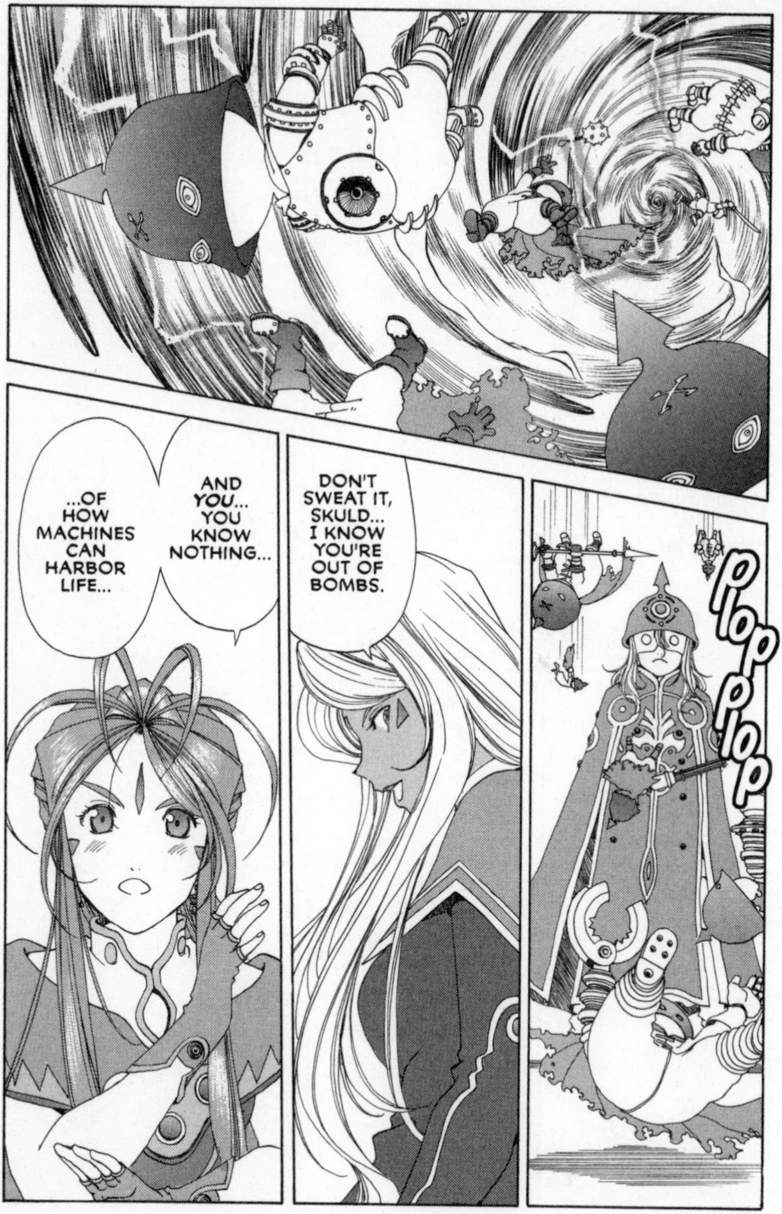
plop plop plop
DON'T SWEAT IT, SKULD... I KNOW YOU'RE OUT OF BOMBS.
AND *YOU*... YOU KNOW NOTHING...
...OF HOW MACHINES CAN HARBOR LIFE...

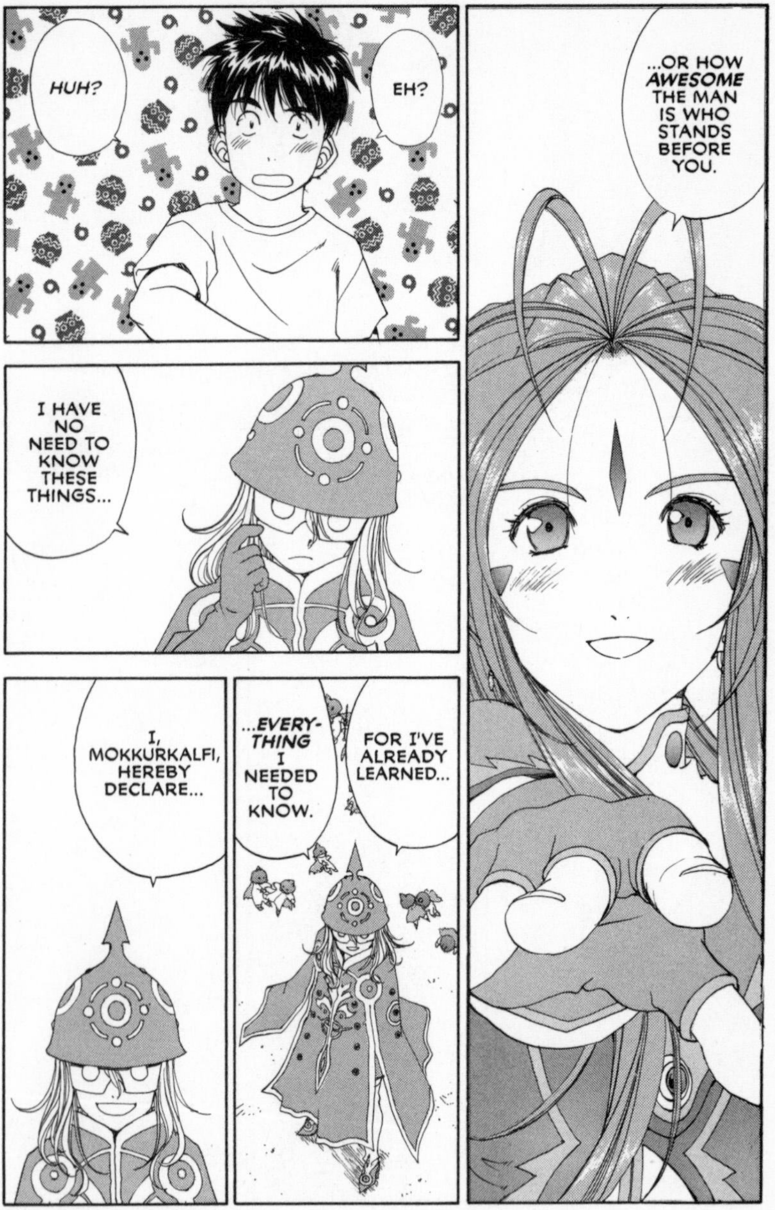
...OR HOW AWESOME THE MAN IS WHO STANDS BEFORE YOU.
EH?
HUH?
I HAVE NO NEED TO KNOW THESE THINGS...
FOR I'VE ALREADY LEARNED...
...EVERY-THING I NEEDED TO KNOW.
I, MOKKURKALFI, HEREBY DECLARE...

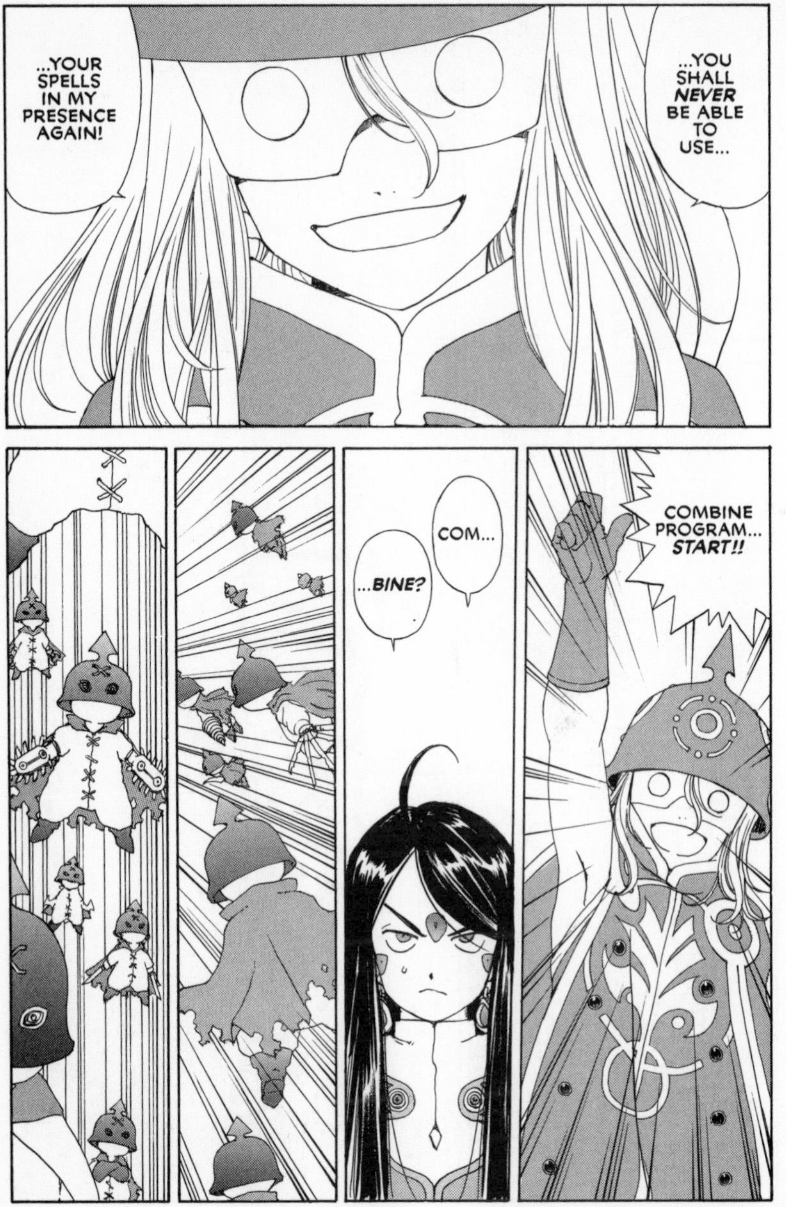
...YOU SHALL *NEVER* BE ABLE TO USE...
...YOUR SPELLS IN MY PRESENCE AGAIN!
COMBINE PROGRAM... *START!!*
COM...
...BINE?

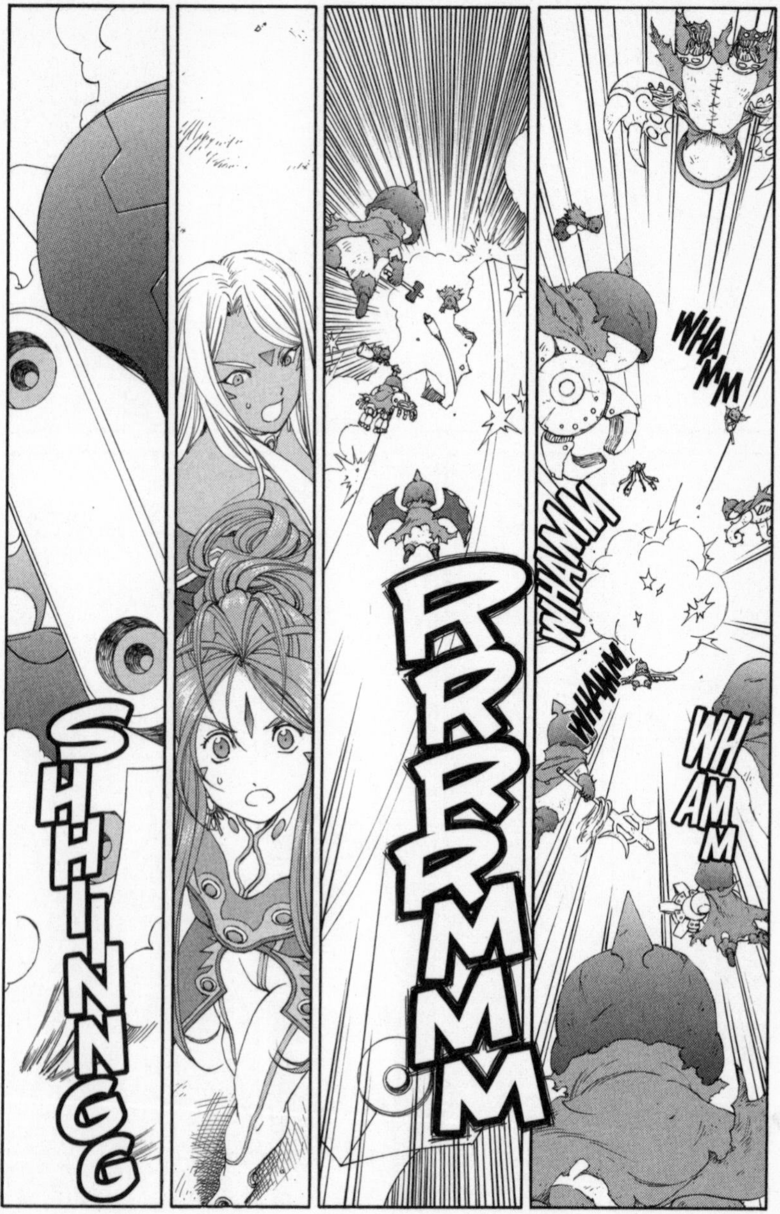
WHAMM
WHAMM
WHAMM
WHAMM
RRRMMM
SHHINGG

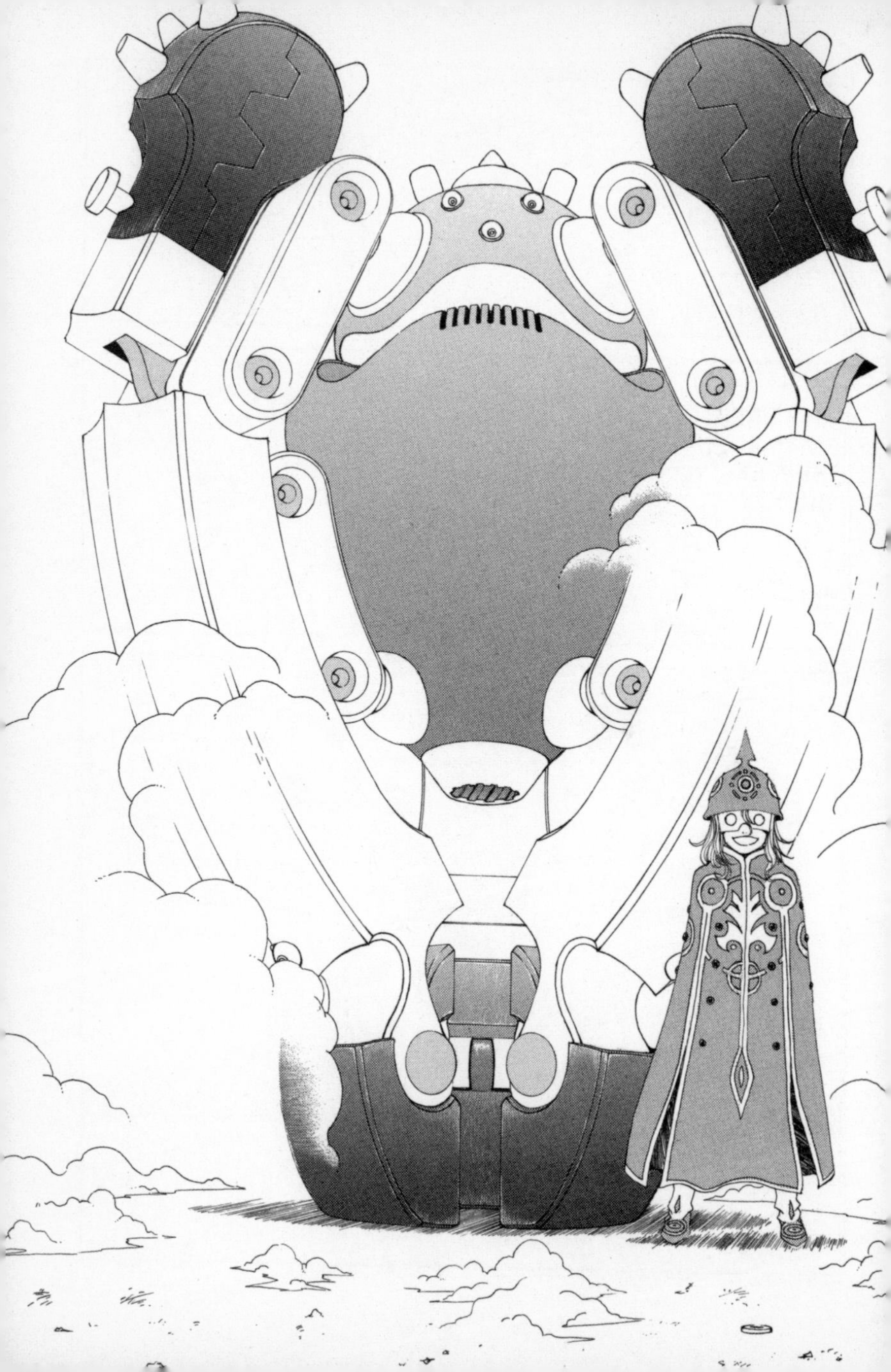

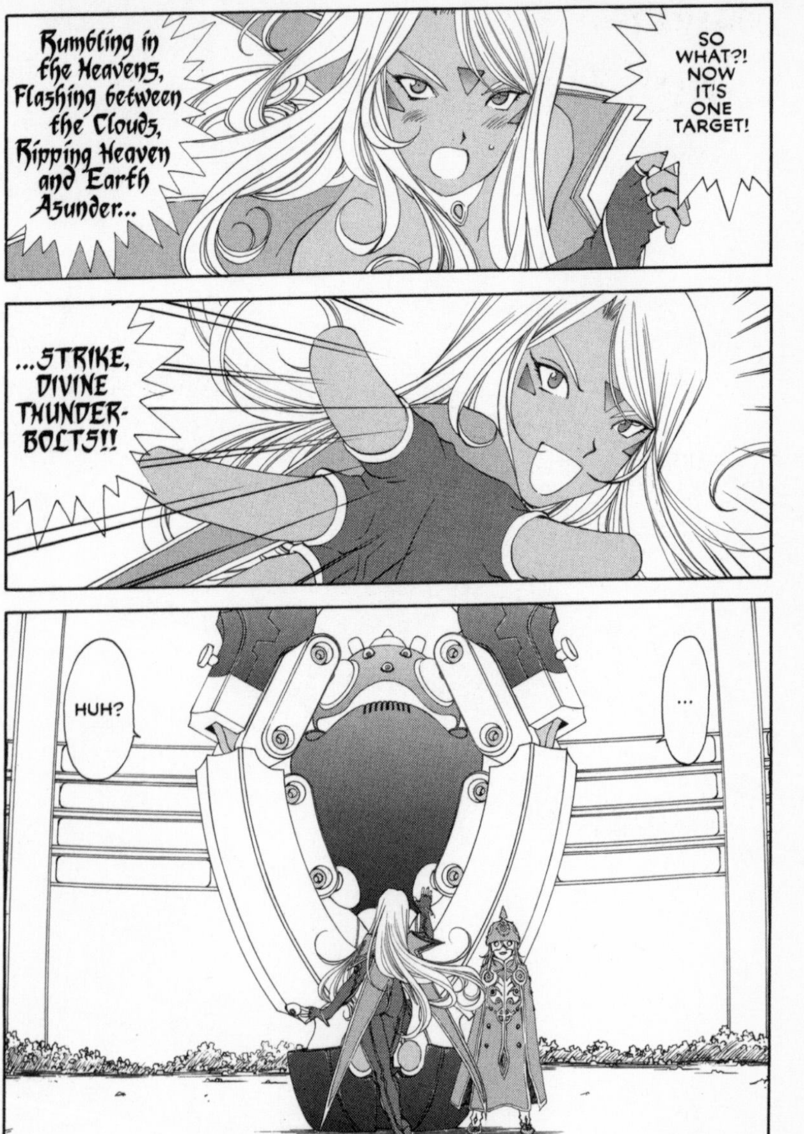
SO WHAT?! NOW IT'S ONE TARGET!
Rumbling in the Heavens, Flashing between the Clouds, Ripping Heaven and Earth Asunder...
...STRIKE, DIVINE THUNDER-BOLTS!!
...
HUH?

CHAPTER 264

Spell Canceling

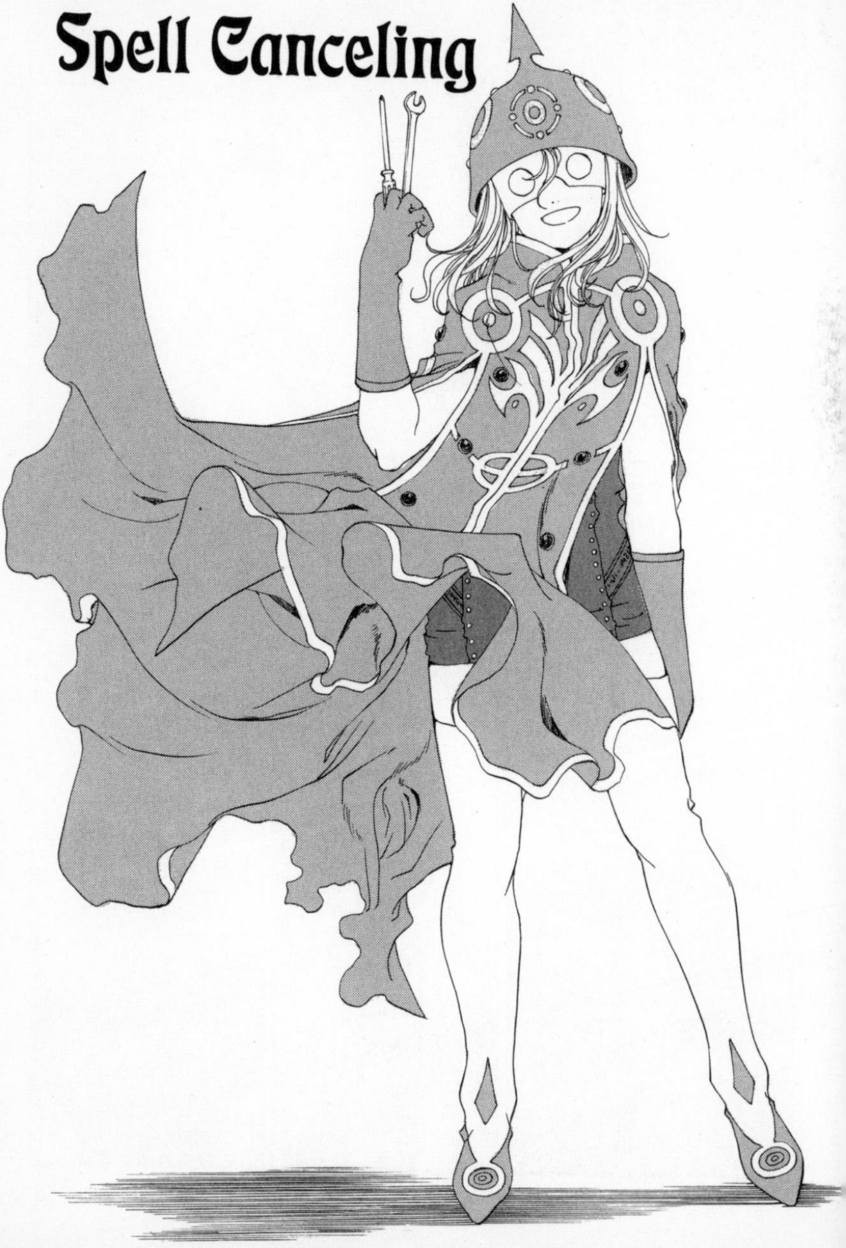

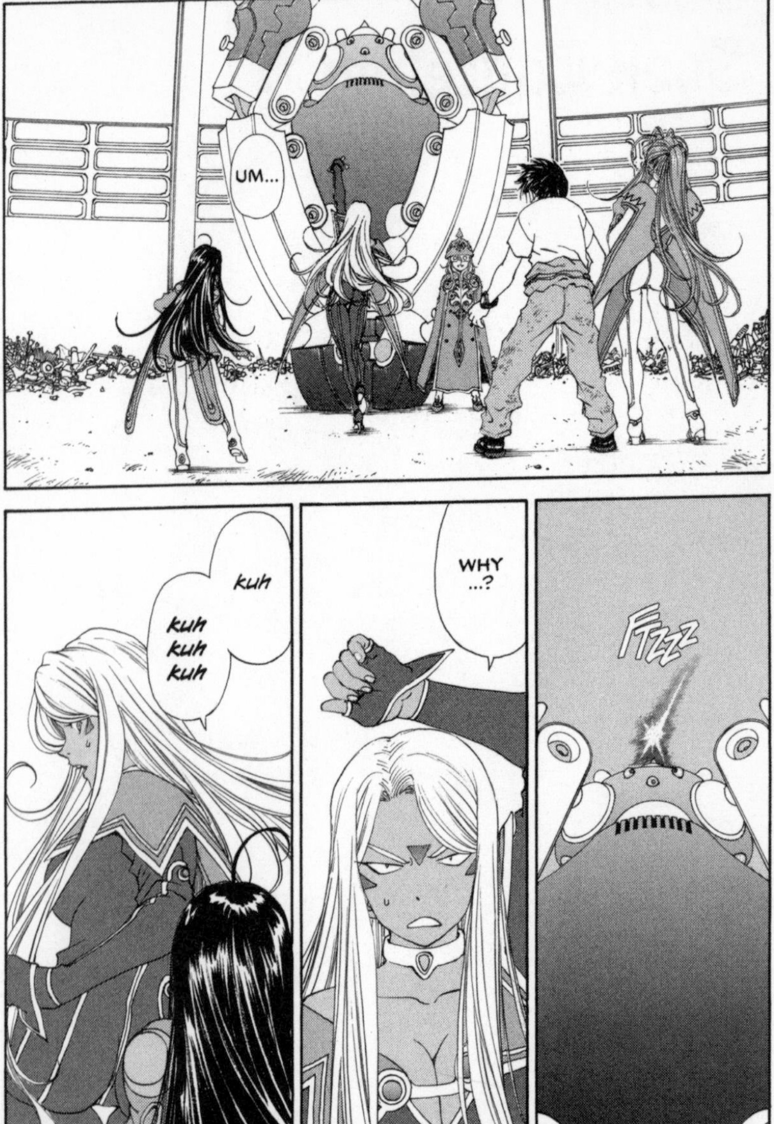
UM...
FTZZZ
WHY ...?
kuh
kuh kuh kuh

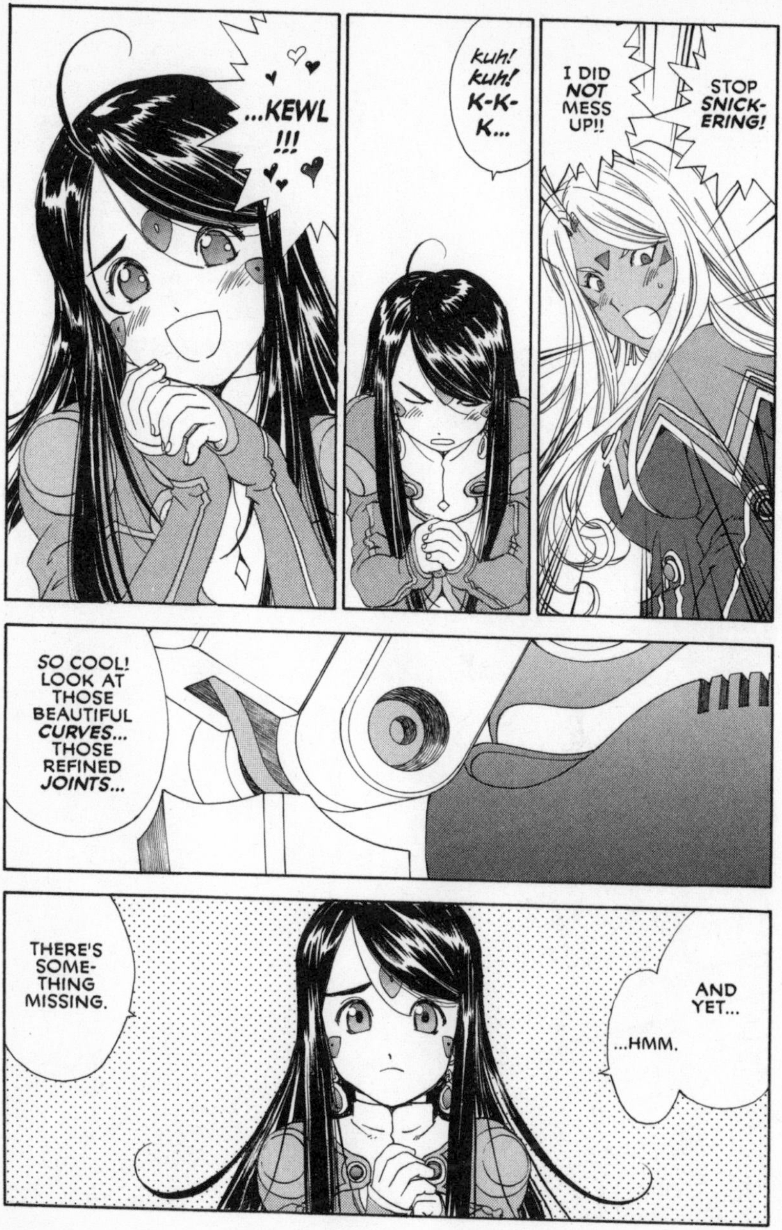
STOP SNICK-ERING!
I DID NOT MESS UP!!
kuh! kuh! K-K-K...
...KEWL !!!
SO COOL! LOOK AT THOSE BEAUTIFUL CURVES... THOSE REFINED JOINTS...
AND YET...
...HMM.
THERE'S SOME-THING MISSING.

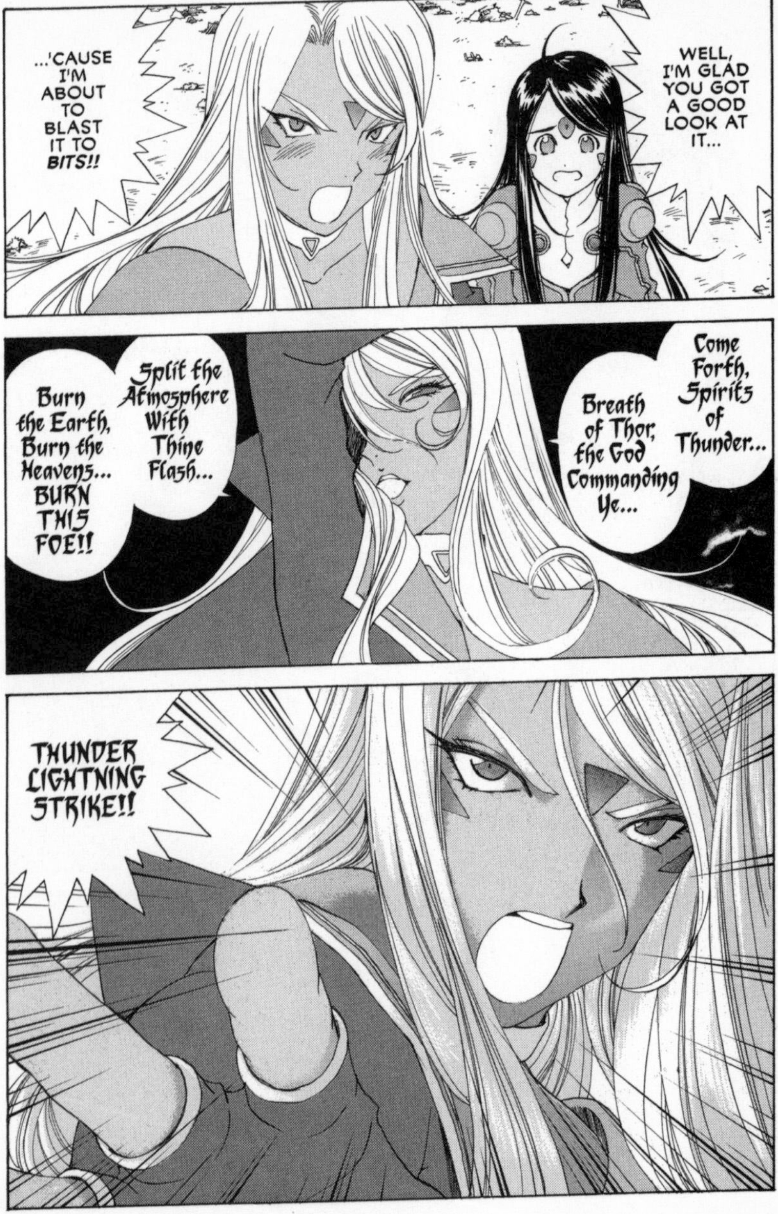
WELL, I'M GLAD YOU GOT A GOOD LOOK AT IT...
...'CAUSE I'M ABOUT TO BLAST IT TO BITS!!
Come Forth, Spirits of Thunder...
Breath of Thor, the God Commanding Ye...
Split the Atmosphere With Thine Flash...
Burn the Earth, Burn the Heavens... BURN THIS FOE!!
THUNDER LIGHTNING STRIKE!!

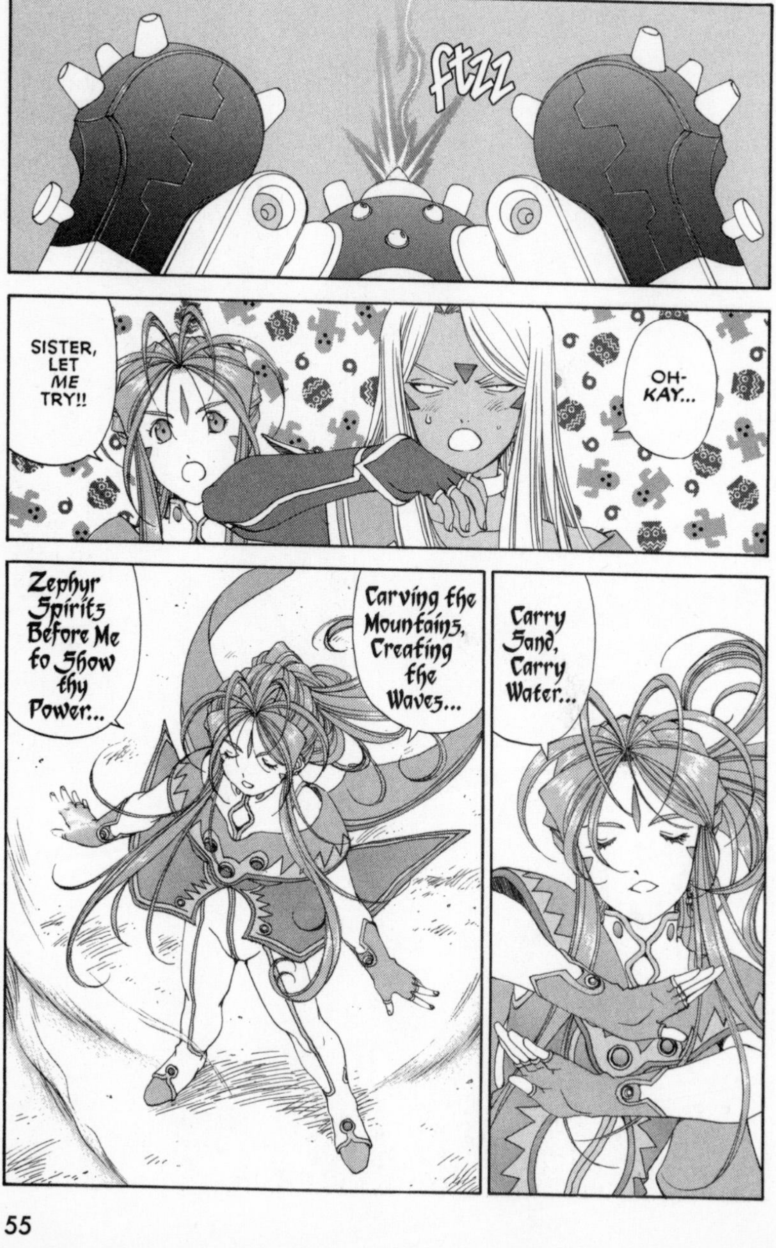
ftzz
SISTER, LET ME TRY!!
OH-KAY...
Zephyr Spirits Before Me to Show thy Power...
Carving the Mountains, Creating the Waves...
Carry Sand, Carry Water...

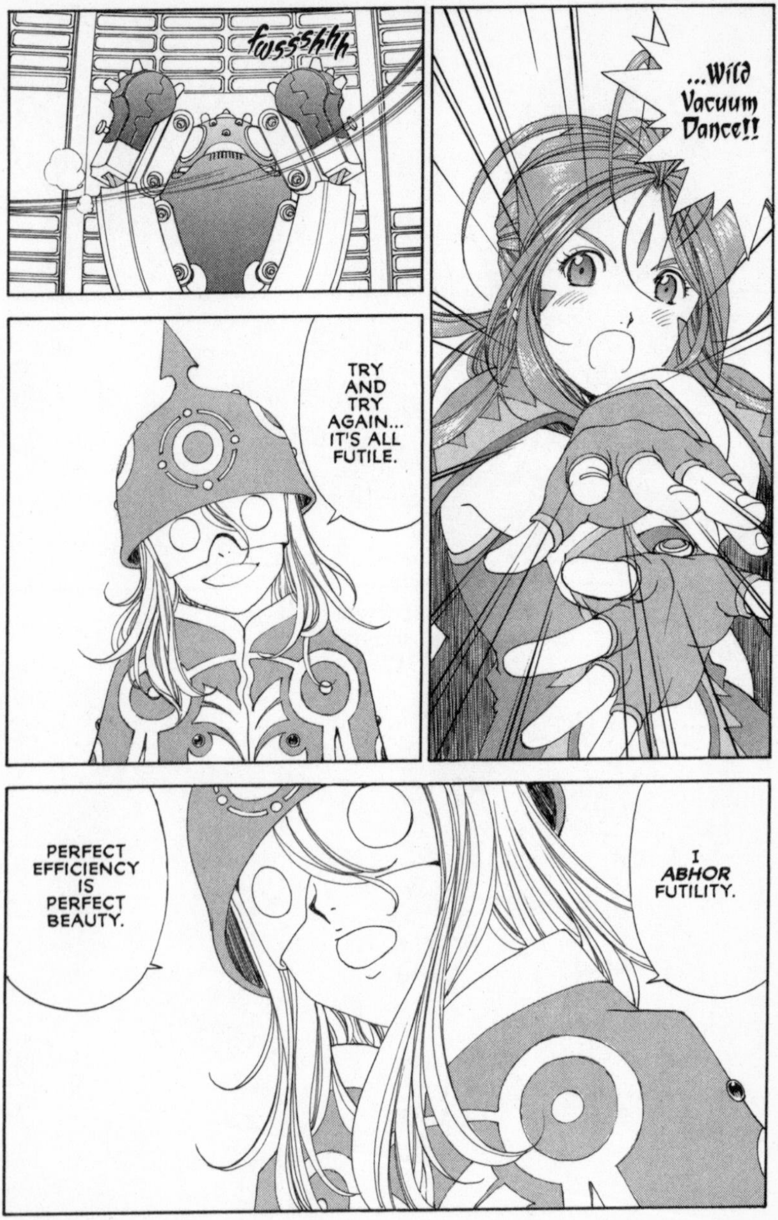

...Wild Vacuum Dance!!
fwssshhh
TRY AND TRY AGAIN... IT'S ALL FUTILE.
I *ABHOR* FUTILITY.
PERFECT EFFICIENCY IS PERFECT BEAUTY.

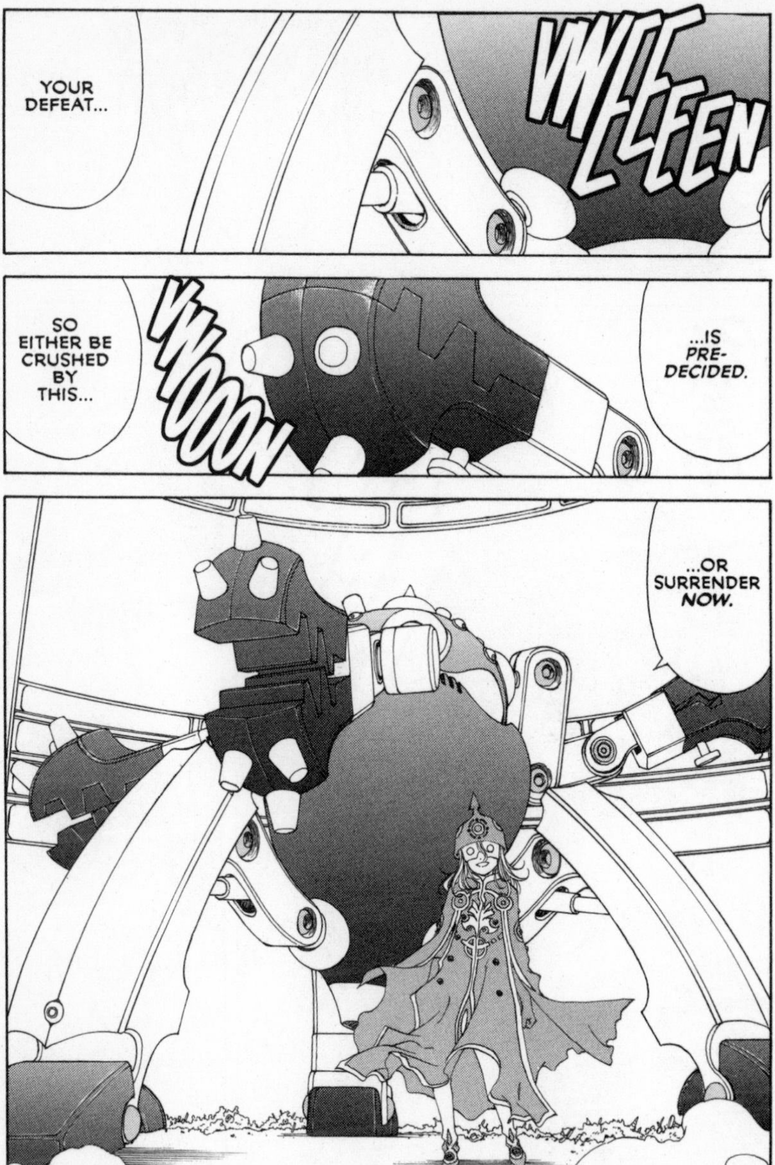
VWEEEEN
YOUR DEFEAT...
...IS *PRE-DECIDED.*
VWOOON
SO EITHER BE CRUSHED BY THIS...
...OR SURRENDER *NOW.*

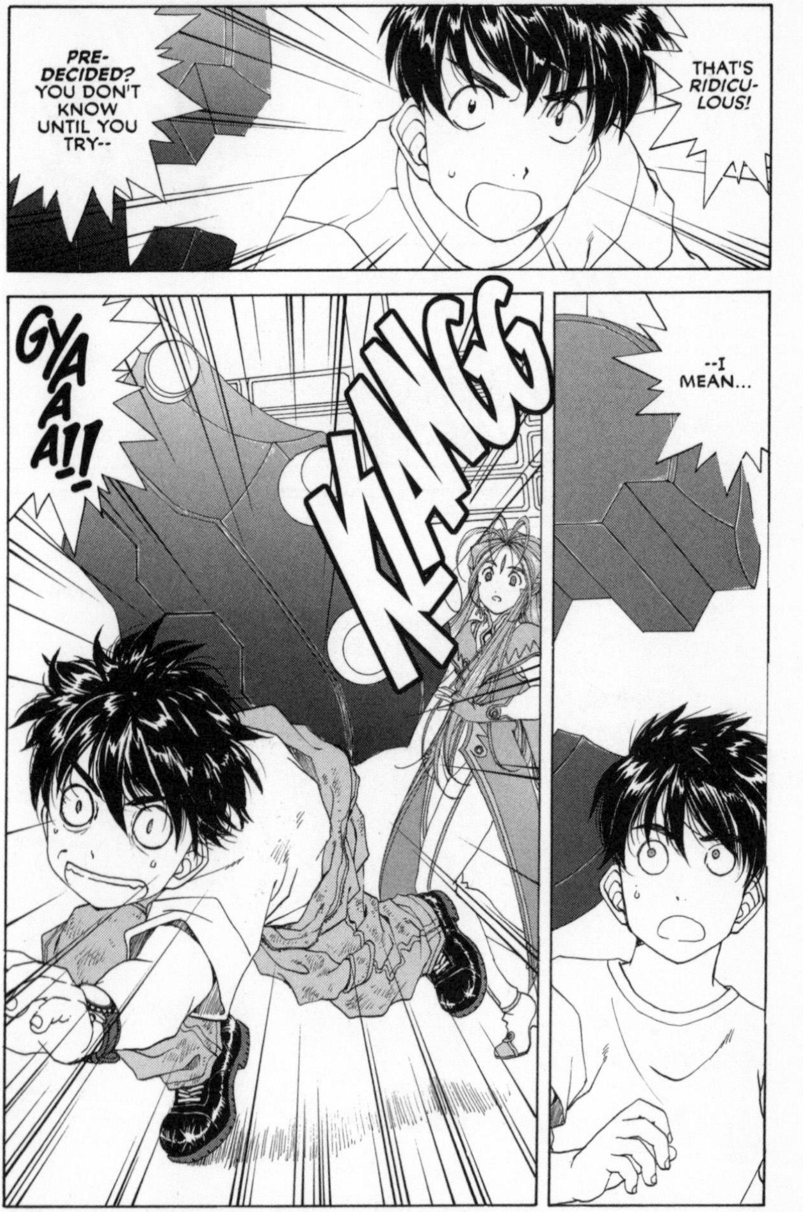
THAT'S RIDICULOUS!
PRE-DECIDED? YOU DON'T KNOW UNTIL YOU TRY--
--I MEAN...
KLANG
GYAAA!!

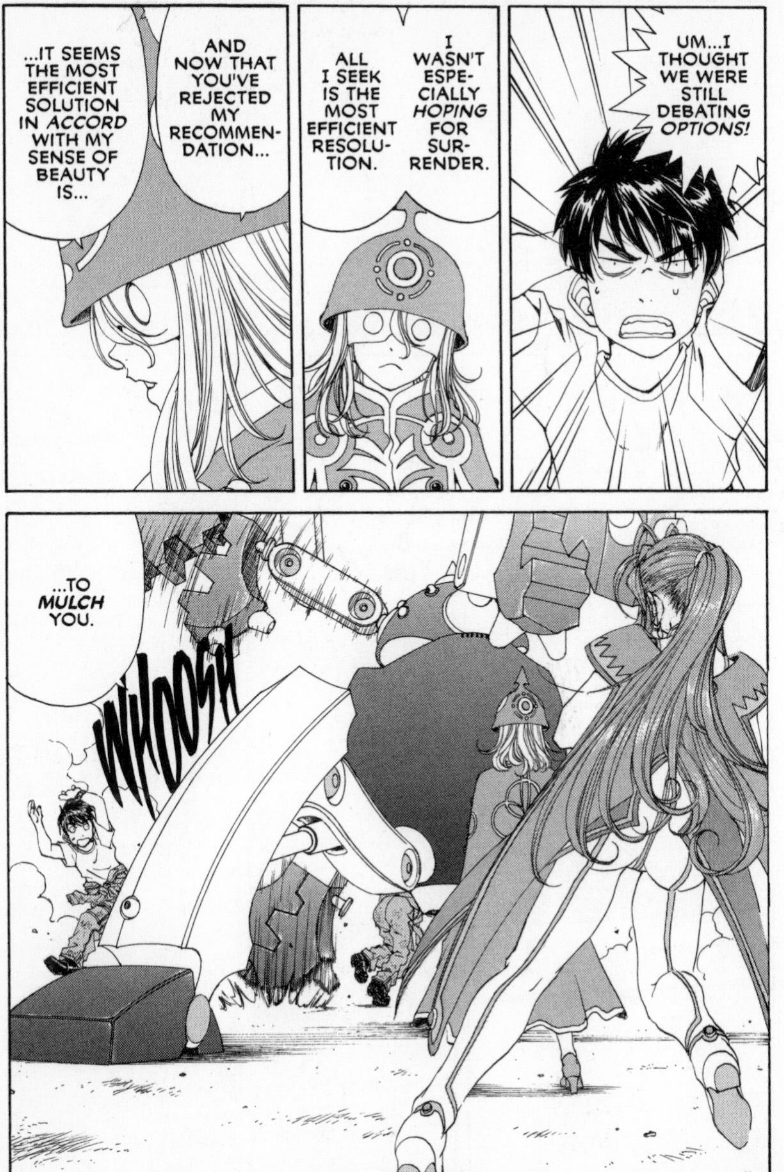
UM...I THOUGHT WE WERE STILL DEBATING *OPTIONS!*
I WASN'T ESPECIALLY *HOPING* FOR SURRENDER.
ALL I SEEK IS THE MOST EFFICIENT RESOLUTION.
AND NOW THAT YOU'VE REJECTED MY RECOMMENDATION...
...IT SEEMS THE MOST EFFICIENT SOLUTION IN *ACCORD* WITH MY SENSE OF BEAUTY IS...
...TO ***MULCH*** YOU.
WHOOSH

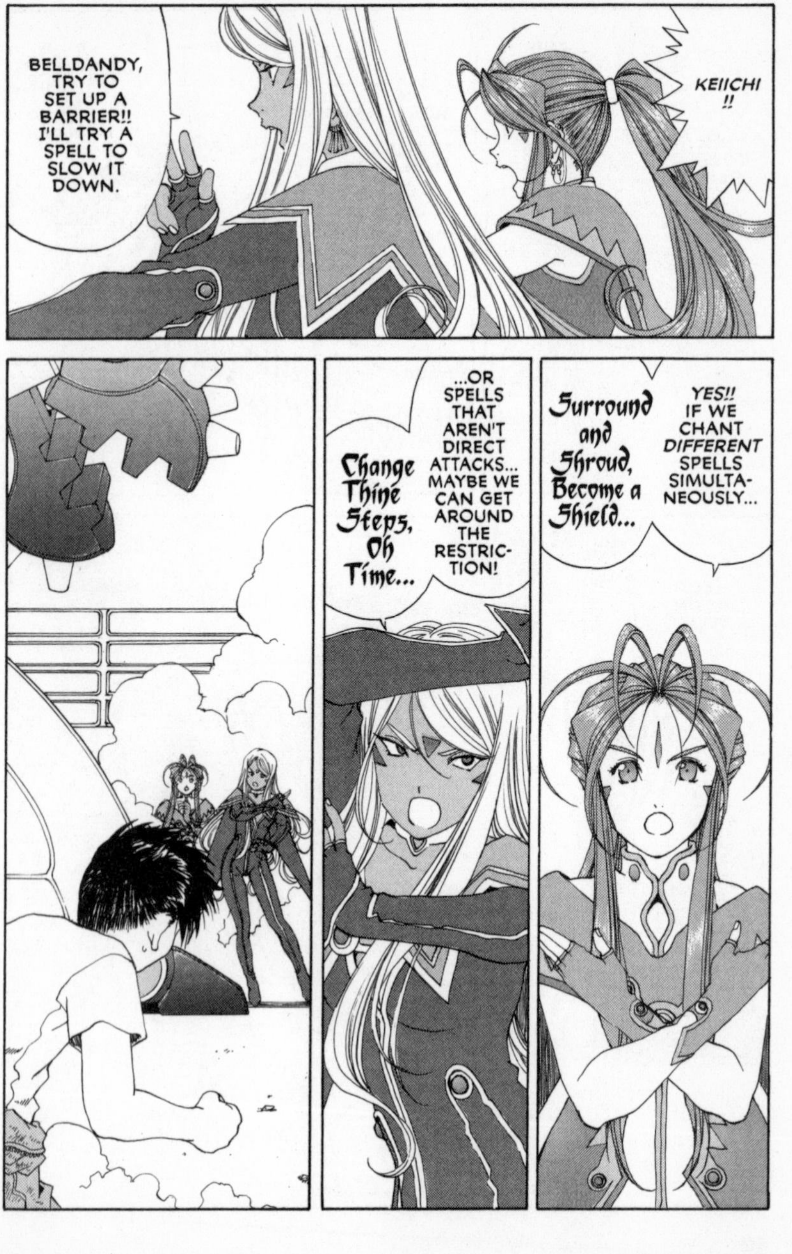
KEIICHI !!
BELLDANDY, TRY TO SET UP A BARRIER!! I'LL TRY A SPELL TO SLOW IT DOWN.
YES!! IF WE CHANT *DIFFERENT* SPELLS SIMULTANEOUSLY...
Surround and Shroud, Become a Shield...
...OR SPELLS THAT AREN'T DIRECT ATTACKS... MAYBE WE CAN GET AROUND THE RESTRICTION!
Change Thine Steps, Oh Time...

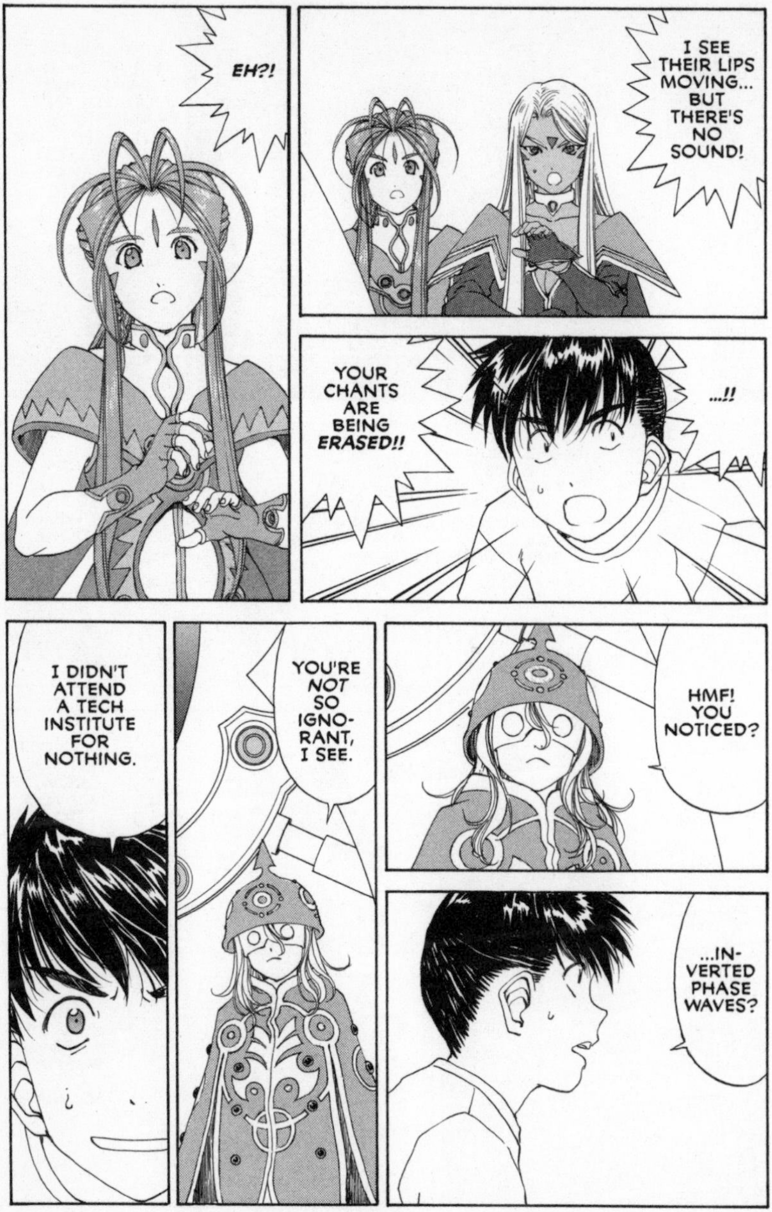
I SEE THEIR LIPS MOVING... BUT THERE'S NO SOUND!
...!!
YOUR CHANTS ARE BEING *ERASED!!*
EH?!
HMF! YOU NOTICED?
...IN-VERTED PHASE WAVES?
YOU'RE *NOT* SO IGNO-RANT, I SEE.
I DIDN'T ATTEND A TECH INSTITUTE FOR NOTHING.

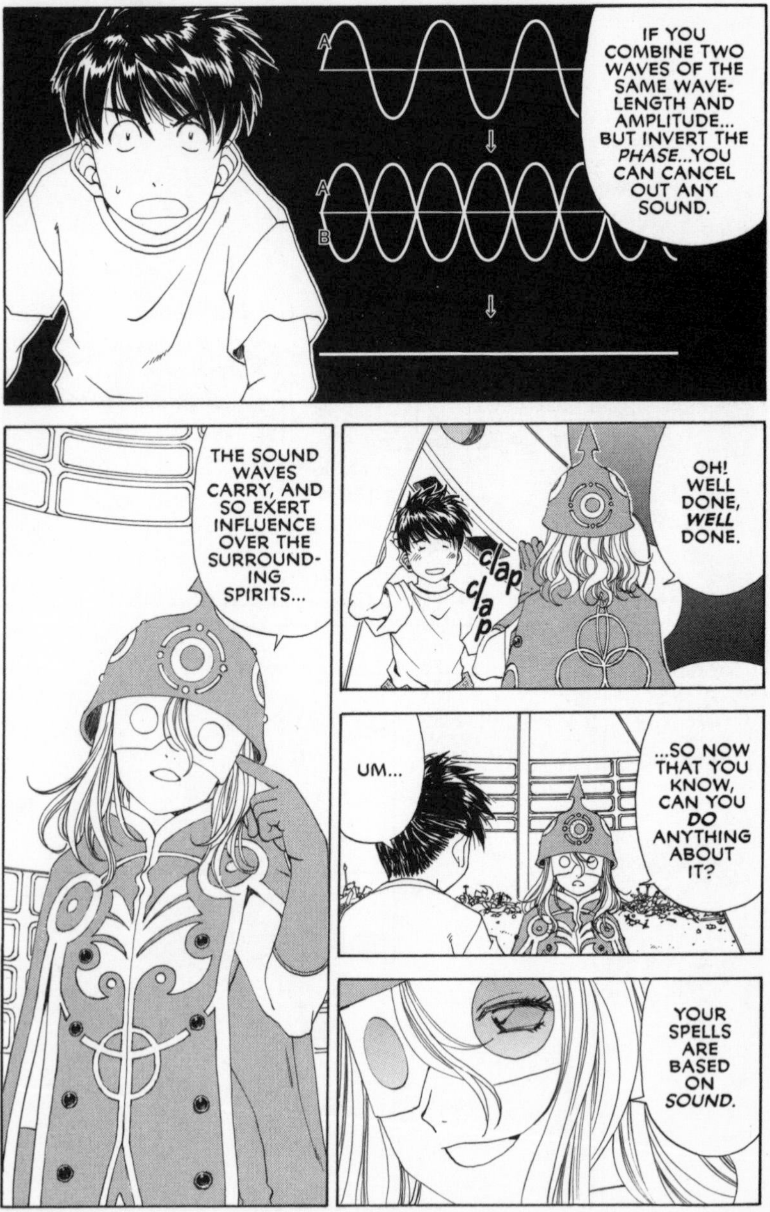
A
IF YOU COMBINE TWO WAVES OF THE SAME WAVE-LENGTH AND AMPLITUDE... BUT INVERT THE *PHASE*...YOU CAN CANCEL OUT ANY SOUND.
A
B
OH! WELL DONE, *WELL* DONE.
clap clap clap
...SO NOW THAT YOU KNOW, CAN YOU *DO* ANYTHING ABOUT IT?
UM...
YOUR SPELLS ARE BASED ON *SOUND.*
THE SOUND WAVES CARRY, AND SO EXERT INFLUENCE OVER THE SURROUNDING SPIRITS...

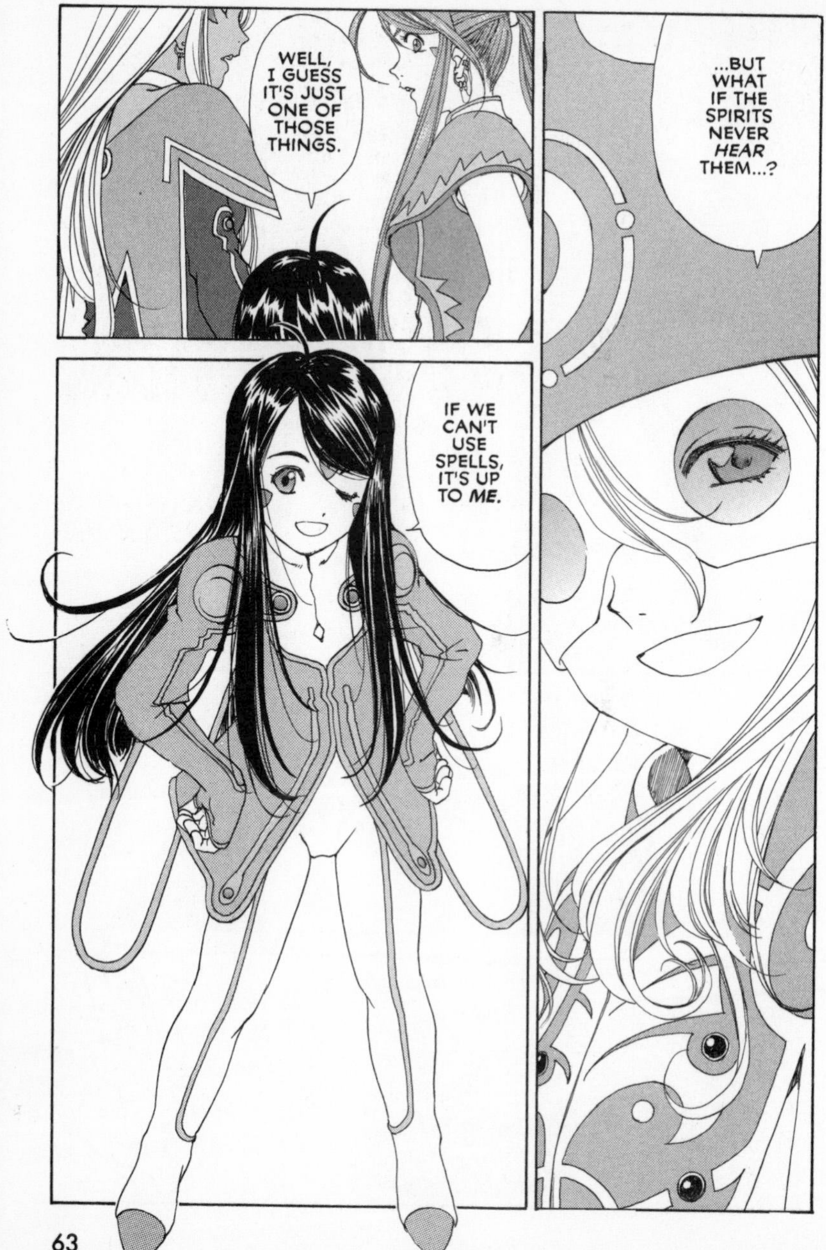
...BUT WHAT IF THE SPIRITS NEVER *HEAR* THEM...?
WELL, I GUESS IT'S JUST ONE OF THOSE THINGS.
IF WE CAN'T USE SPELLS, IT'S UP TO *ME*.

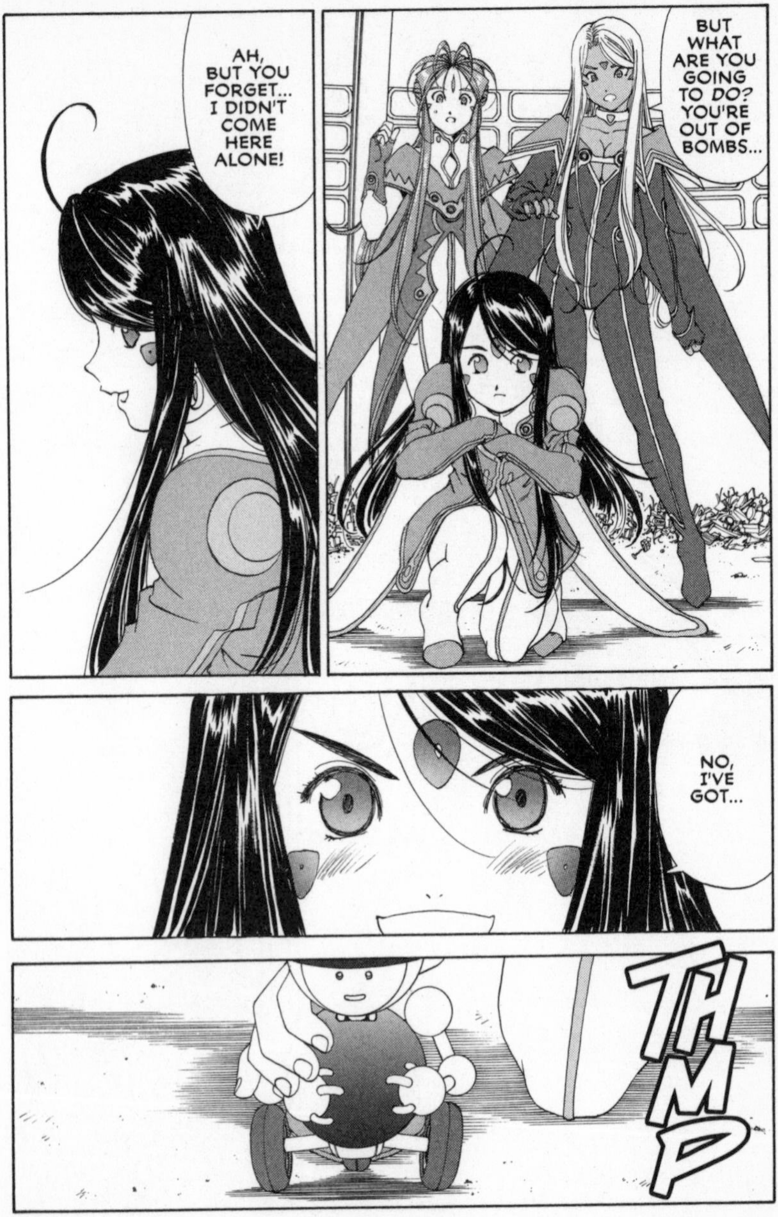
BUT WHAT ARE YOU GOING TO *DO?* YOU'RE OUT OF BOMBS...
AH, BUT YOU FORGET... I DIDN'T COME HERE ALONE!
NO, I'VE GOT...
THMP

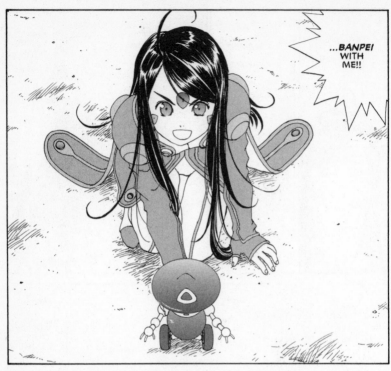

...BANPEI WITH ME!!
...
pffftt EXCUSE ME...?
COULD YOU GET ANY MORE LAME ...?
WHAT'S SO LAME ABOUT BANPEI?

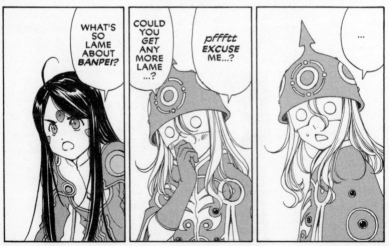

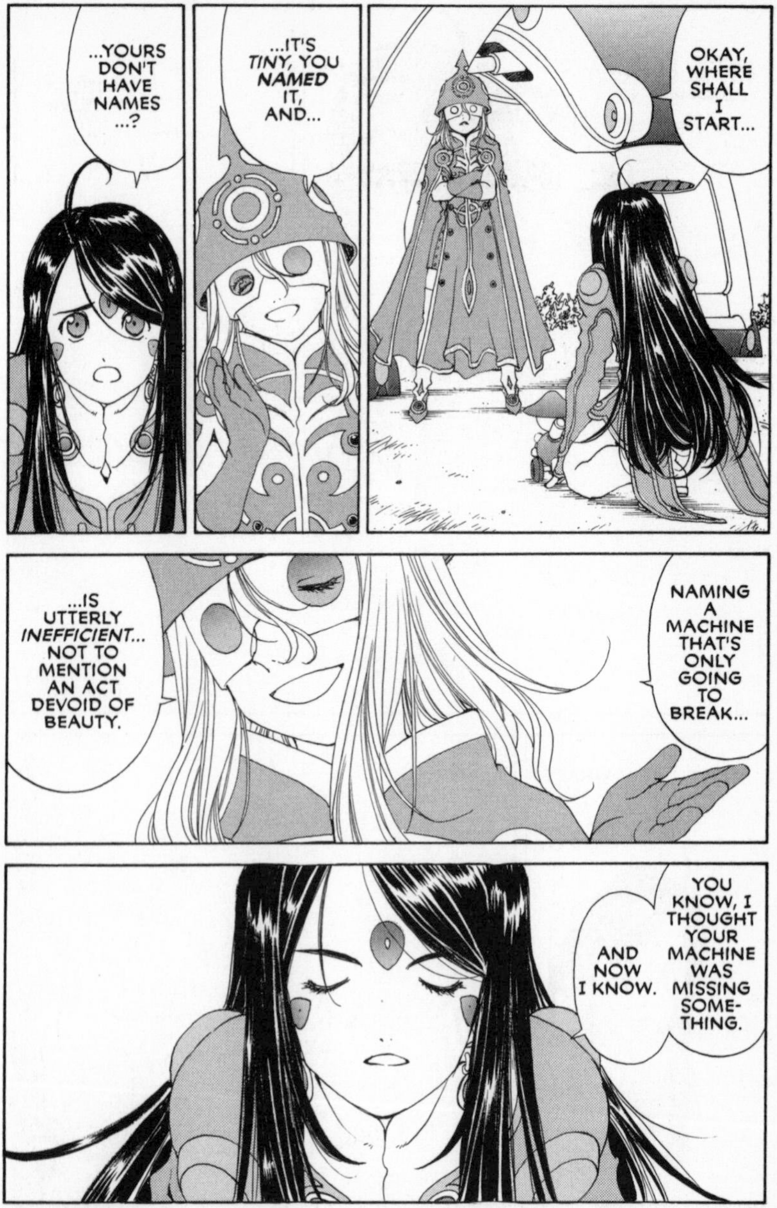
OKAY, WHERE SHALL I START...
...IT'S *TINY*, YOU **NAMED** IT, AND...
...YOURS DON'T HAVE NAMES ...?
NAMING A MACHINE THAT'S ONLY GOING TO BREAK...
...IS UTTERLY *INEFFICIENT*... NOT TO MENTION AN ACT DEVOID OF BEAUTY.
YOU KNOW, I THOUGHT YOUR MACHINE WAS MISSING SOME-THING.
AND NOW I KNOW.

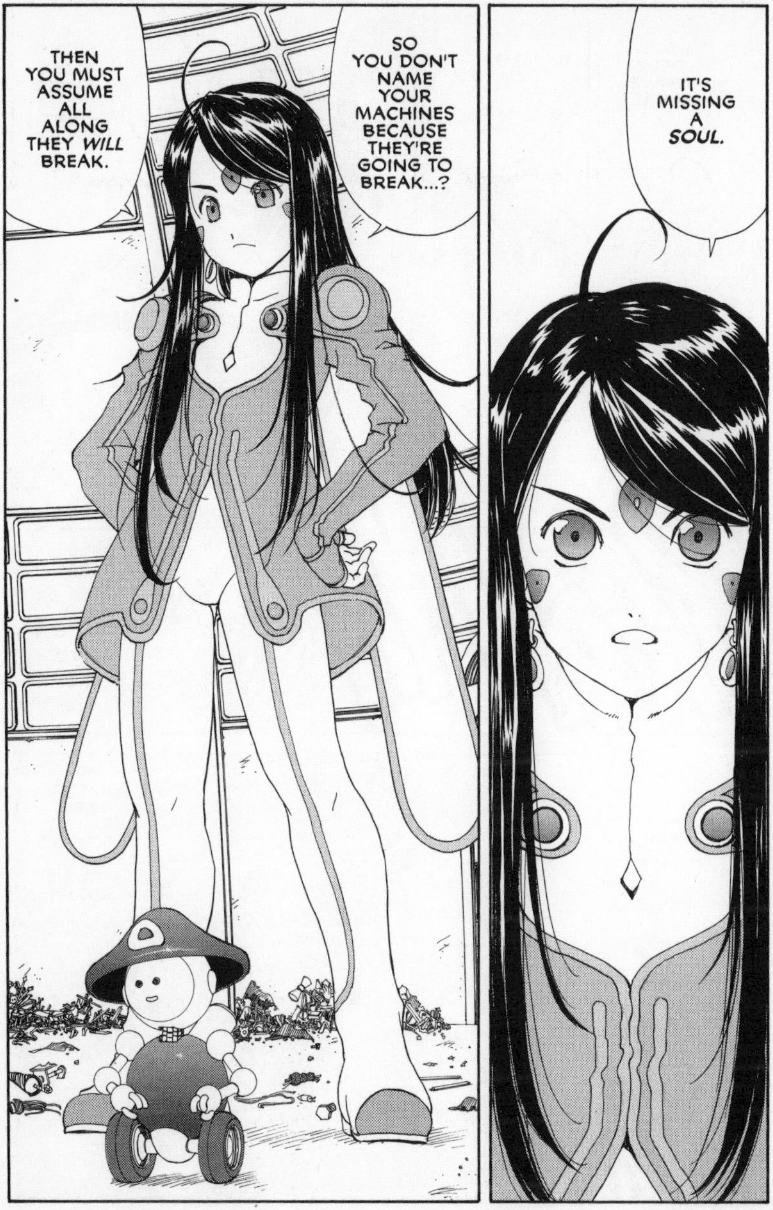
IT'S MISSING A *SOUL.*
SO YOU DON'T NAME YOUR MACHINES BECAUSE THEY'RE GOING TO BREAK...?
THEN YOU MUST ASSUME ALL ALONG THEY *WILL* BREAK.

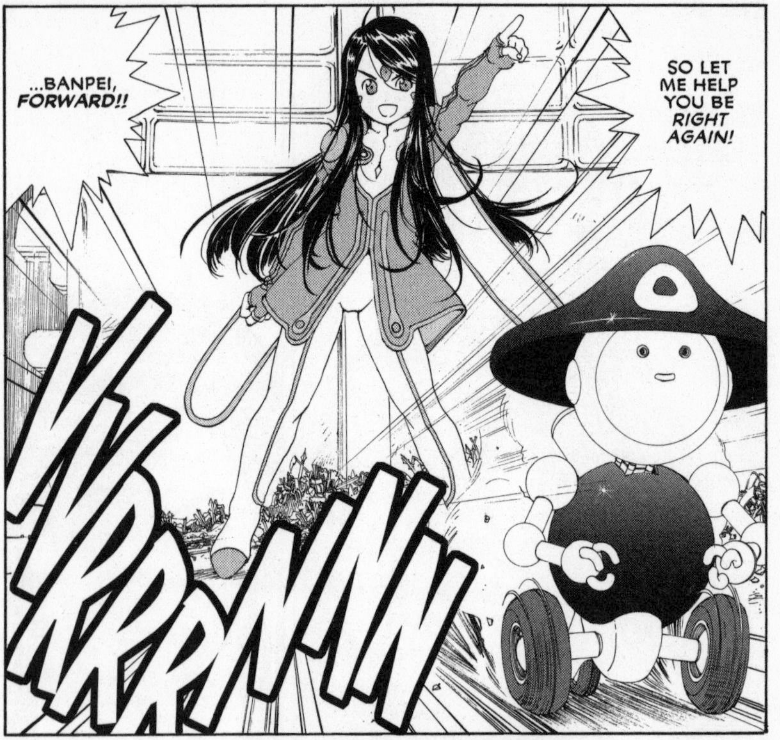
SO LET ME HELP YOU BE *RIGHT AGAIN!*
...BANPEI, *FORWARD!!*

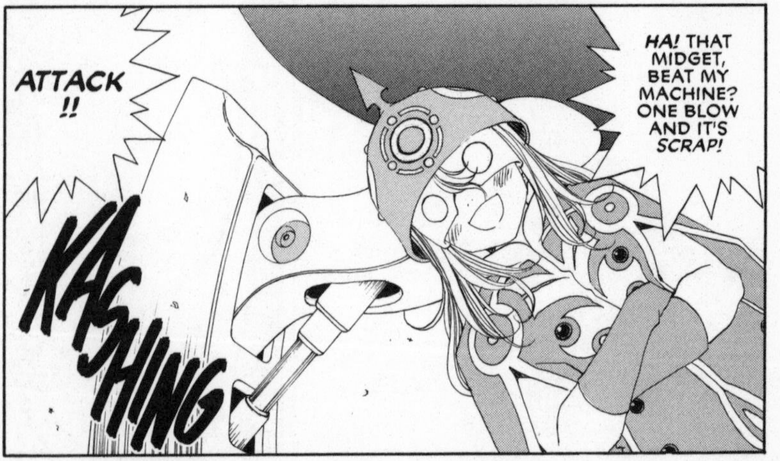
HA! THAT MIDGET, BEAT MY MACHINE? ONE BLOW AND IT'S *SCRAP!*
ATTACK !!
KASHING

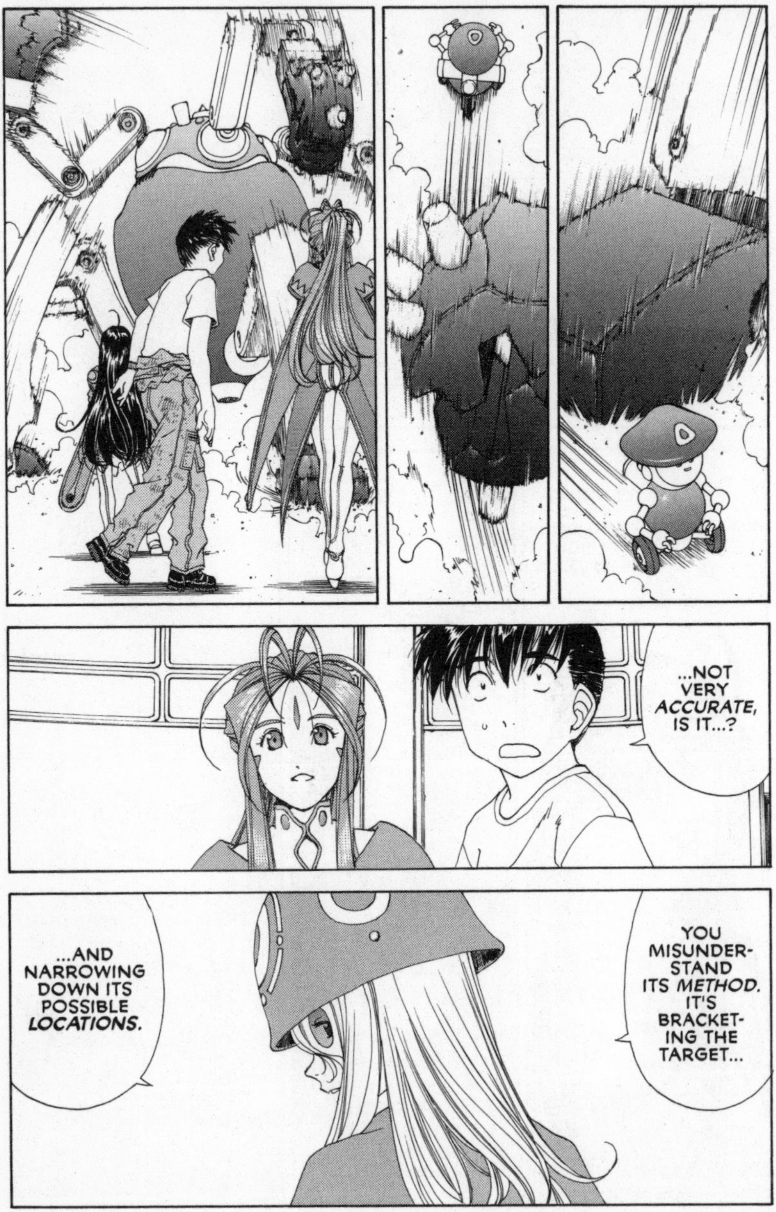
...NOT VERY ACCURATE, IS IT...?
YOU MISUNDERSTAND ITS METHOD. IT'S BRACKETING THE TARGET...
...AND NARROWING DOWN ITS POSSIBLE LOCATIONS.

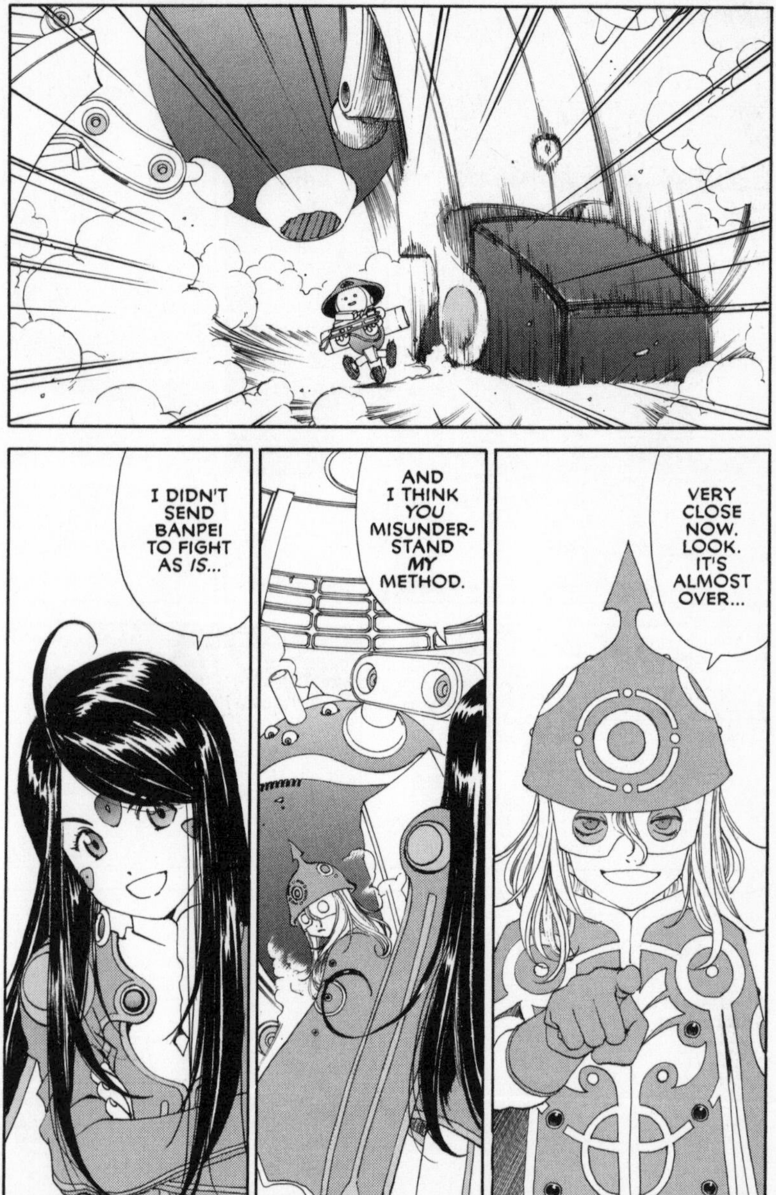
VERY CLOSE NOW. LOOK. IT'S ALMOST OVER...
AND I THINK *YOU* MISUNDER-STAND *MY* METHOD.
I DIDN'T SEND BANPEI TO FIGHT AS *IS*...

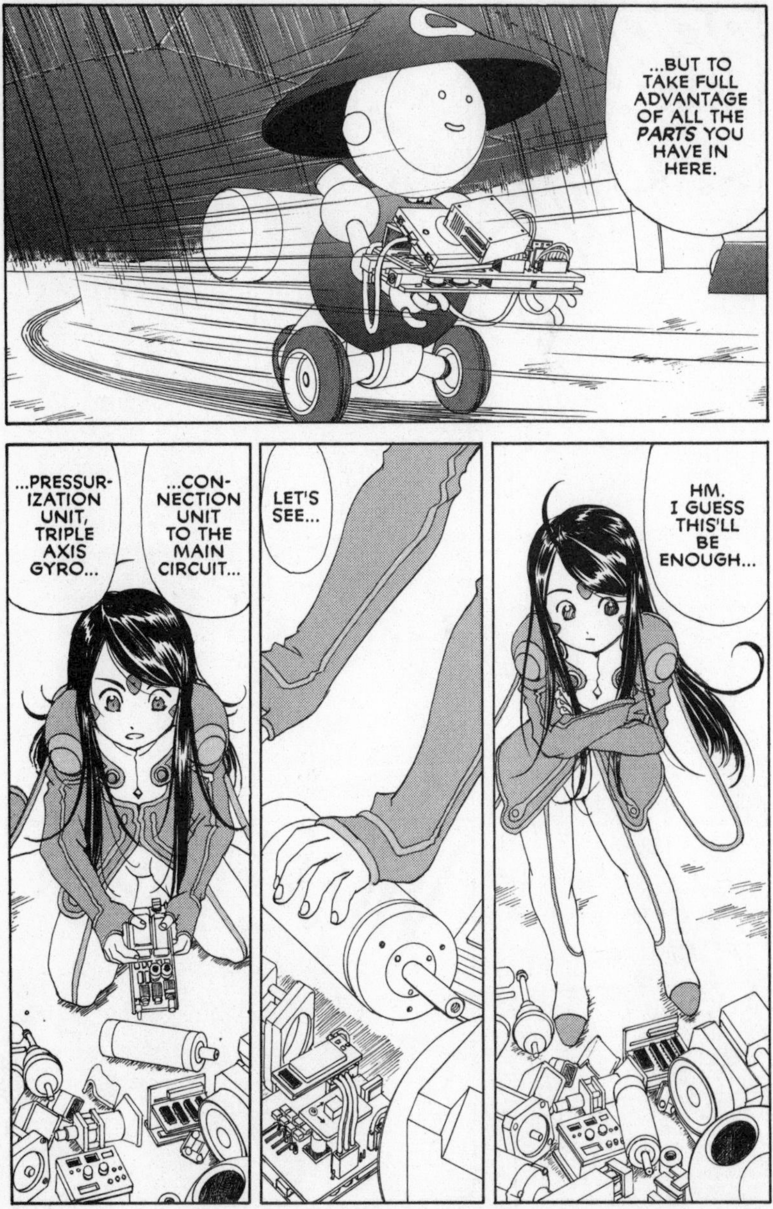
...BUT TO TAKE FULL ADVANTAGE OF ALL THE *PARTS* YOU HAVE IN HERE.
HM. I GUESS THIS'LL BE ENOUGH...
LET'S SEE...
...CONNECTION UNIT TO THE MAIN CIRCUIT...
...PRESSURIZATION UNIT, TRIPLE AXIS GYRO...

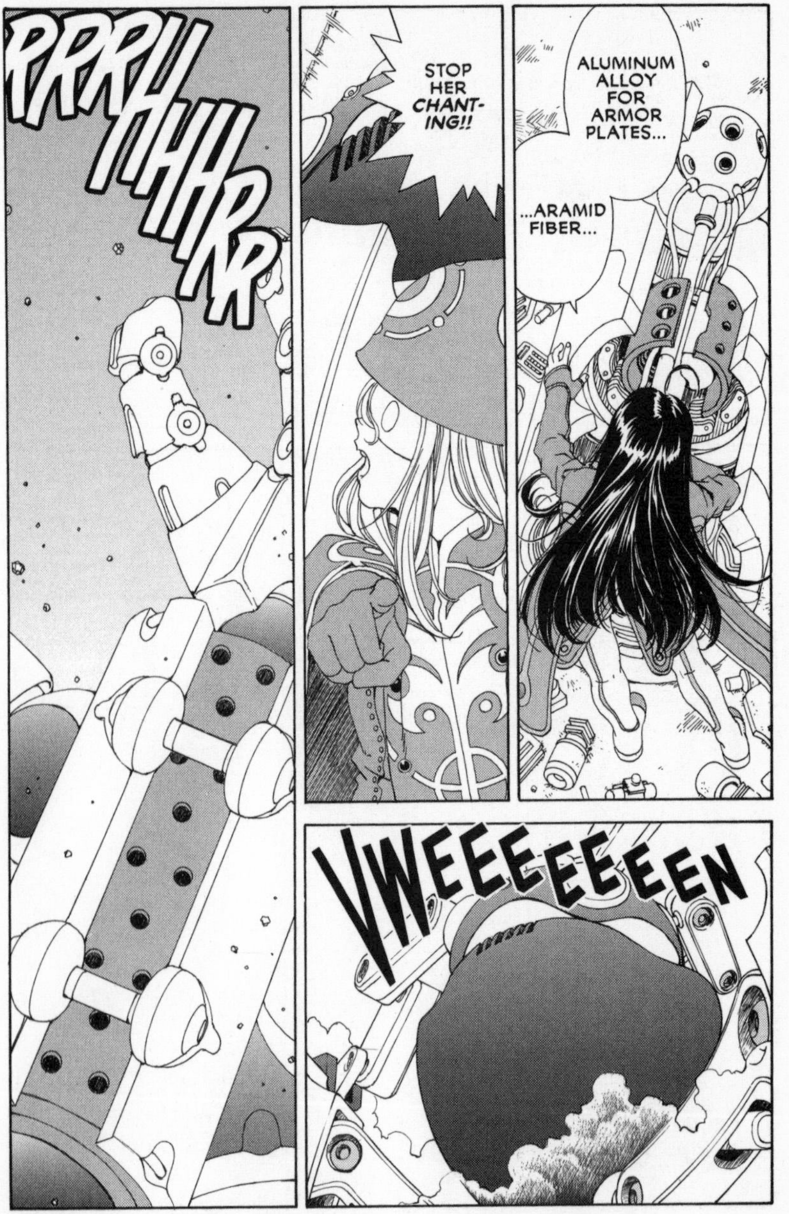
ALUMINUM ALLOY FOR ARMOR PLATES...
...ARAMID FIBER...
STOP HER CHANT-ING!!
VWEEEEEEEN
RRRUHHRR

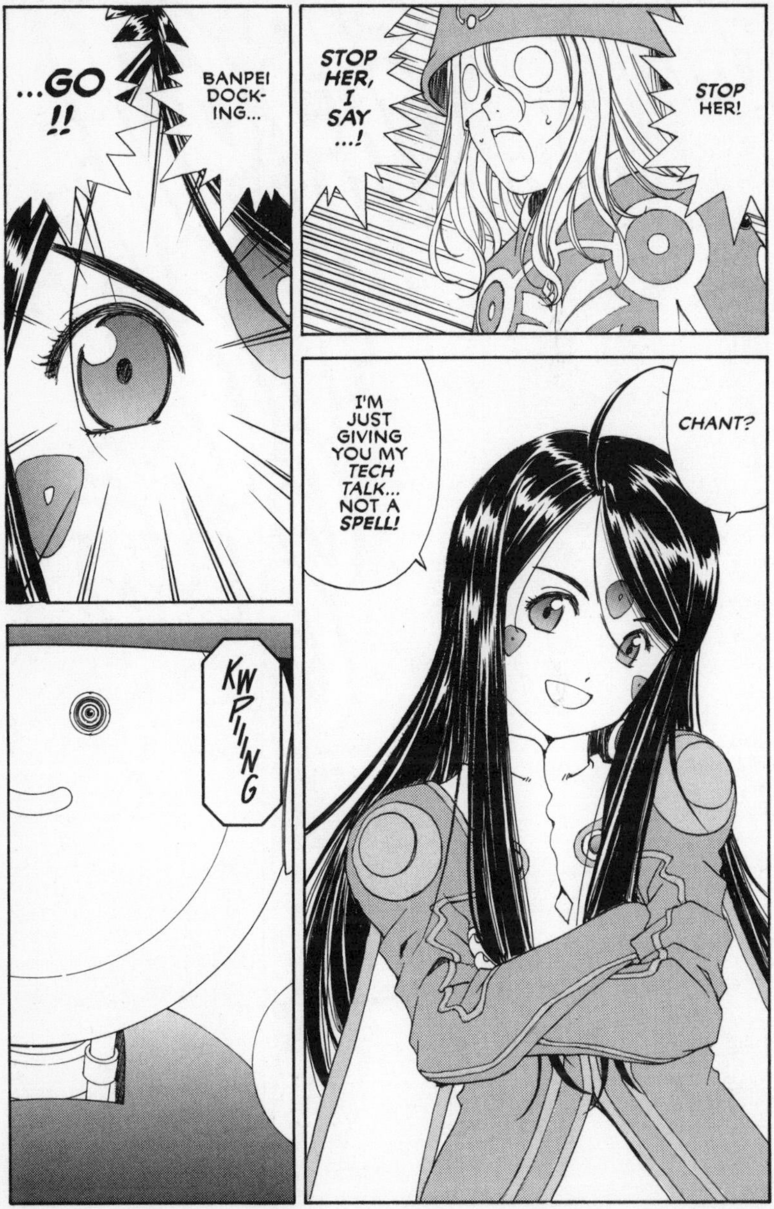
STOP HER!
STOP HER, I SAY ...!
BANPEI DOCKING...
...GO !!
CHANT?
I'M JUST GIVING YOU MY TECH TALK... NOT A SPELL!
KWPIIING

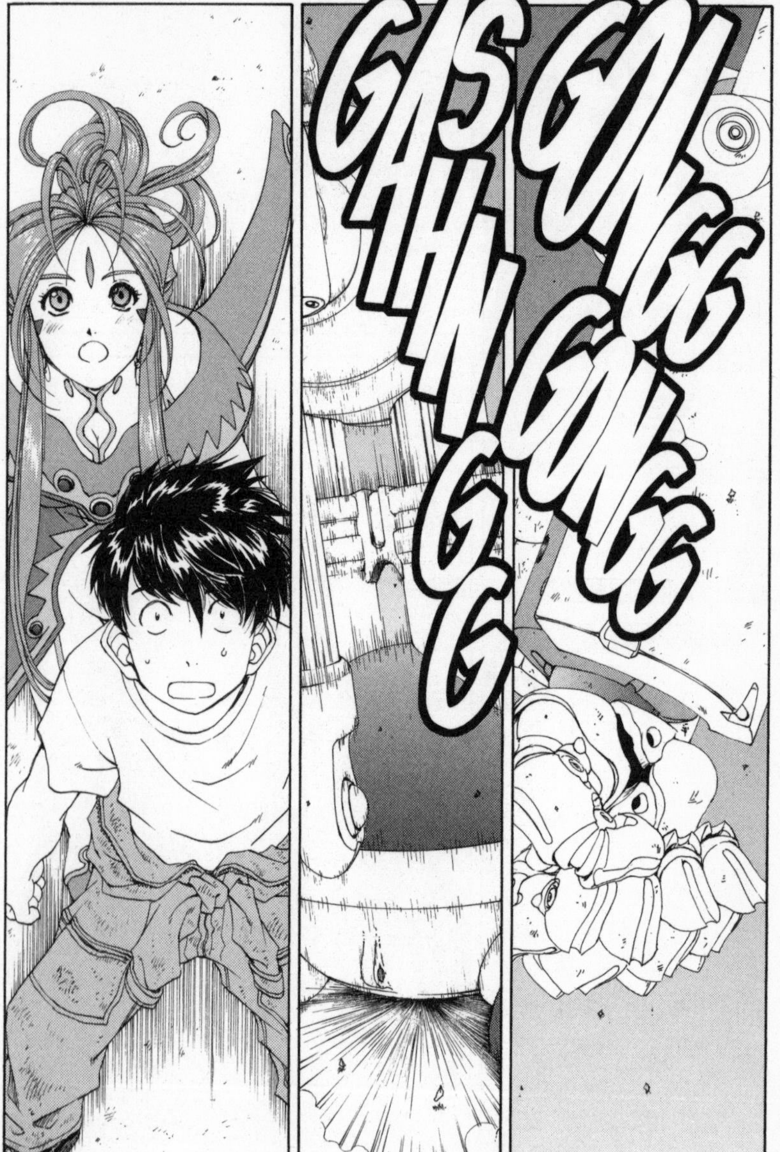
GASAHNGG
GONGG GONGG

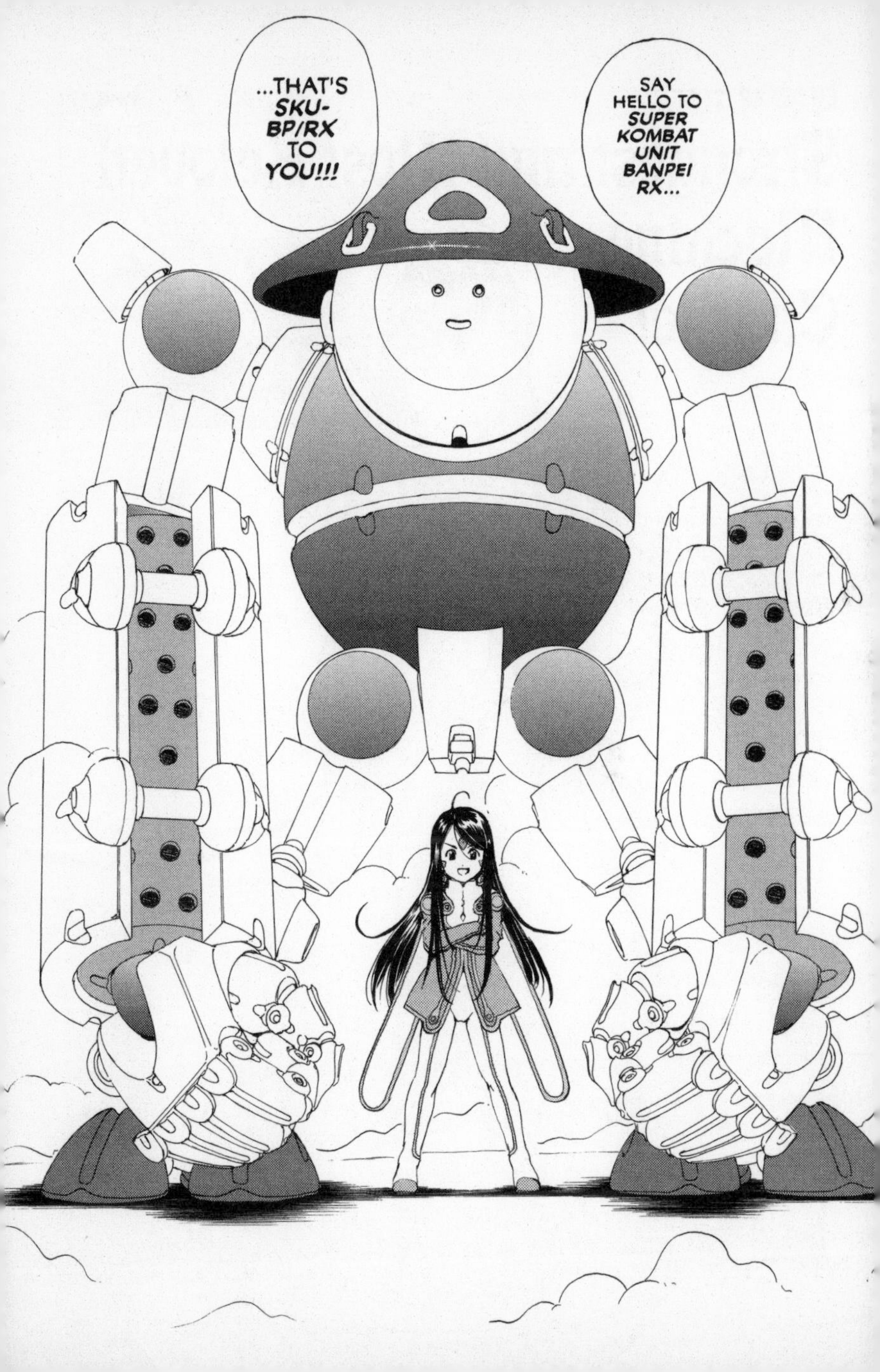
SAY HELLO TO SUPER KOMBAT UNIT BANPEI RX...
...THAT'S SKU-BP/RX TO YOU!!!

CHAPTER 265

Strongest and Most Beloved Machine, Charge!

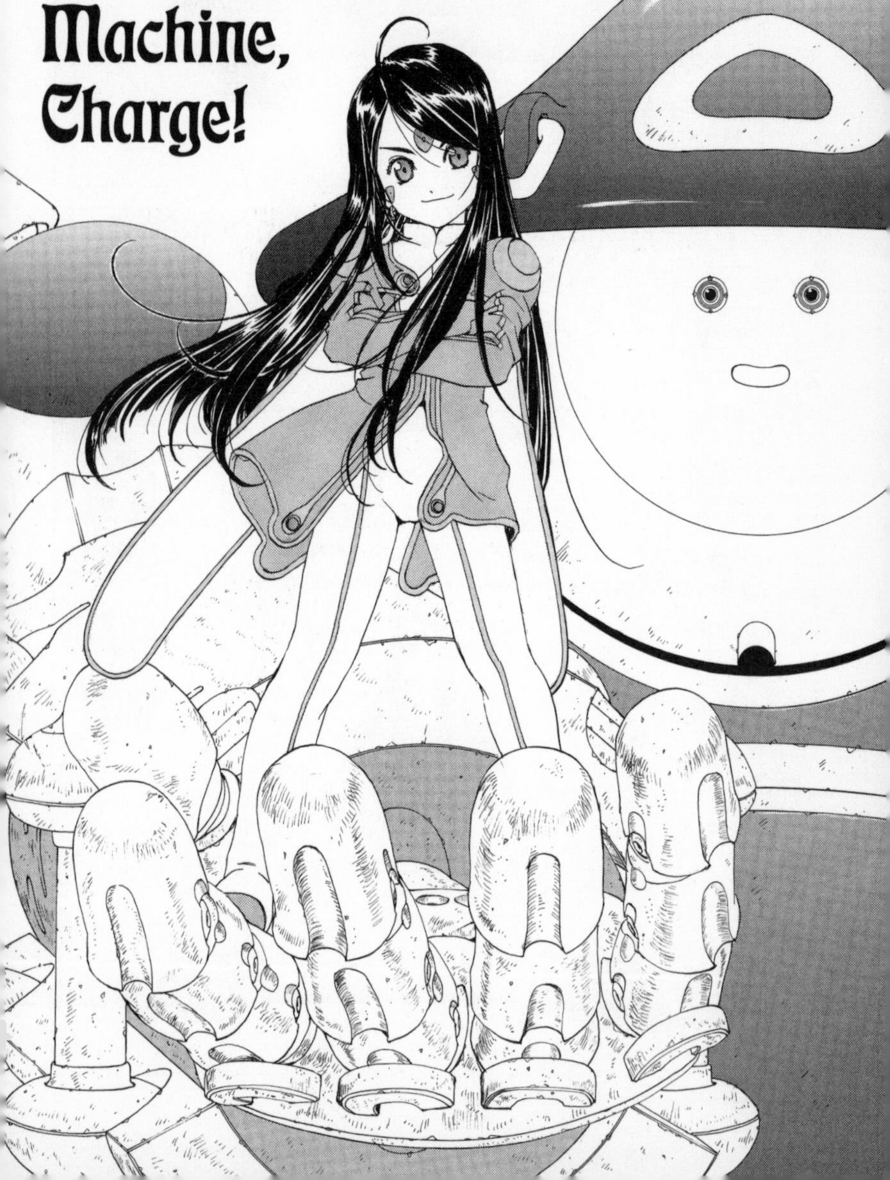

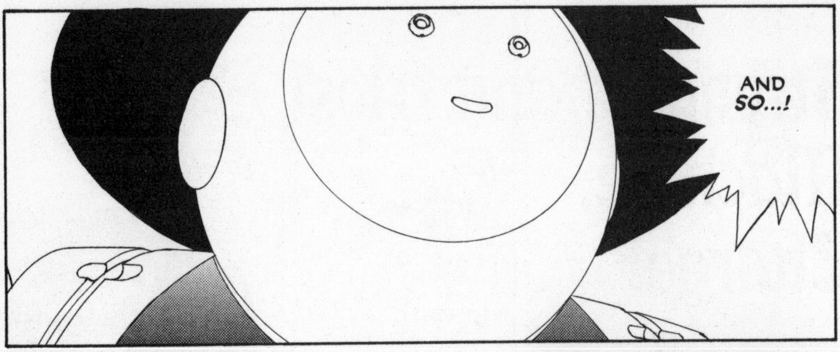
AND *SO*...!

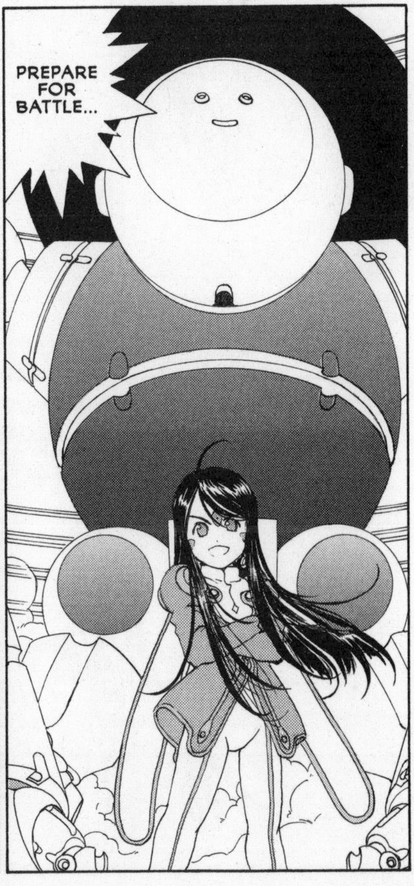
PREPARE FOR BATTLE...

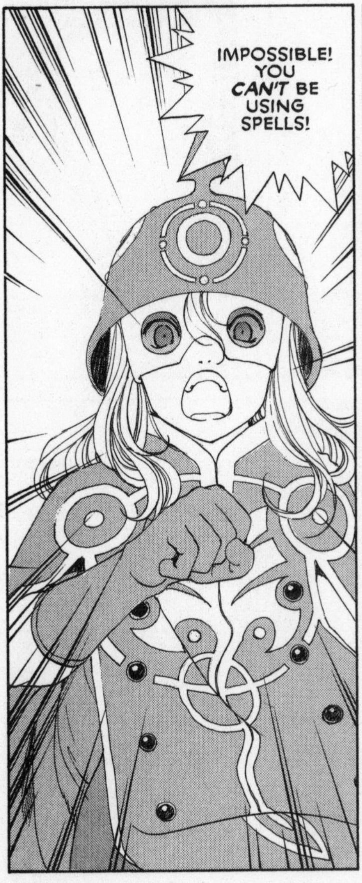
IMPOSSIBLE! YOU *CAN'T* BE USING SPELLS!

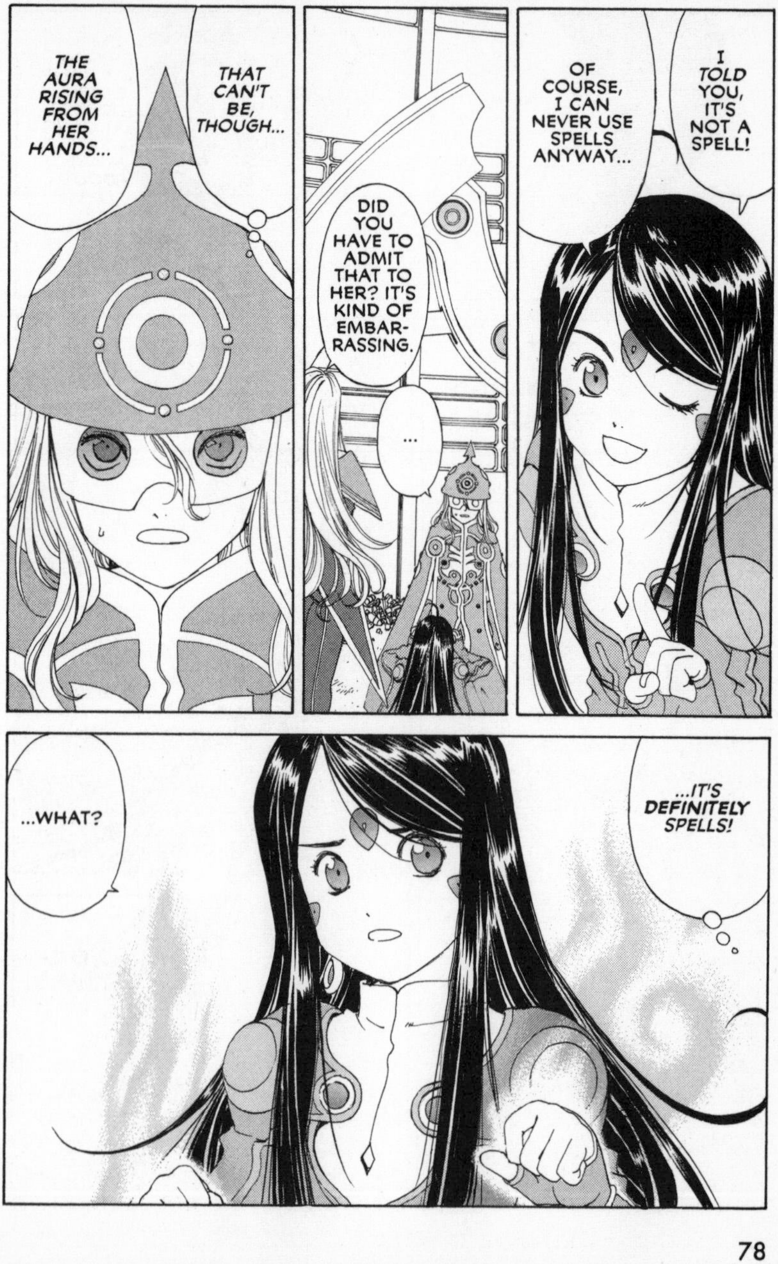
I TOLD YOU, IT'S NOT A SPELL!
OF COURSE, I CAN NEVER USE SPELLS ANYWAY...
DID YOU HAVE TO ADMIT THAT TO HER? IT'S KIND OF EMBAR-RASSING.
...
THAT CAN'T BE, THOUGH...
THE AURA RISING FROM HER HANDS...
...IT'S DEFINITELY SPELLS!
...WHAT?

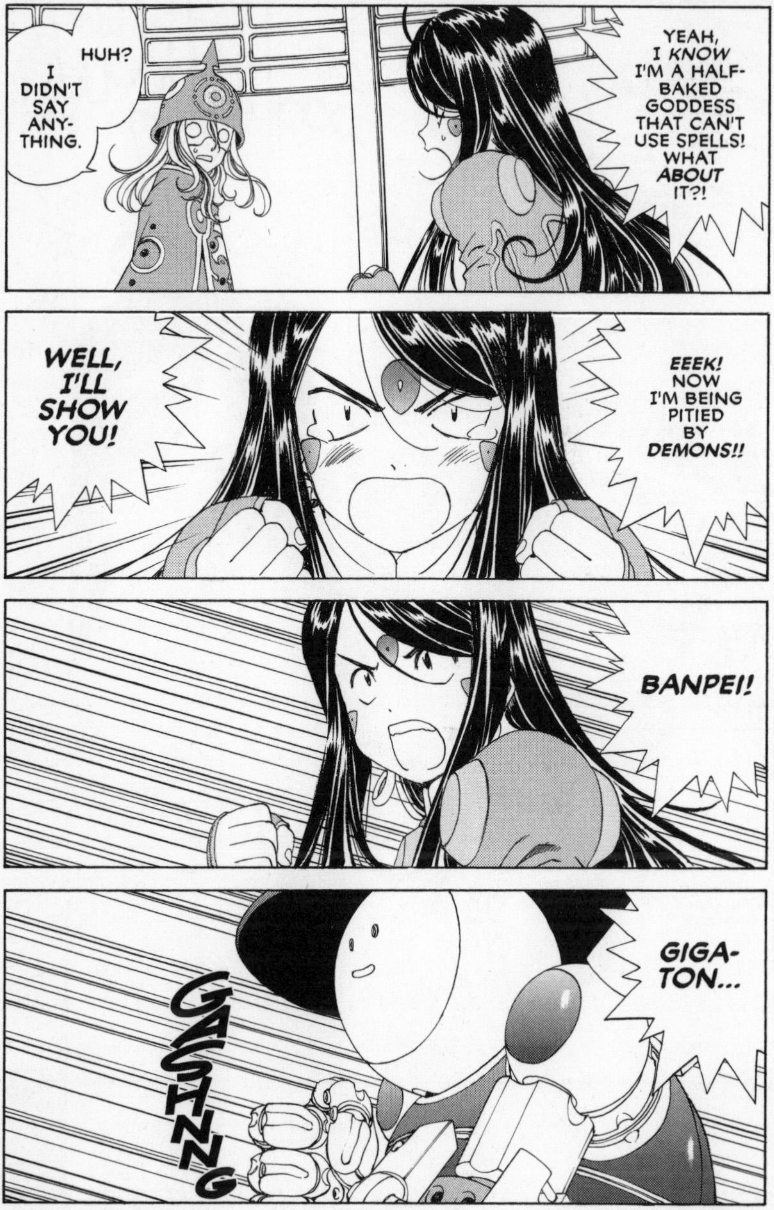
YEAH, I KNOW I'M A HALF-BAKED GODDESS THAT CAN'T USE SPELLS! WHAT ABOUT IT?!
HUH? I DIDN'T SAY ANY-THING.
EEEK! NOW I'M BEING PITIED BY DEMONS!!
WELL, I'LL SHOW YOU!
BANPEI!
GIGA-TON...
GASHNG

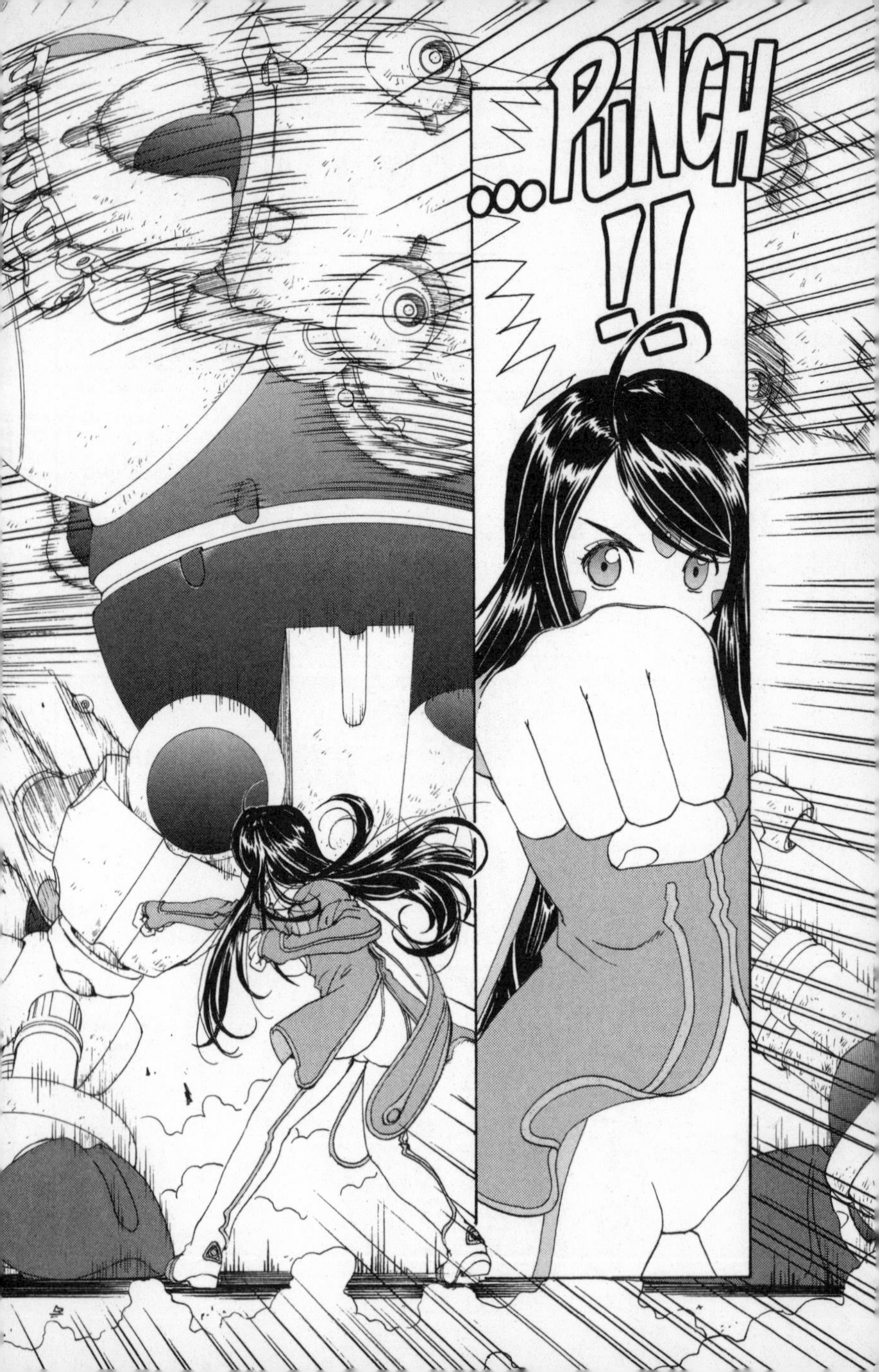
...PUNCH!!

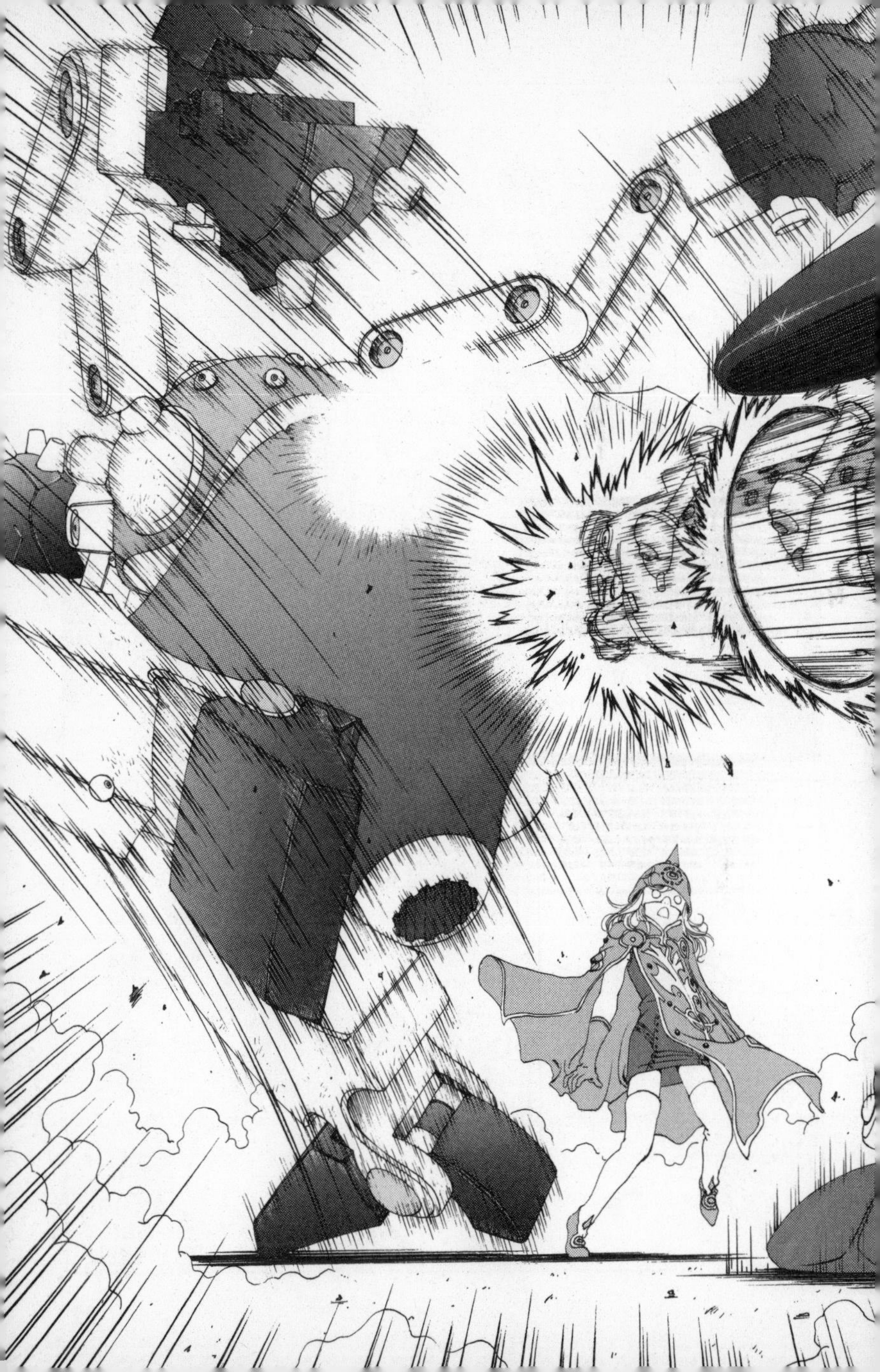

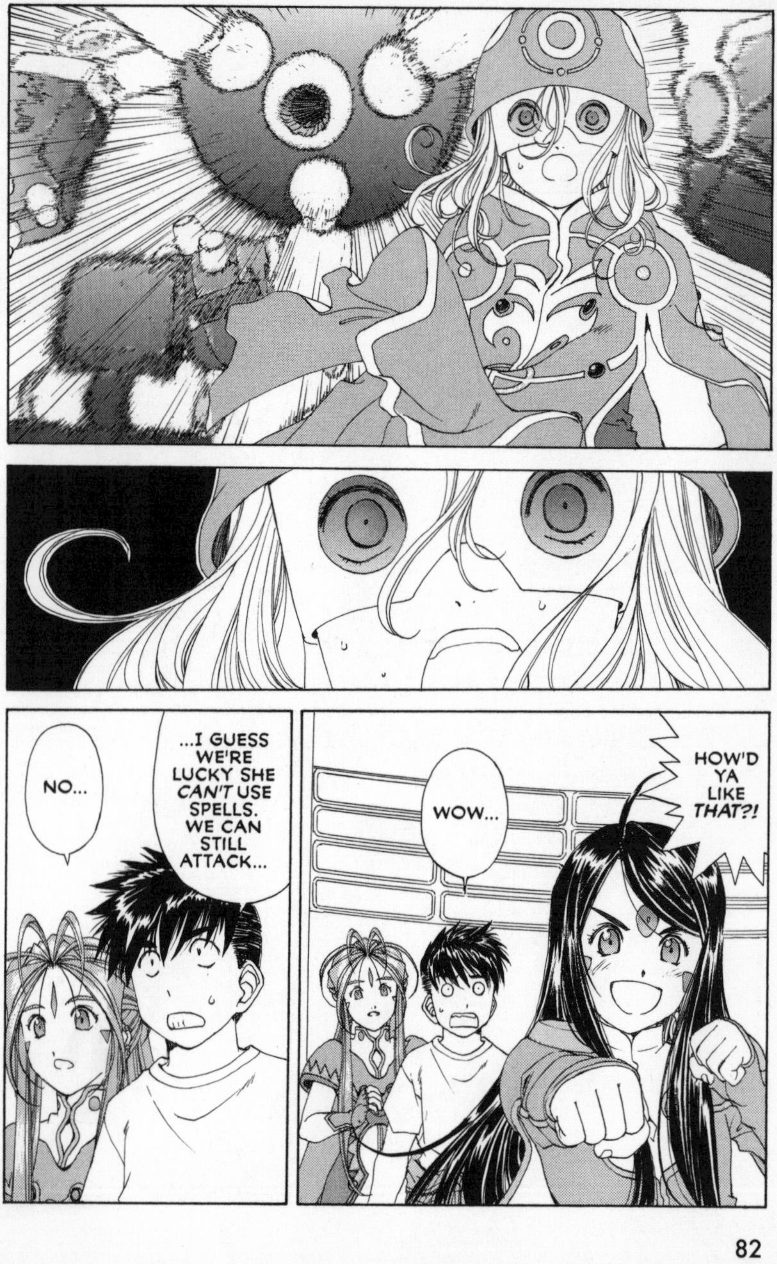
HOW'D YA LIKE *THAT?!*
WOW...
...I GUESS WE'RE LUCKY SHE *CAN'T* USE SPELLS. WE CAN STILL ATTACK...
NO...

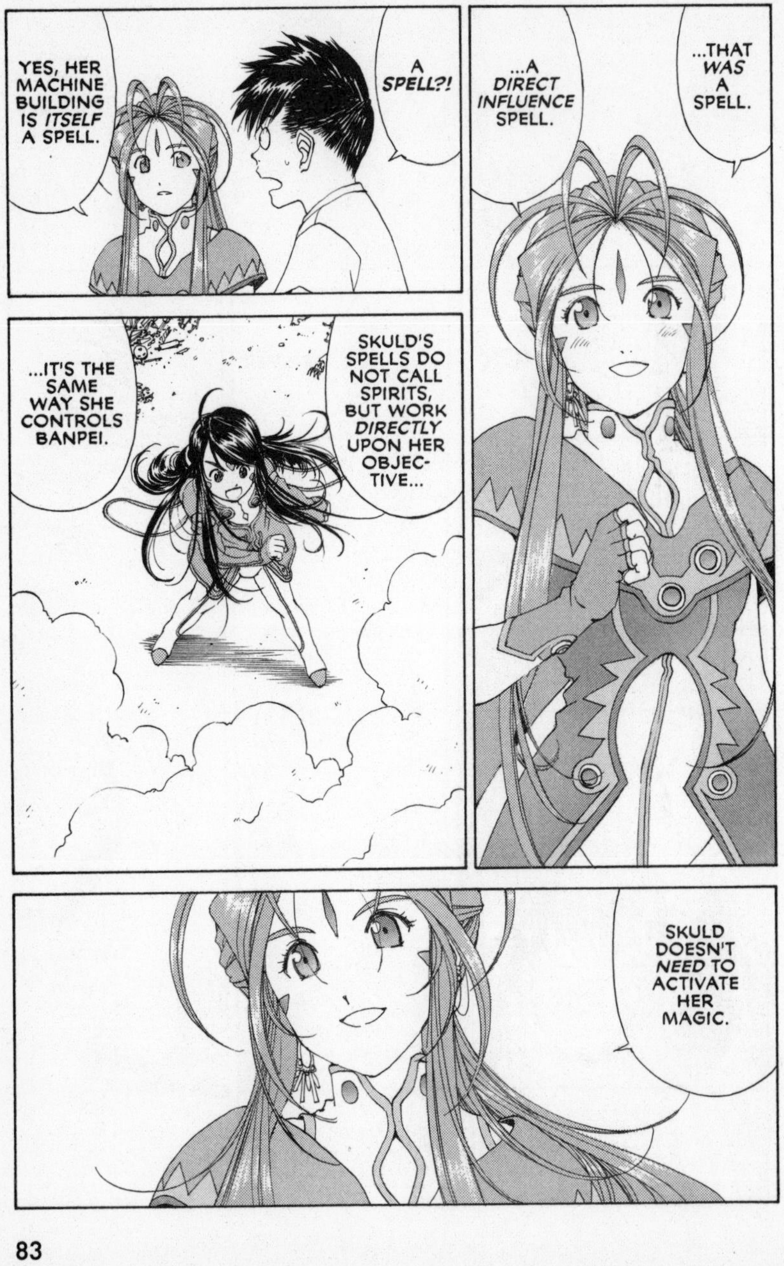
...THAT *WAS* A SPELL.
...A *DIRECT INFLUENCE* SPELL.
A *SPELL?!*
YES, HER MACHINE BUILDING IS *ITSELF* A SPELL.
SKULD'S SPELLS DO NOT CALL SPIRITS, BUT WORK *DIRECTLY* UPON HER OBJECTIVE...
...IT'S THE SAME WAY SHE CONTROLS BANPEI.
SKULD DOESN'T *NEED* TO ACTIVATE HER MAGIC.

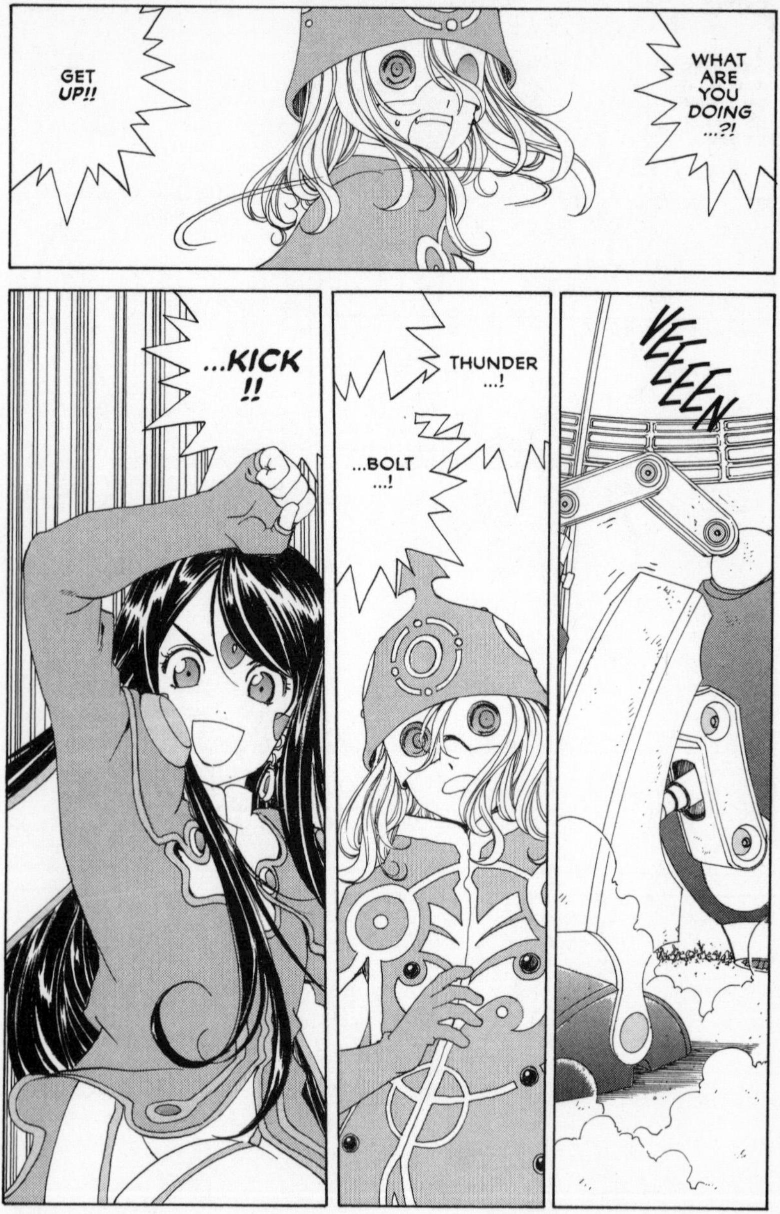
WHAT ARE YOU DOING ...?!
GET UP!!
VEEEEN
THUNDER ...!
...BOLT ...!
...KICK !!

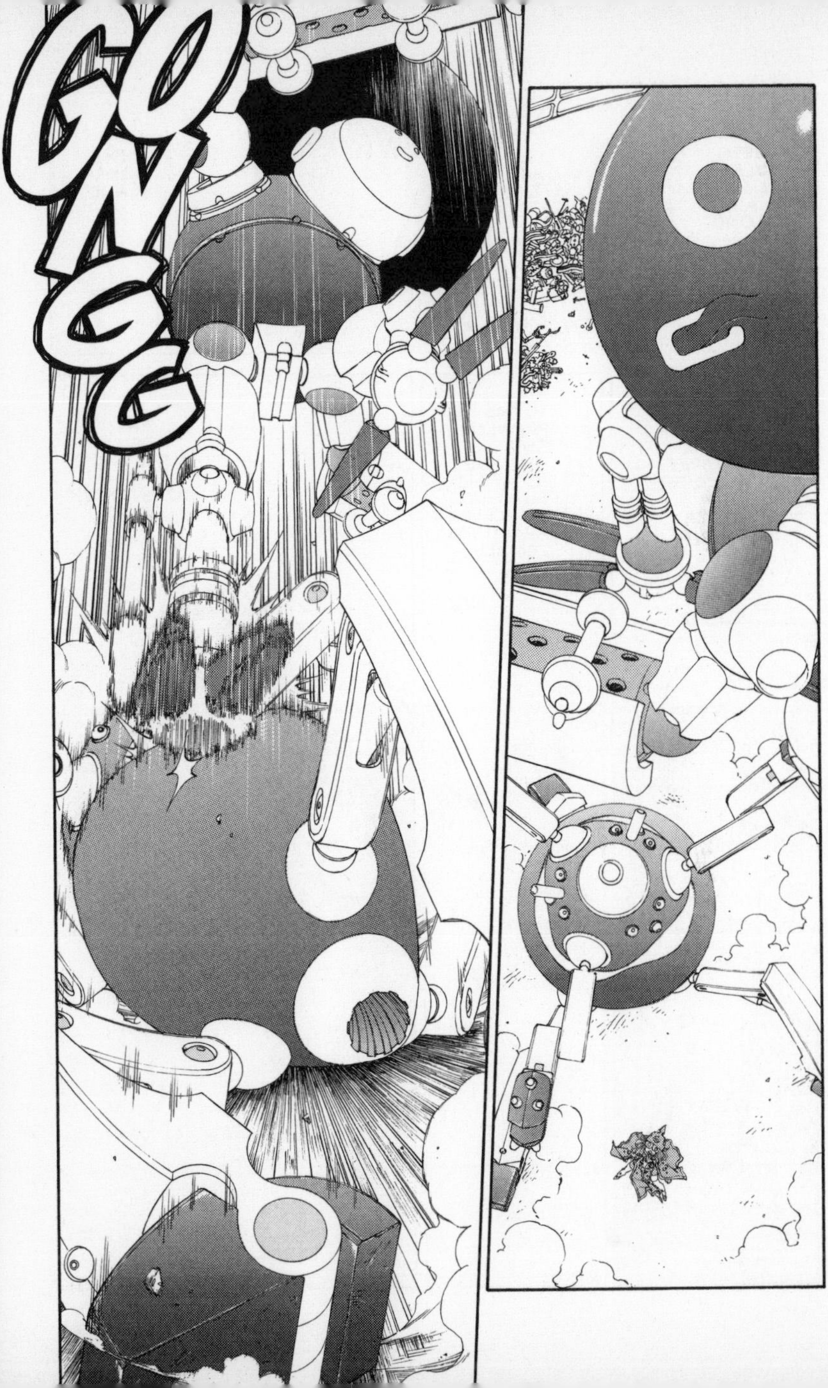
GONGG

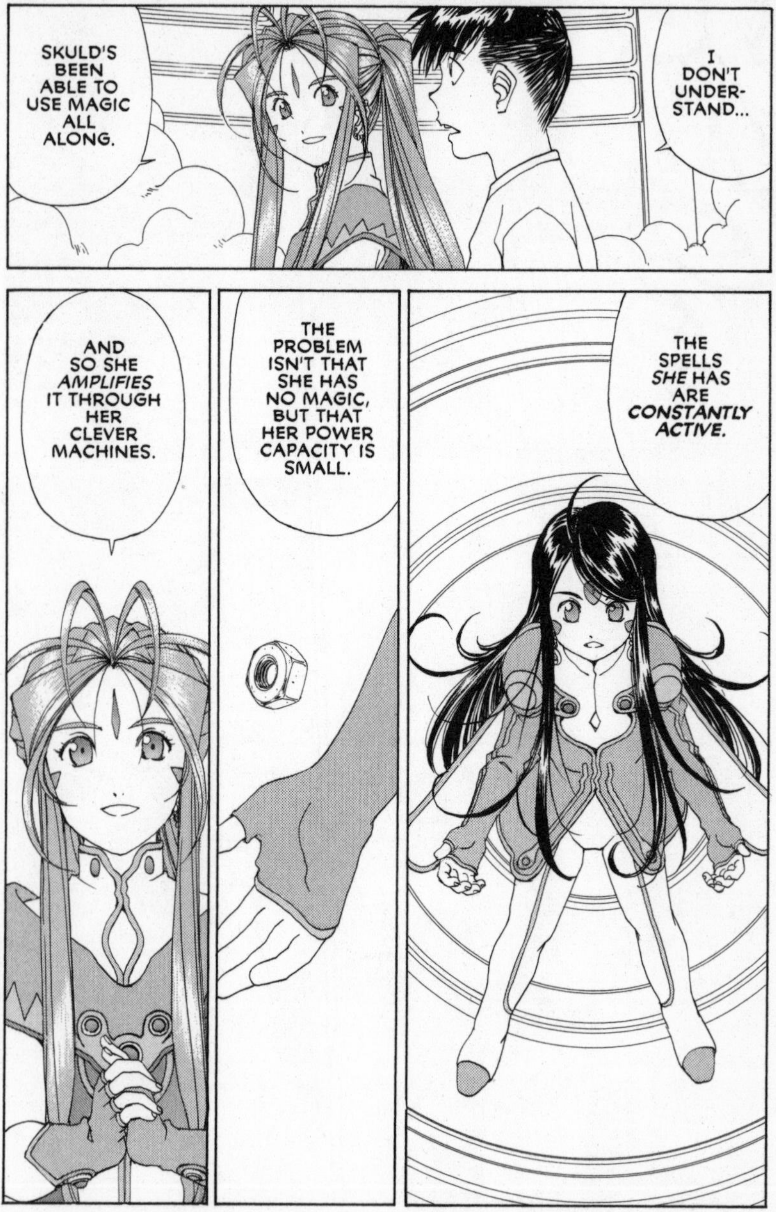
I DON'T UNDERSTAND...
SKULD'S BEEN ABLE TO USE MAGIC ALL ALONG.
THE SPELLS *SHE* HAS ARE *CONSTANTLY ACTIVE.*
THE PROBLEM ISN'T THAT SHE HAS NO MAGIC, BUT THAT HER POWER CAPACITY IS SMALL.
AND SO SHE *AMPLIFIES* IT THROUGH HER CLEVER MACHINES.

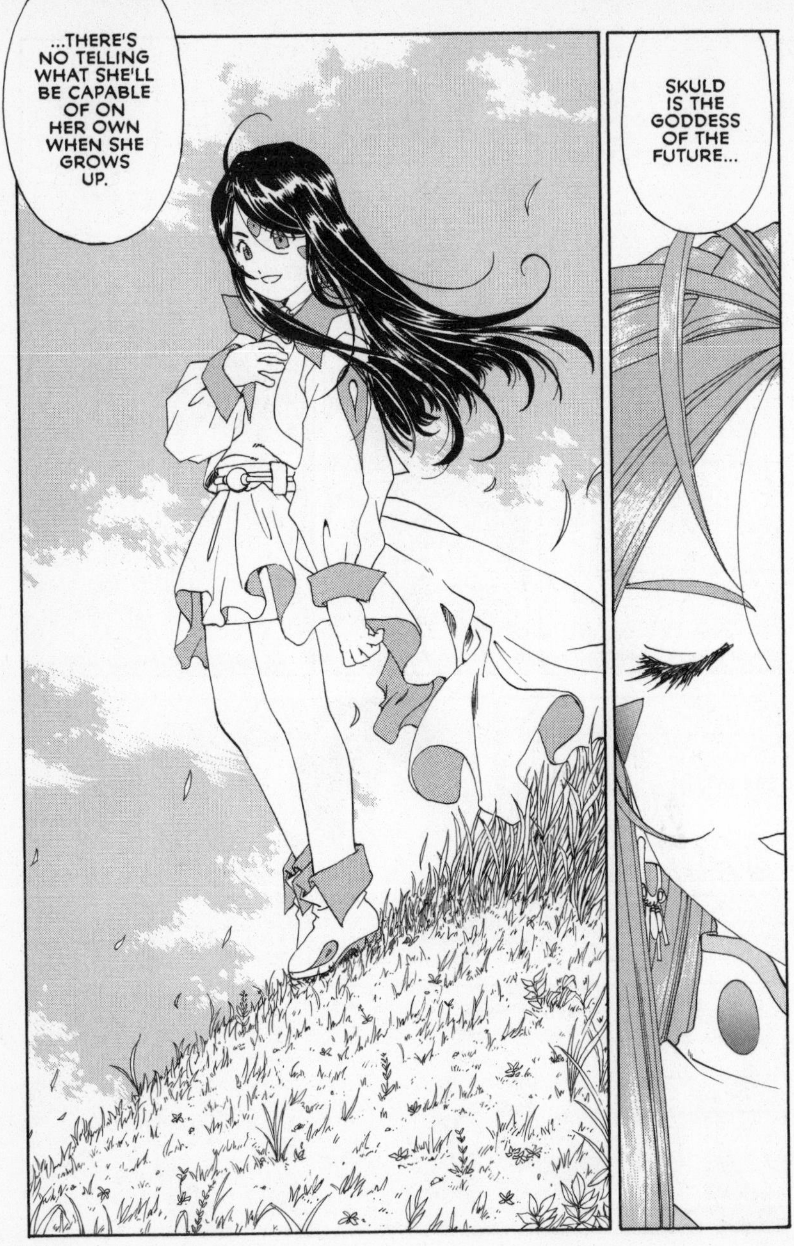
SKULD IS THE GODDESS OF THE FUTURE...
...THERE'S NO TELLING WHAT SHE'LL BE CAPABLE OF ON HER OWN WHEN SHE GROWS UP.

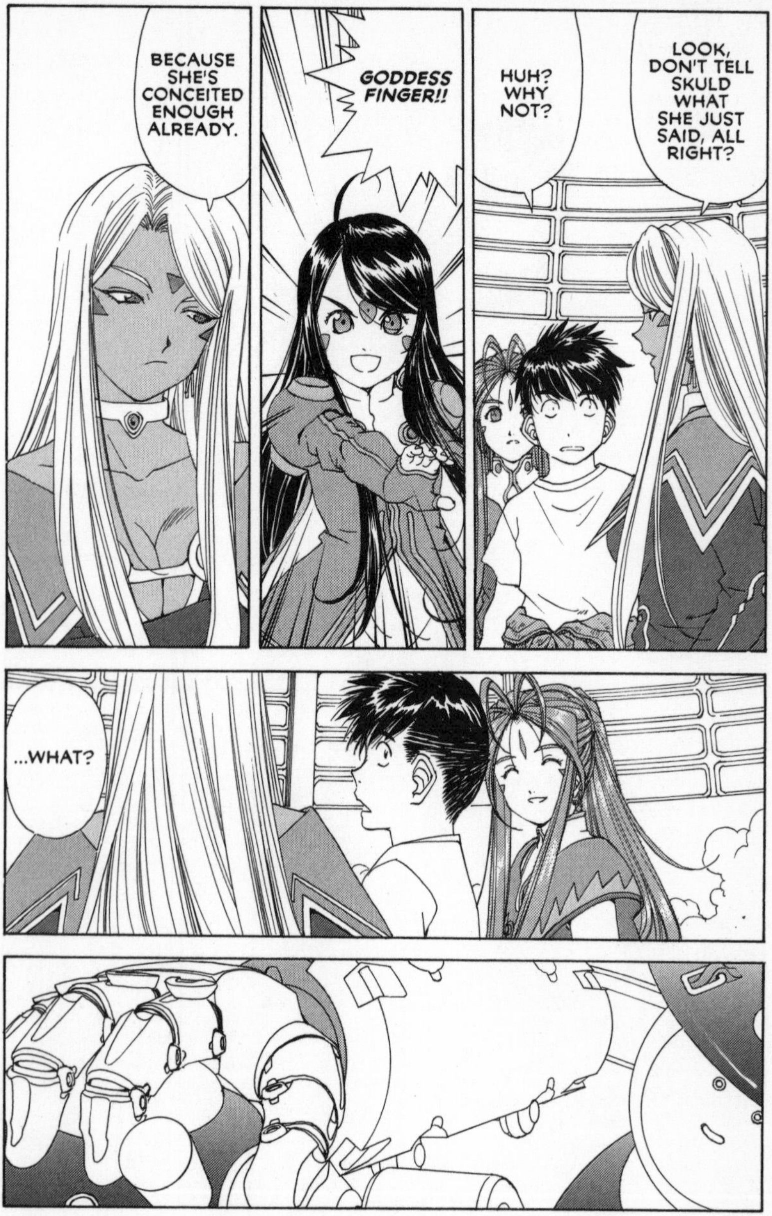
LOOK, DON'T TELL SKULD WHAT SHE JUST SAID, ALL RIGHT?
HUH? WHY NOT?
GODDESS FINGER!!
BECAUSE SHE'S CONCEITED ENOUGH ALREADY.
...WHAT?

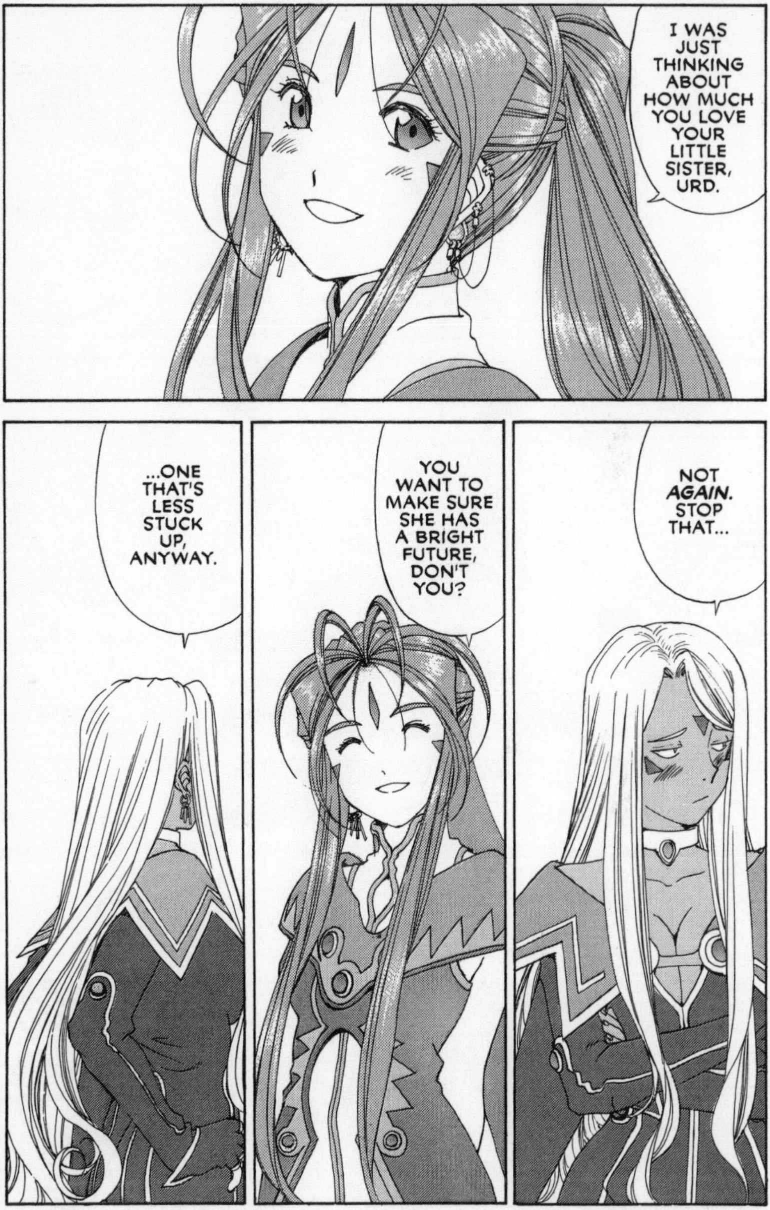
I WAS JUST THINKING ABOUT HOW MUCH YOU LOVE YOUR LITTLE SISTER, URD.
NOT *AGAIN.* STOP THAT...
YOU WANT TO MAKE SURE SHE HAS A BRIGHT FUTURE, DON'T YOU?
...ONE THAT'S LESS STUCK UP, ANYWAY.

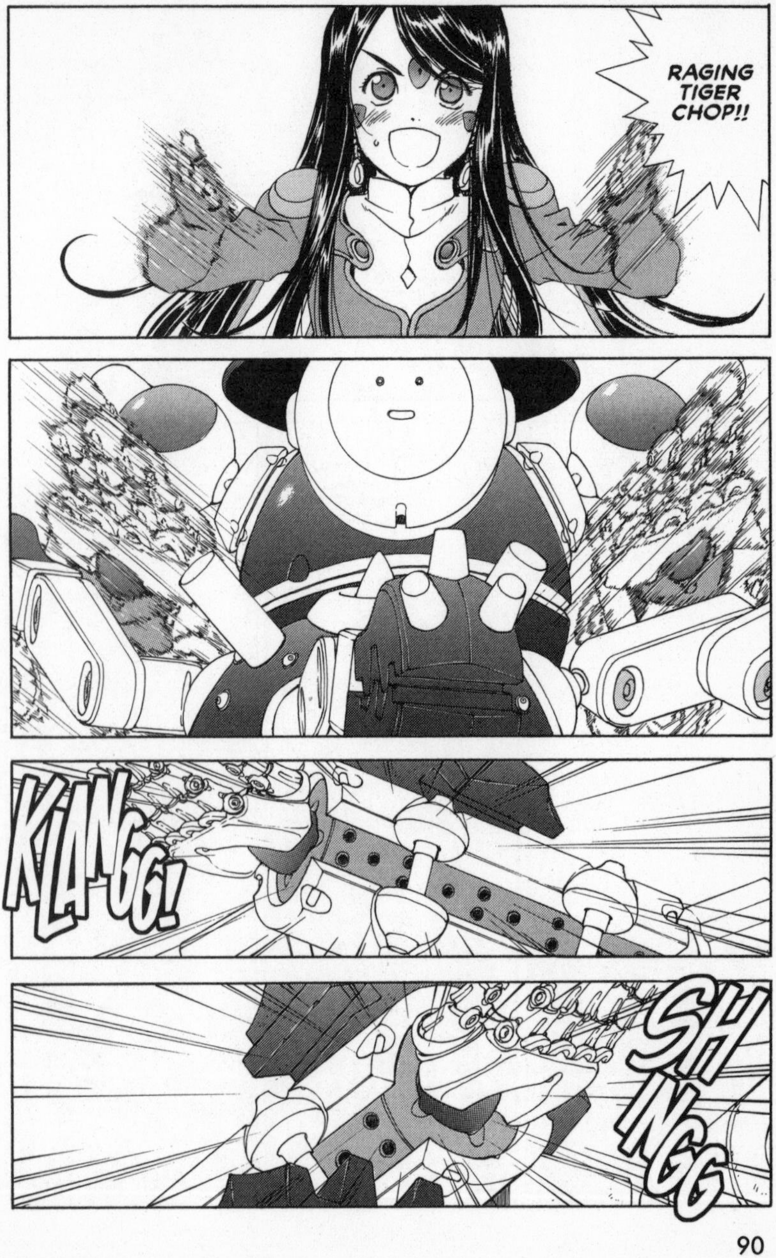
RAGING TIGER CHOP!!
KLANGG!
SHINGG

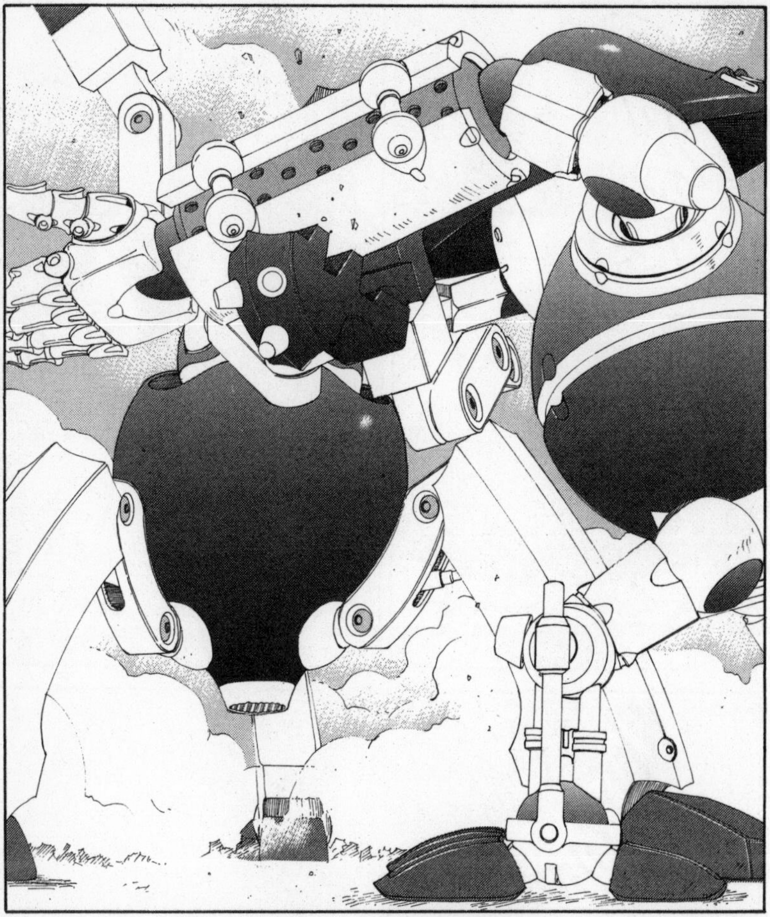

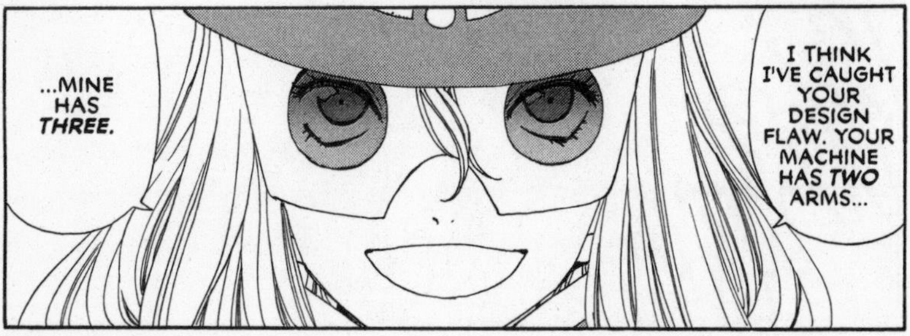
I THINK I'VE CAUGHT YOUR DESIGN FLAW. YOUR MACHINE HAS *TWO* ARMS...
...MINE HAS *THREE.*

...ONE FREE.

WHICH MEANS I'VE STILL GOT...

UM...!

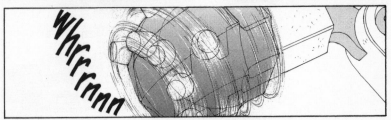

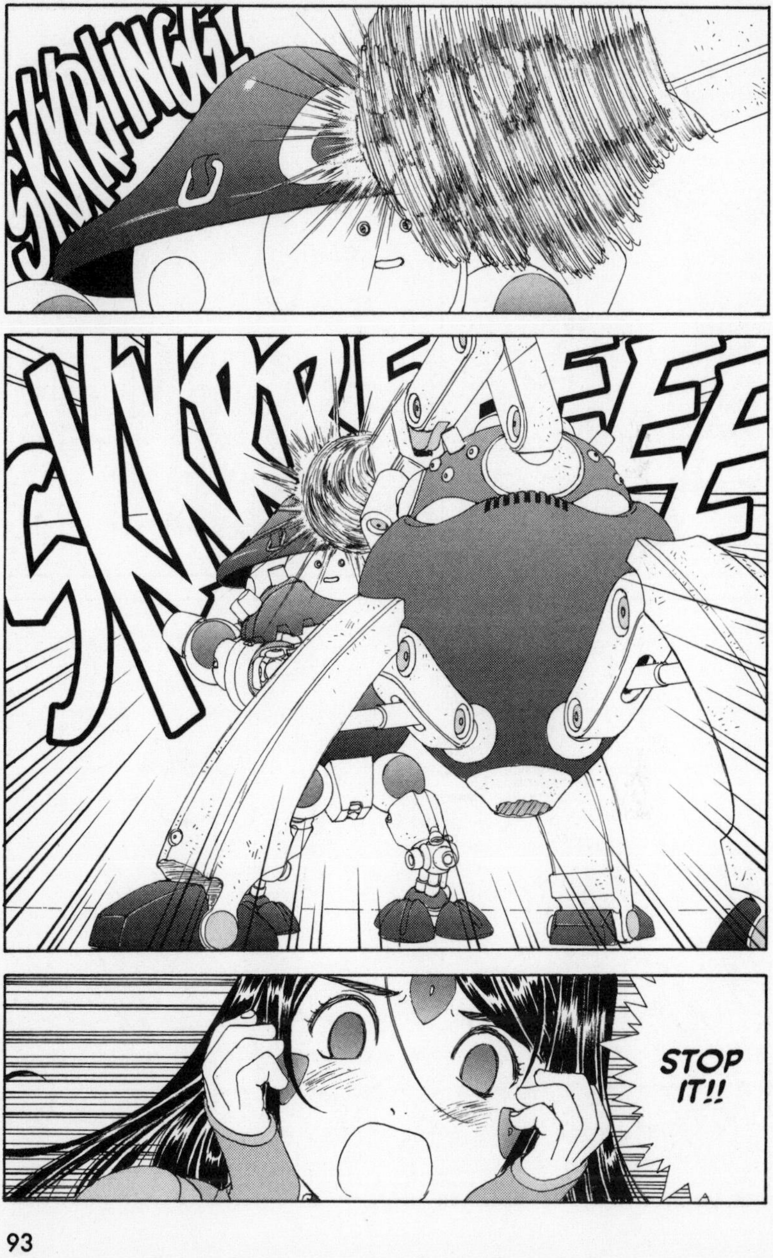
SKRIINGG!
SKRREEEE
STOP IT!!

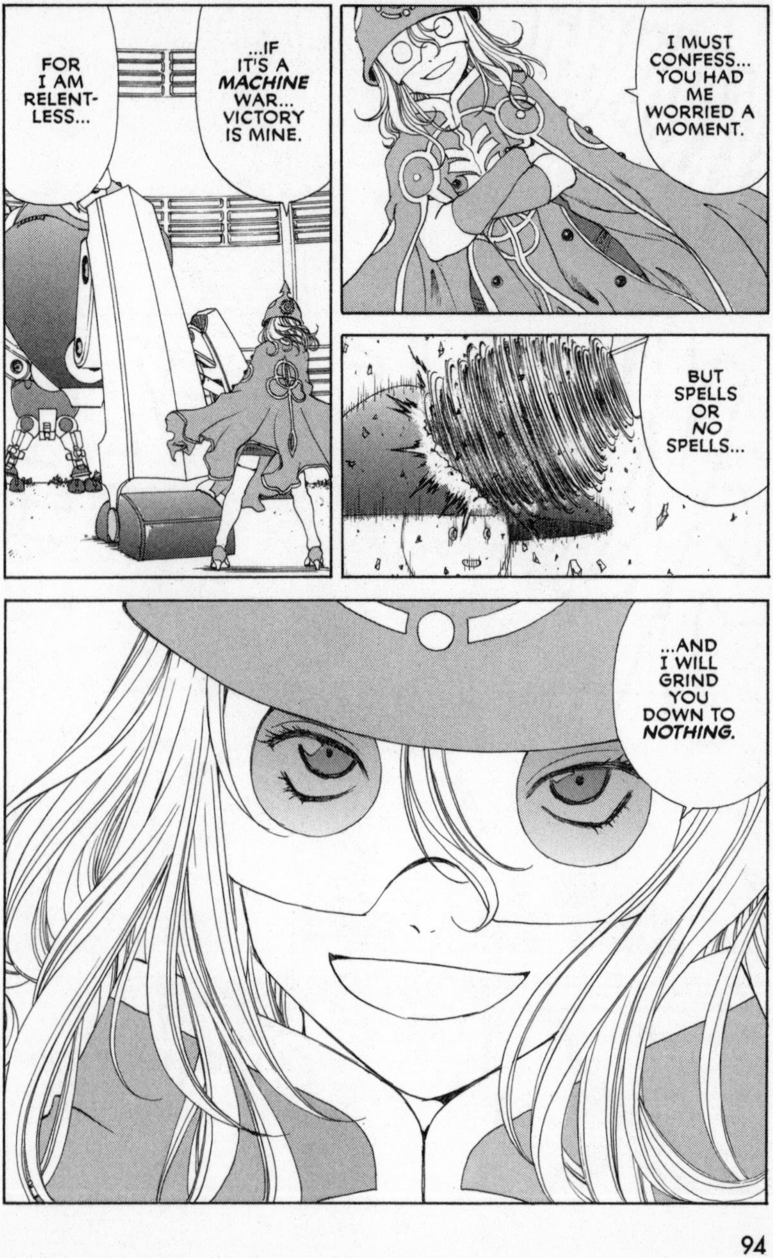
I MUST CONFESS... YOU HAD ME WORRIED A MOMENT.
BUT SPELLS OR *NO* SPELLS...
...IF IT'S A *MACHINE* WAR... VICTORY IS MINE.
FOR I AM RELENT-LESS...
...AND I WILL GRIND YOU DOWN TO *NOTHING*.

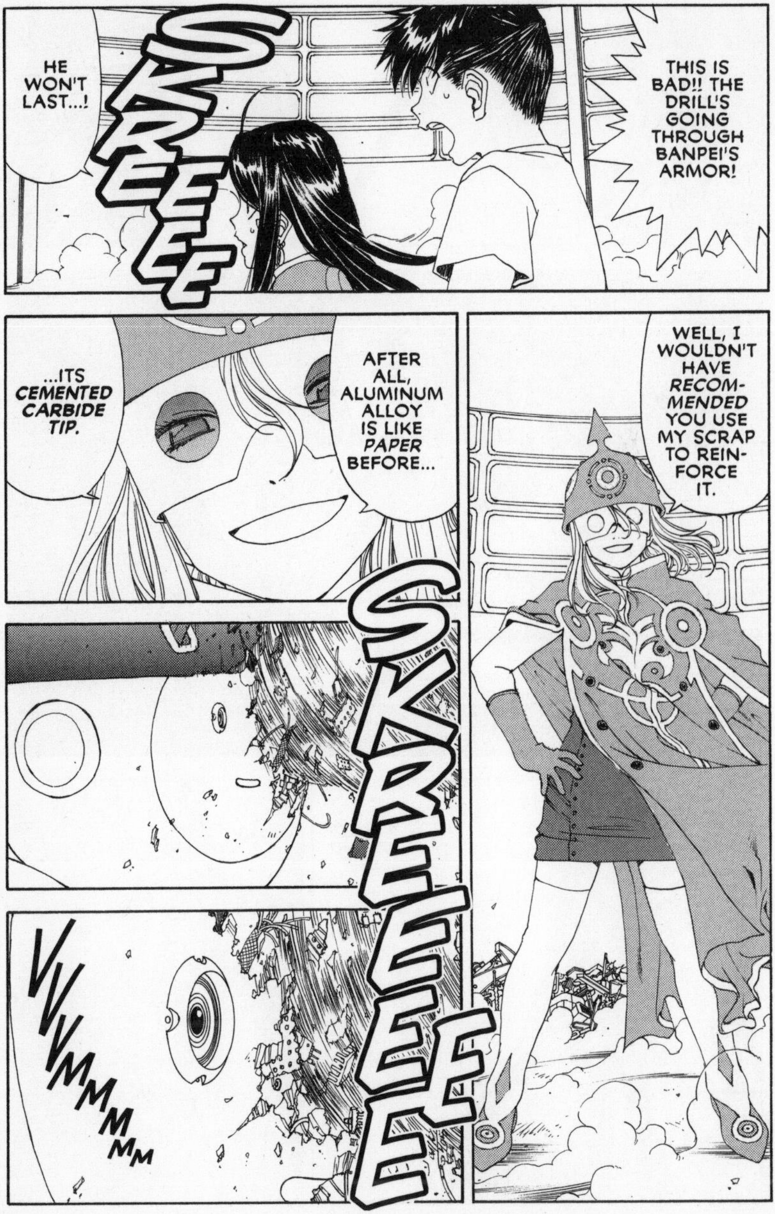
THIS IS BAD!! THE DRILL'S GOING THROUGH BANPEI'S ARMOR!
SKREEEE
HE WON'T LAST...!
WELL, I WOULDN'T HAVE *RECOMMENDED* YOU USE MY SCRAP TO REINFORCE IT.
AFTER ALL, ALUMINUM ALLOY IS LIKE *PAPER* BEFORE...
...ITS *CEMENTED CARBIDE* TIP.
SKREEEEEE
VVVMMMMM

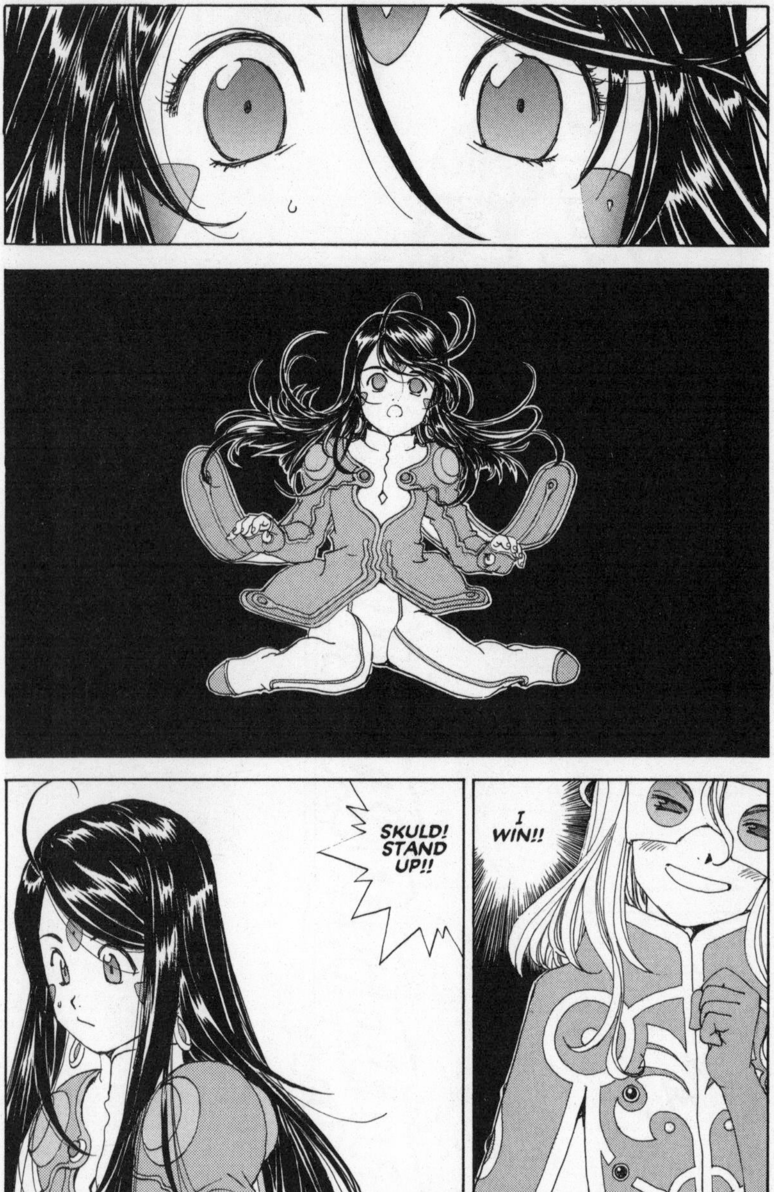
I WIN!!
SKULD! STAND UP!!

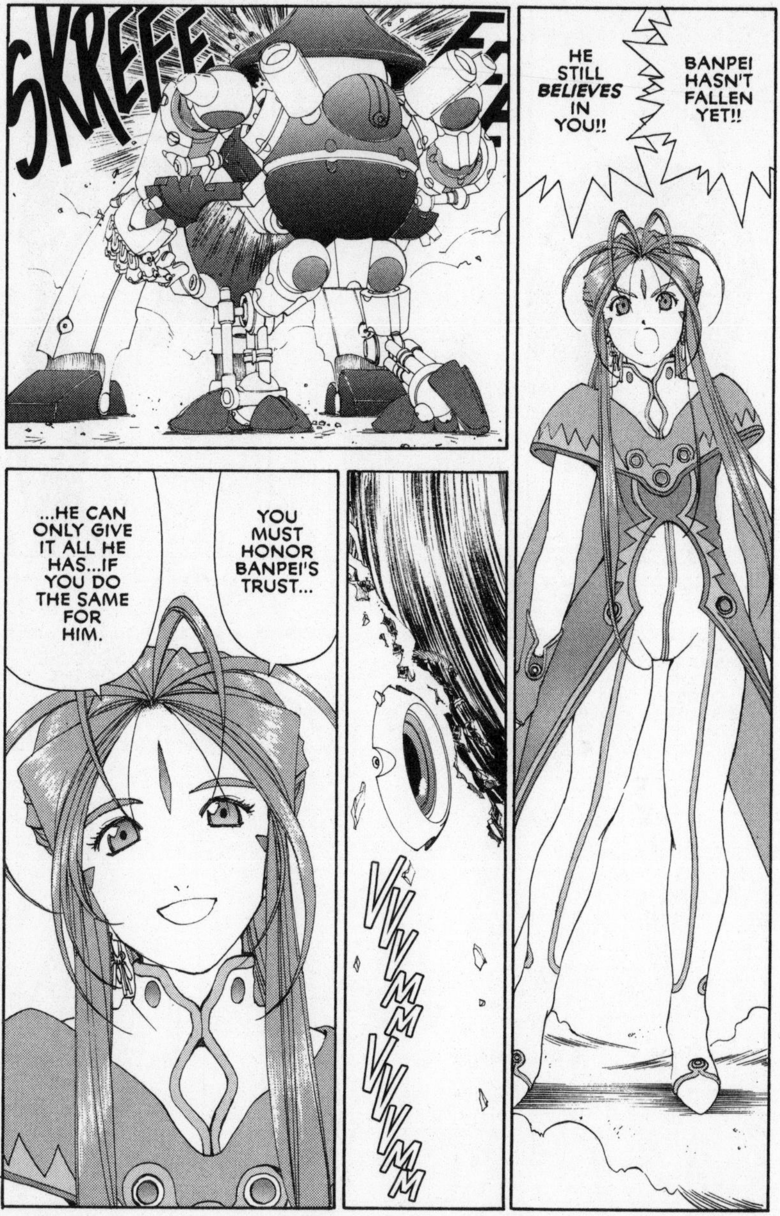
BANPEI HASN'T FALLEN YET!!
HE STILL *BELIEVES* IN YOU!!
SKREEE
YOU MUST HONOR BANPEI'S TRUST...
...HE CAN ONLY GIVE IT ALL HE HAS...IF YOU DO THE SAME FOR HIM.
VVVMM
VVVMM

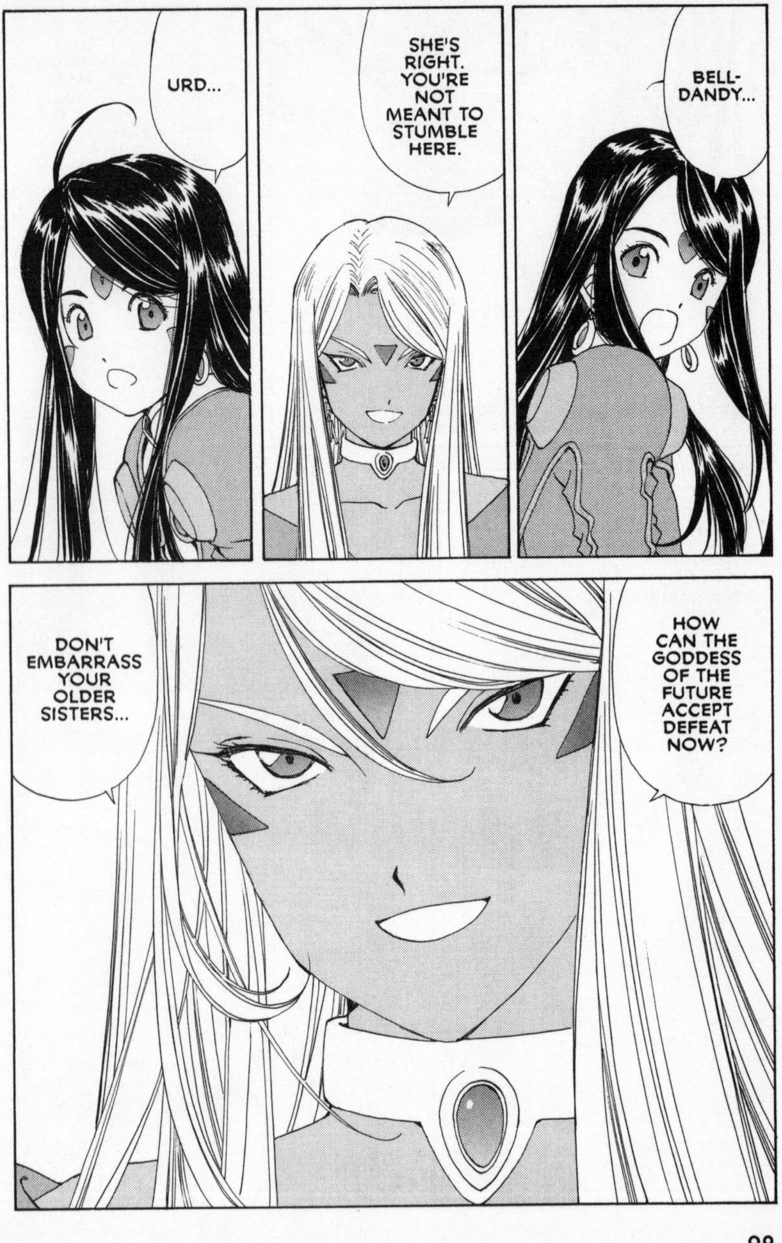
BELL-DANDY...
SHE'S RIGHT. YOU'RE NOT MEANT TO STUMBLE HERE.
URD...
HOW CAN THE GODDESS OF THE FUTURE ACCEPT DEFEAT NOW?
DON'T EMBARRASS YOUR OLDER SISTERS...

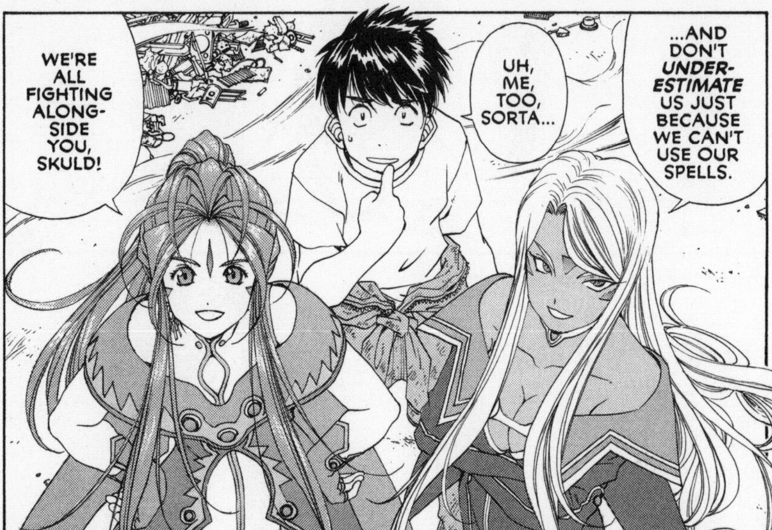
...AND DON'T *UNDER-ESTIMATE* US JUST BECAUSE WE CAN'T USE OUR SPELLS.
UH, ME, TOO, SORTA...
WE'RE ALL FIGHTING ALONG-SIDE YOU, SKULD!

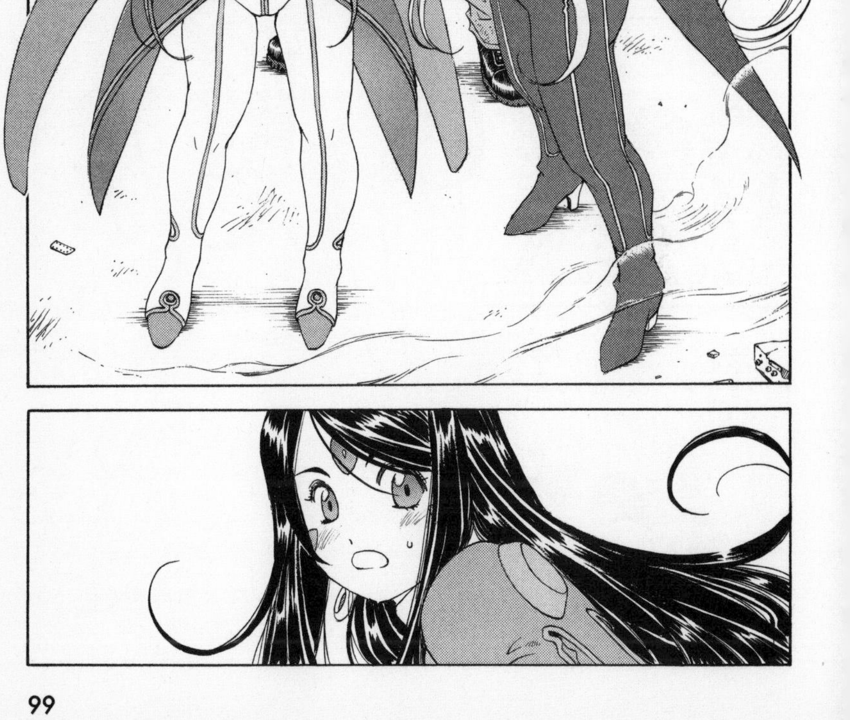

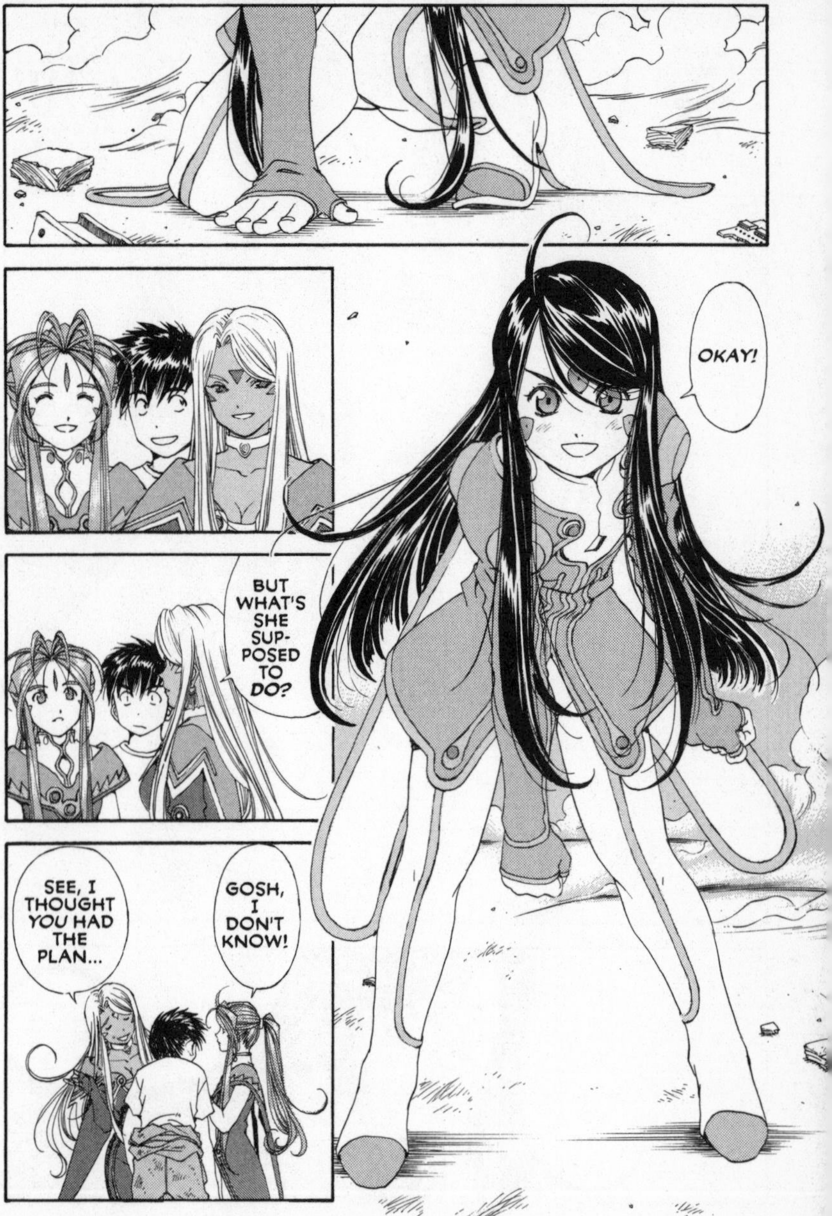
OKAY!
BUT WHAT'S SHE SUP-POSED TO *DO?*
GOSH, I DON'T KNOW!
SEE, I THOUGHT *YOU* HAD THE PLAN...

CHAPTER 266

Counterattack Cut 'n' Grind

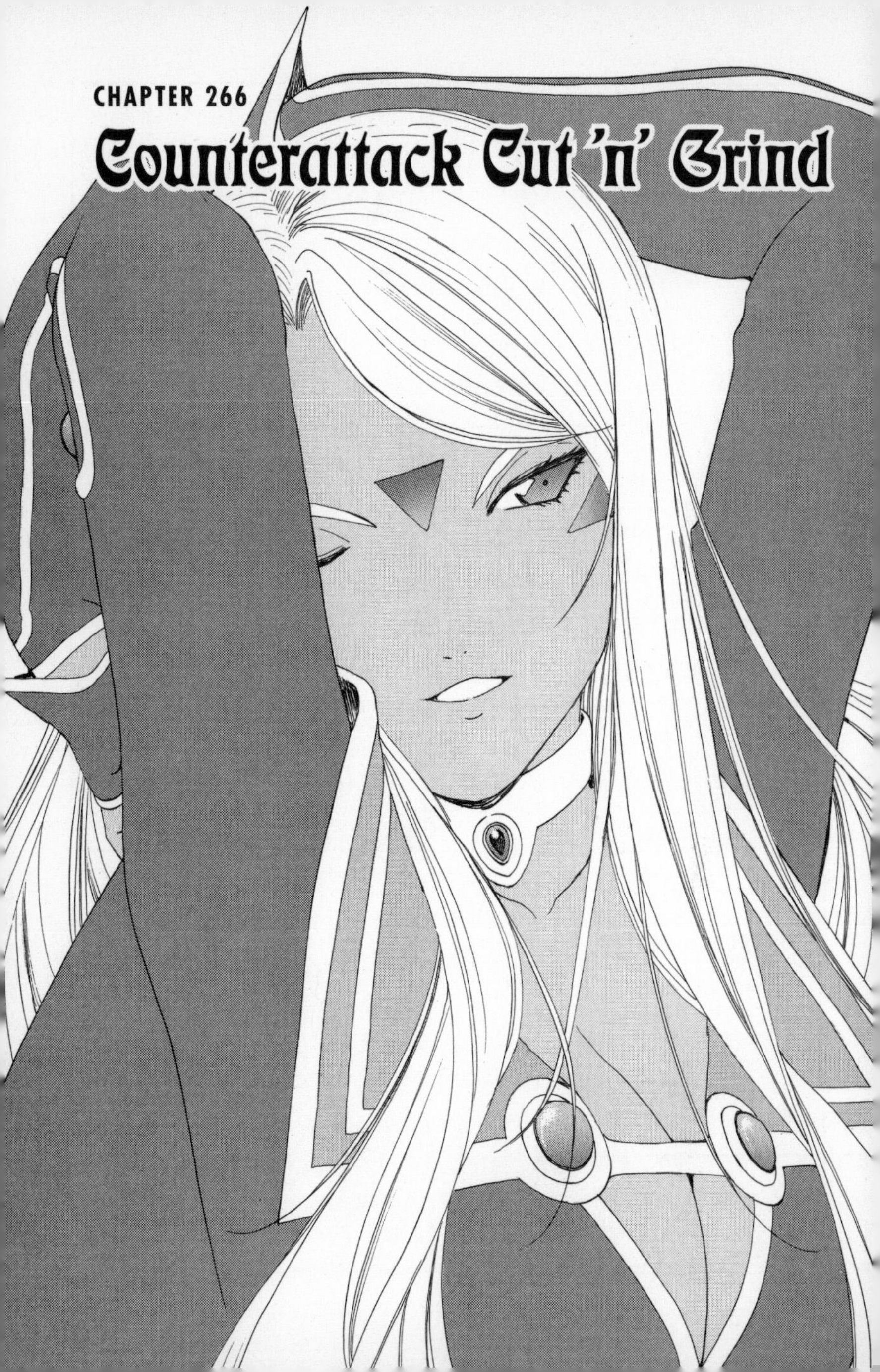

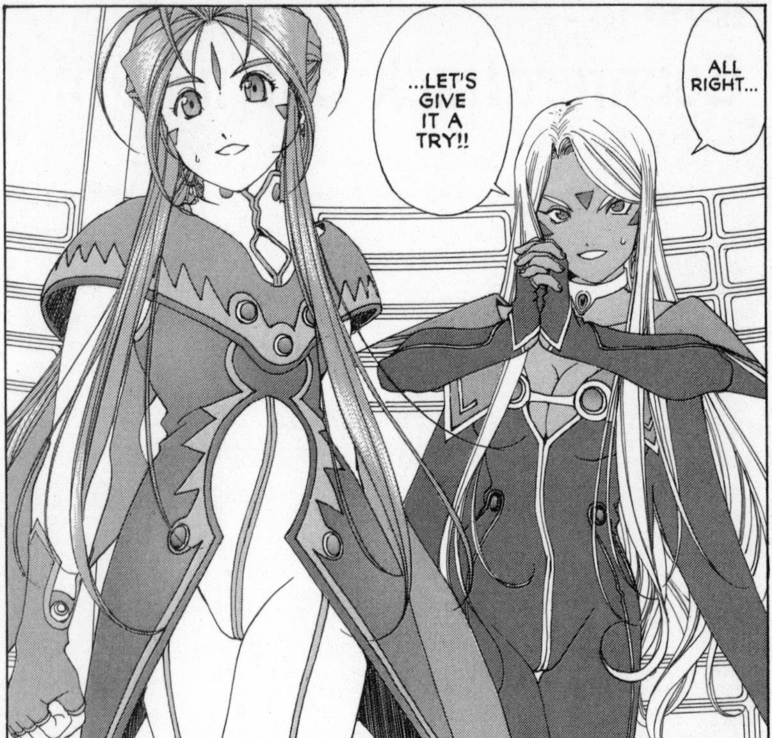
ALL RIGHT...
...LET'S GIVE IT A TRY!!

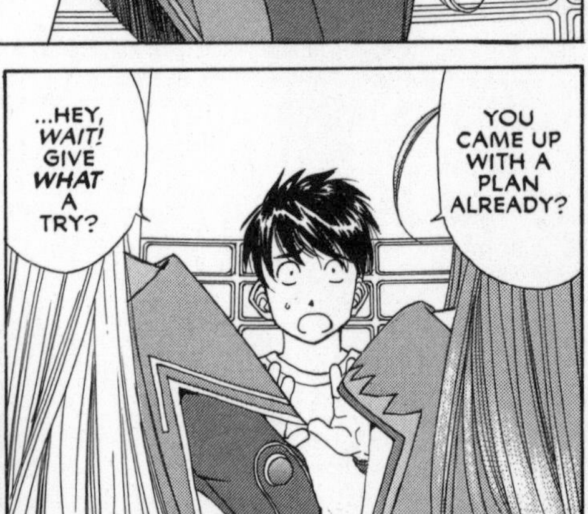
YOU CAME UP WITH A PLAN ALREADY?
...HEY, *WAIT!* GIVE *WHAT* A TRY?

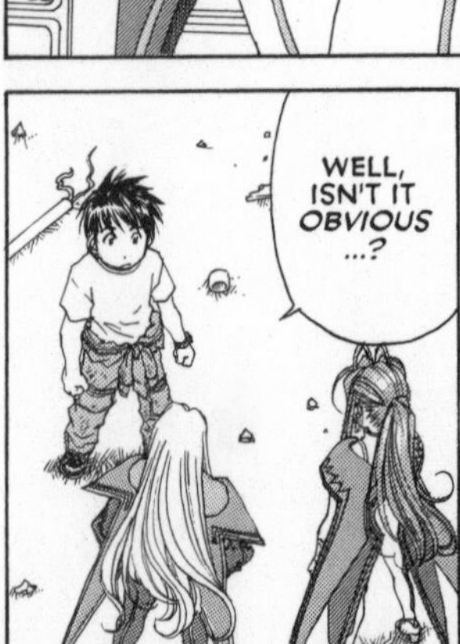
WELL, ISN'T IT *OBVIOUS* ...?

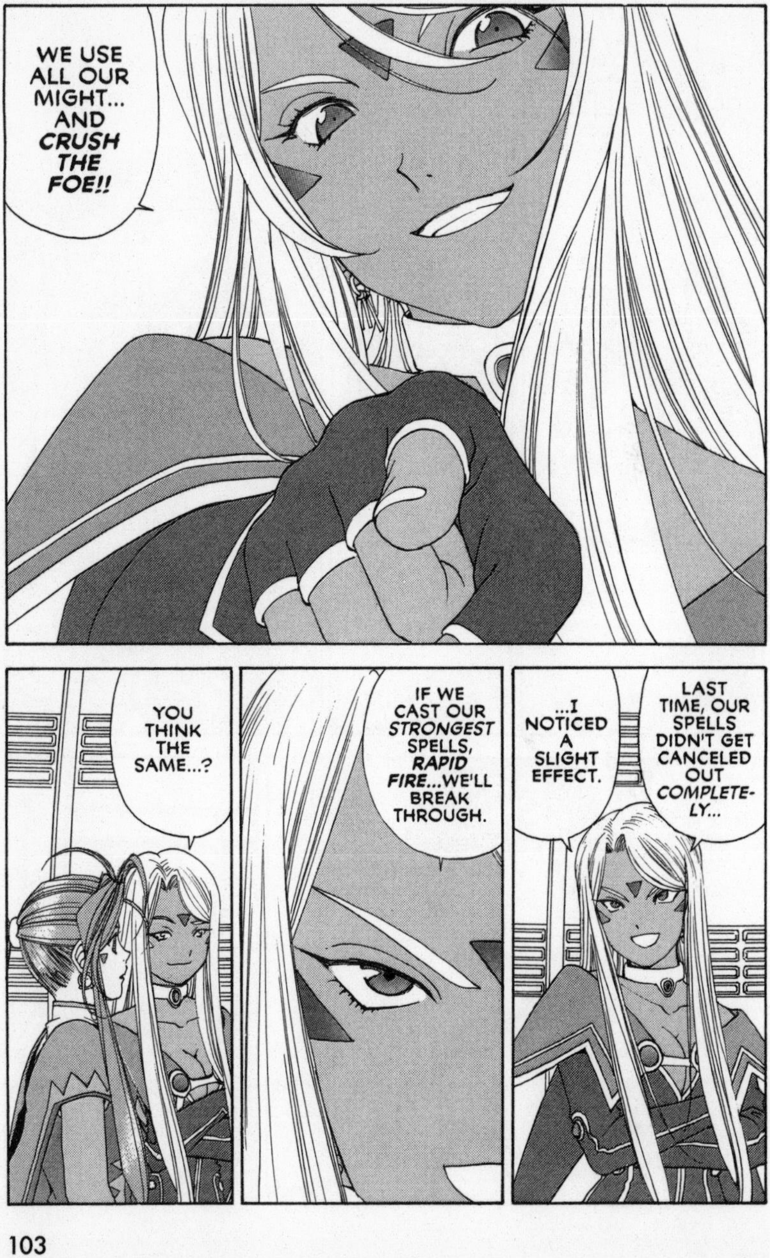
WE USE ALL OUR MIGHT... AND *CRUSH THE FOE!!*
LAST TIME, OUR SPELLS DIDN'T GET CANCELED OUT *COMPLETE-LY...*
...I NOTICED A SLIGHT EFFECT.
IF WE CAST OUR *STRONGEST* SPELLS, ***RAPID FIRE...*** WE'LL BREAK THROUGH.
YOU THINK THE SAME...?

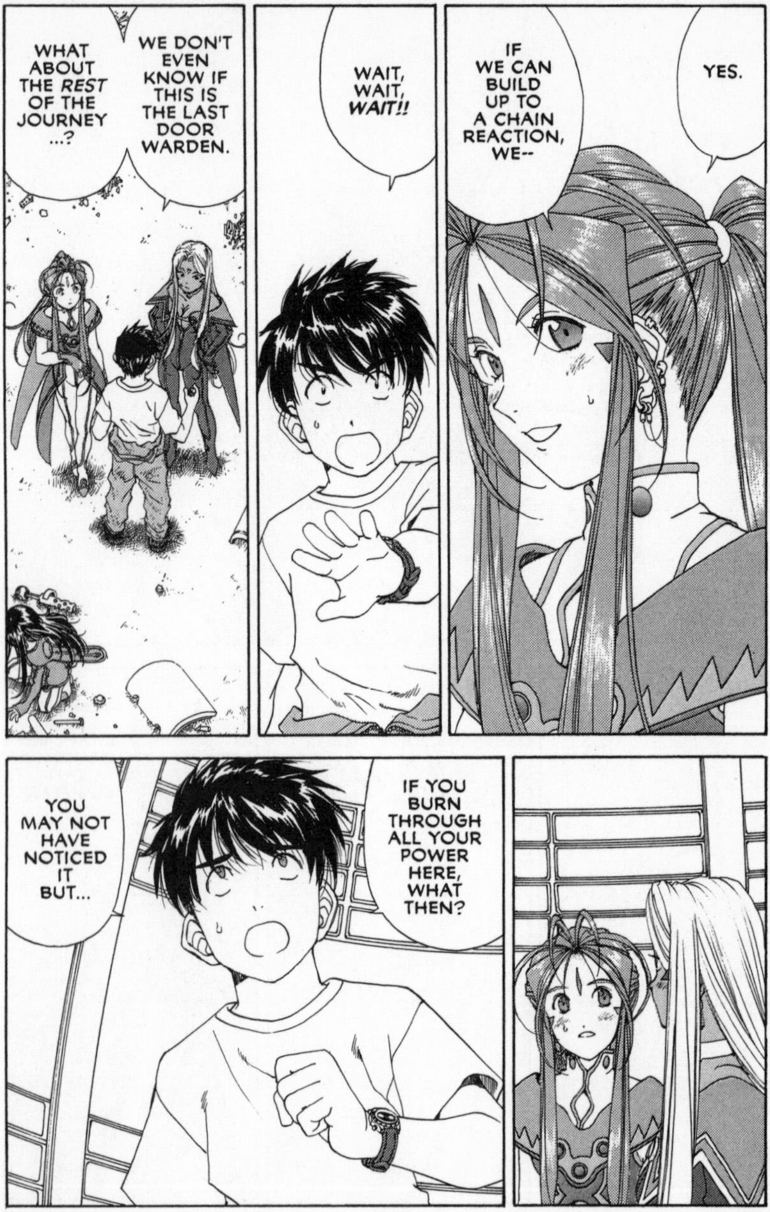
YES.
IF WE CAN BUILD UP TO A CHAIN REACTION, WE--
WAIT, WAIT, *WAIT!!*
WE DON'T EVEN KNOW IF THIS IS THE LAST DOOR WARDEN.
WHAT ABOUT THE *REST* OF THE JOURNEY ...?
IF YOU BURN THROUGH ALL YOUR POWER HERE, WHAT THEN?
YOU MAY NOT HAVE NOTICED IT BUT...

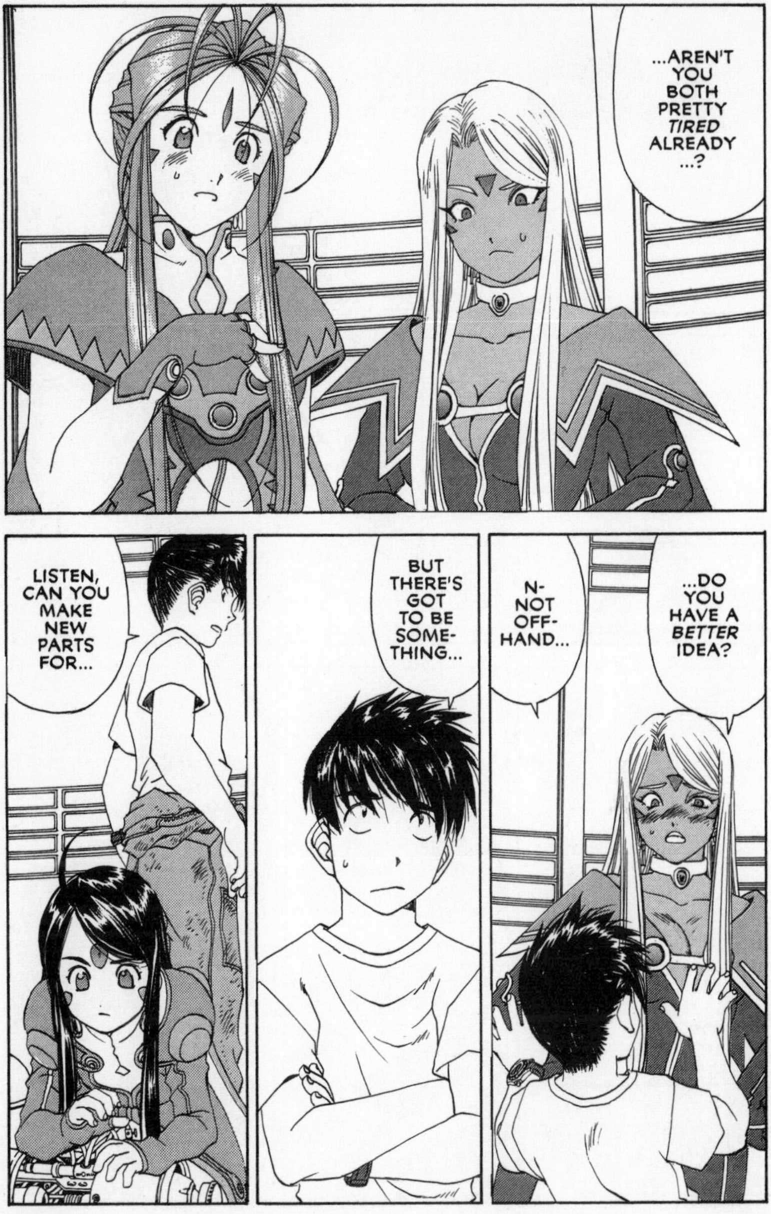
...AREN'T YOU BOTH PRETTY *TIRED* ALREADY ...?
...DO YOU HAVE A *BETTER* IDEA?
N-NOT OFF-HAND...
BUT THERE'S GOT TO BE SOME-THING...
LISTEN, CAN YOU MAKE NEW PARTS FOR...

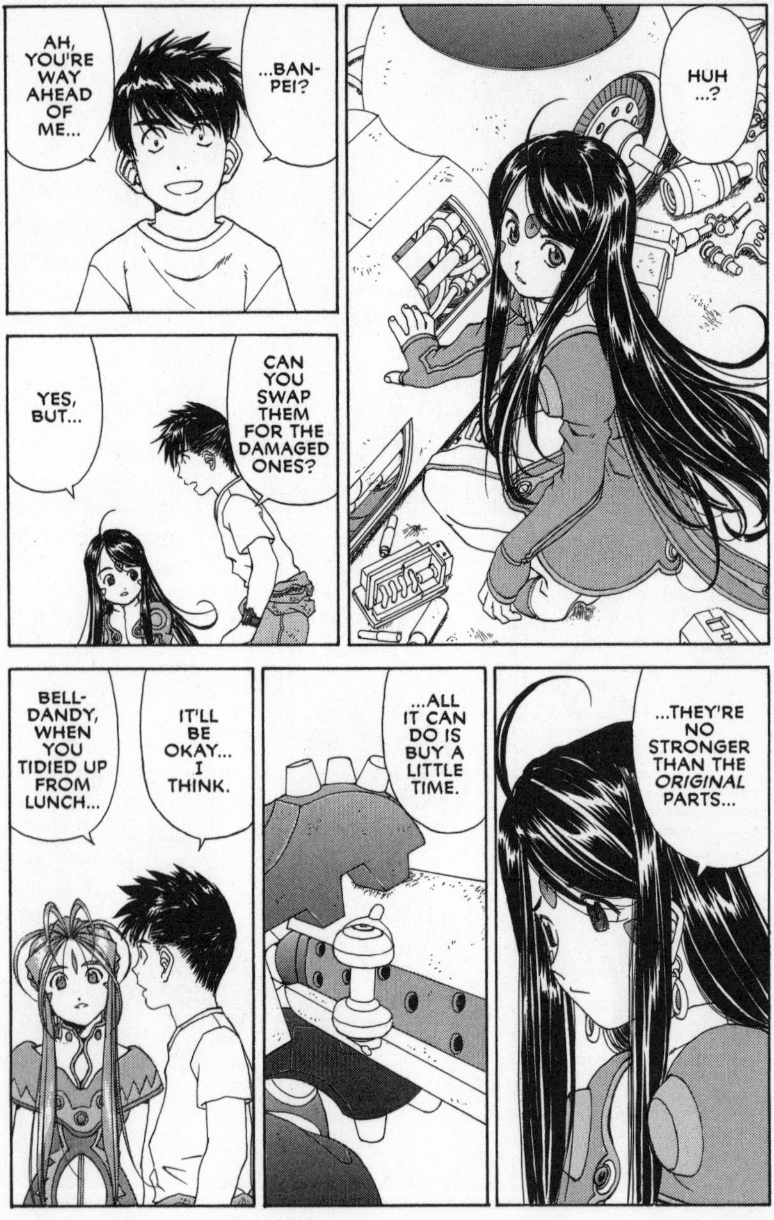
HUH ...?
...BAN-PEI?
AH, YOU'RE WAY AHEAD OF ME...
CAN YOU SWAP THEM FOR THE DAMAGED ONES?
YES, BUT...
...THEY'RE NO STRONGER THAN THE *ORIGINAL* PARTS...
...ALL IT CAN DO IS BUY A LITTLE TIME.
IT'LL BE OKAY... I THINK.
BELL-DANDY, WHEN YOU TIDIED UP FROM LUNCH...

...THOSE OXYGEN ABSORB- ERS...
WERE THERE ANY MORE?
EH?
OH, YES.
I WAS GOING TO DISPOSE OF THIS PROPERLY LATER...
GREAT! I DON'T KNOW IF IT'LL WORK, BUT...
...
BODY TEMPER- ATURE...

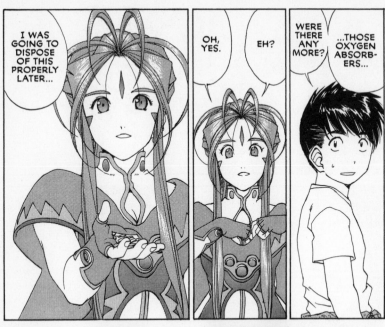

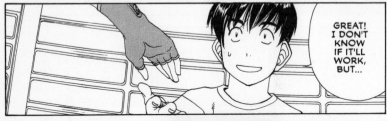

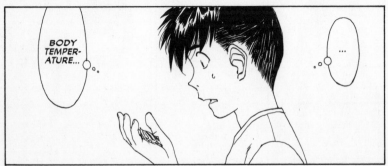

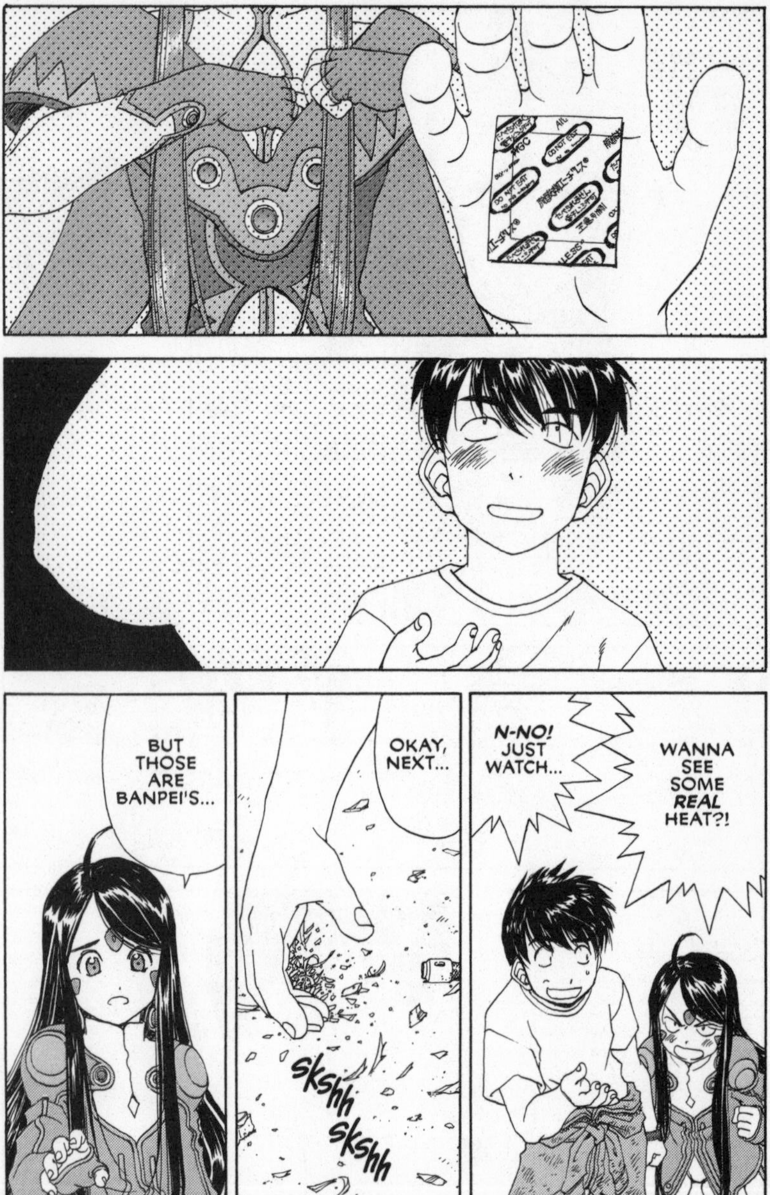

WANNA SEE SOME *REAL* HEAT?!
N-NO! JUST WATCH...
OKAY, NEXT...
SKSHH
SKSHH
BUT THOSE ARE BANPEI'S...

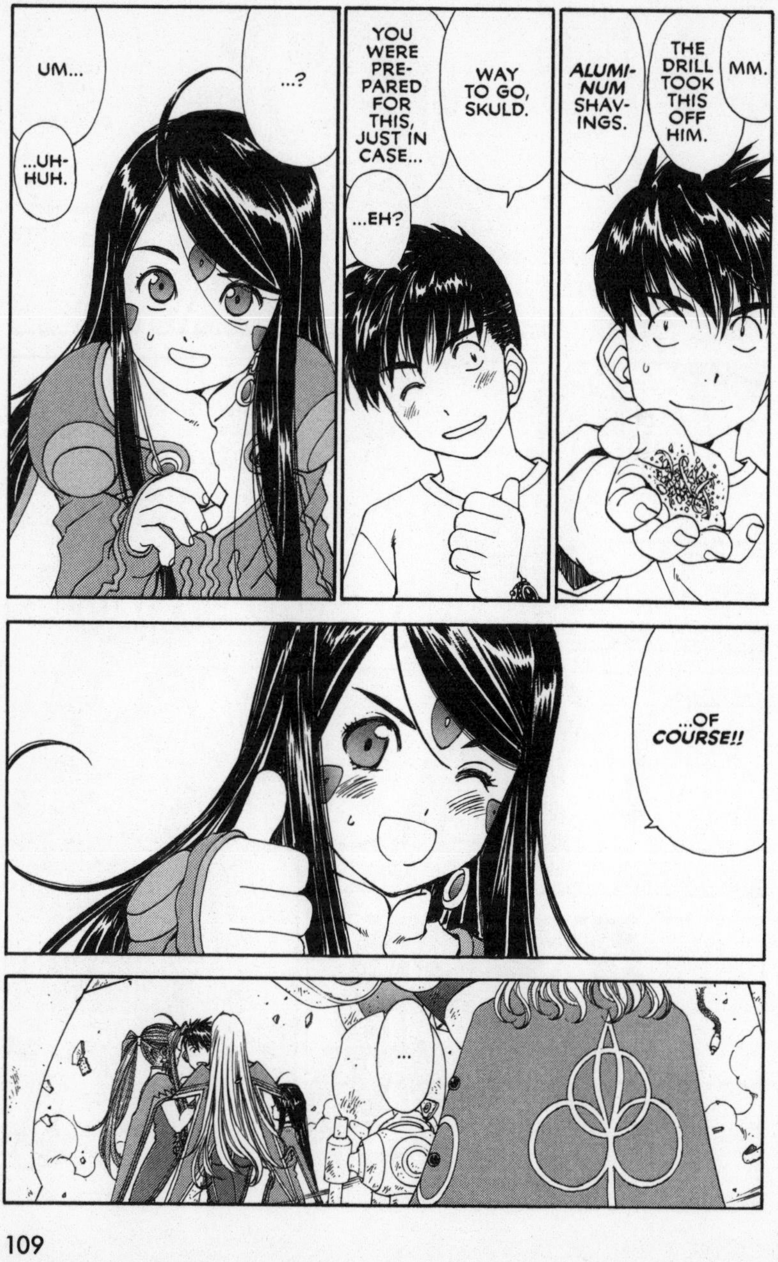
MM.
THE DRILL TOOK THIS OFF HIM.
ALUMINUM SHAVINGS.
WAY TO GO, SKULD.
YOU WERE PREPARED FOR THIS, JUST IN CASE...
...EH?
...?
UM...
...UH-HUH.
...OF *COURSE!!*
...

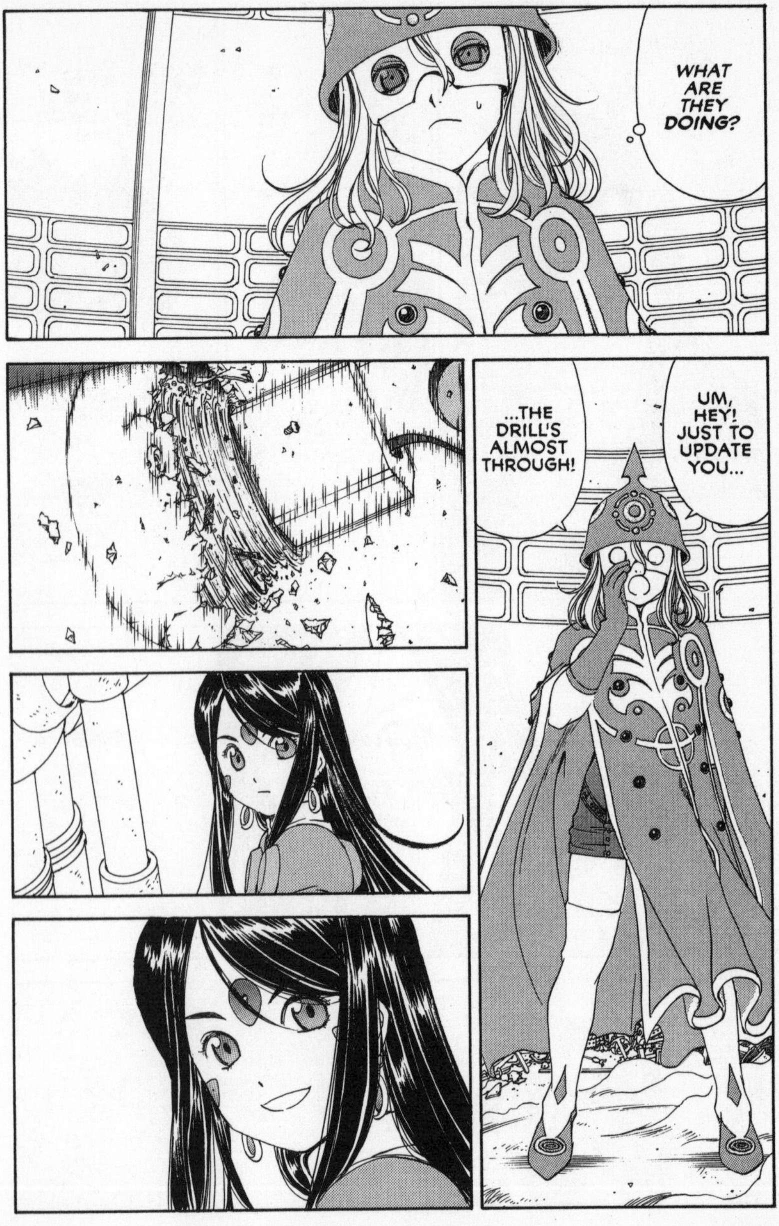
WHAT ARE THEY DOING?
UM, HEY! JUST TO UPDATE YOU...
...THE DRILL'S ALMOST THROUGH!

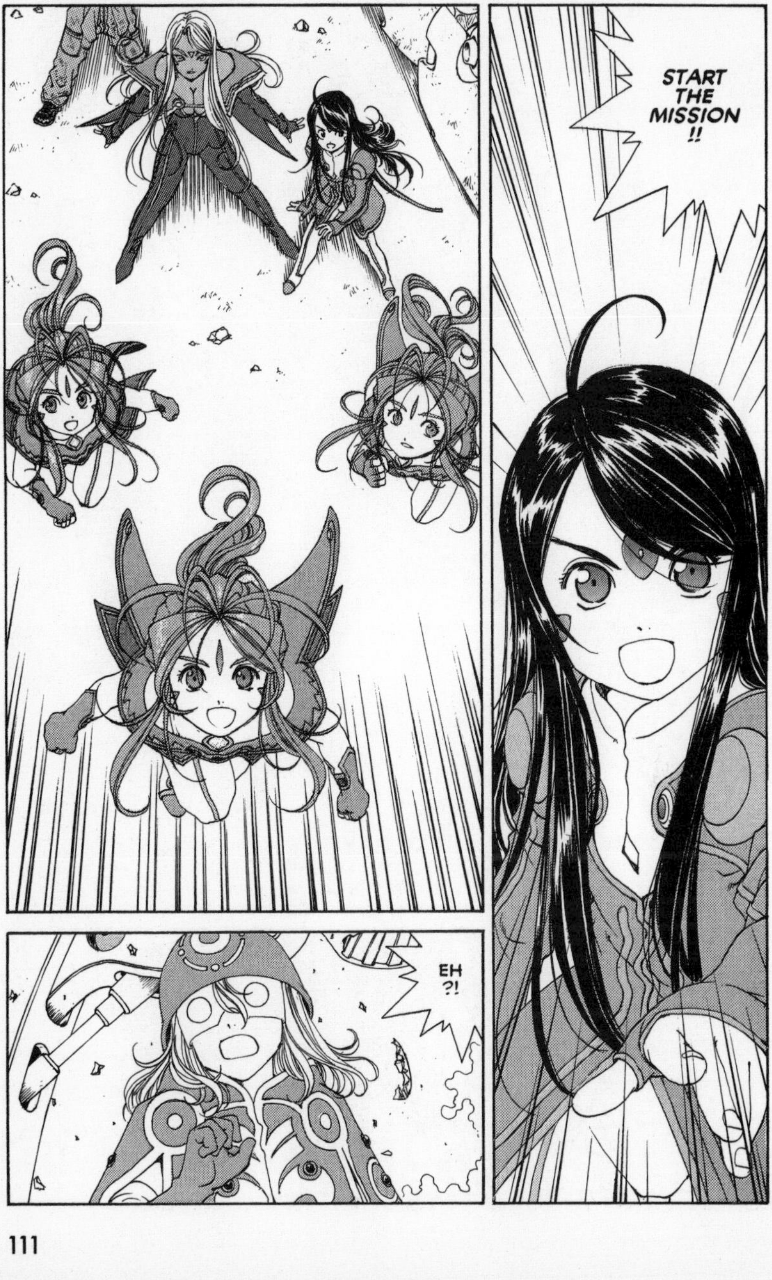
START THE MISSION !!
EH ?!

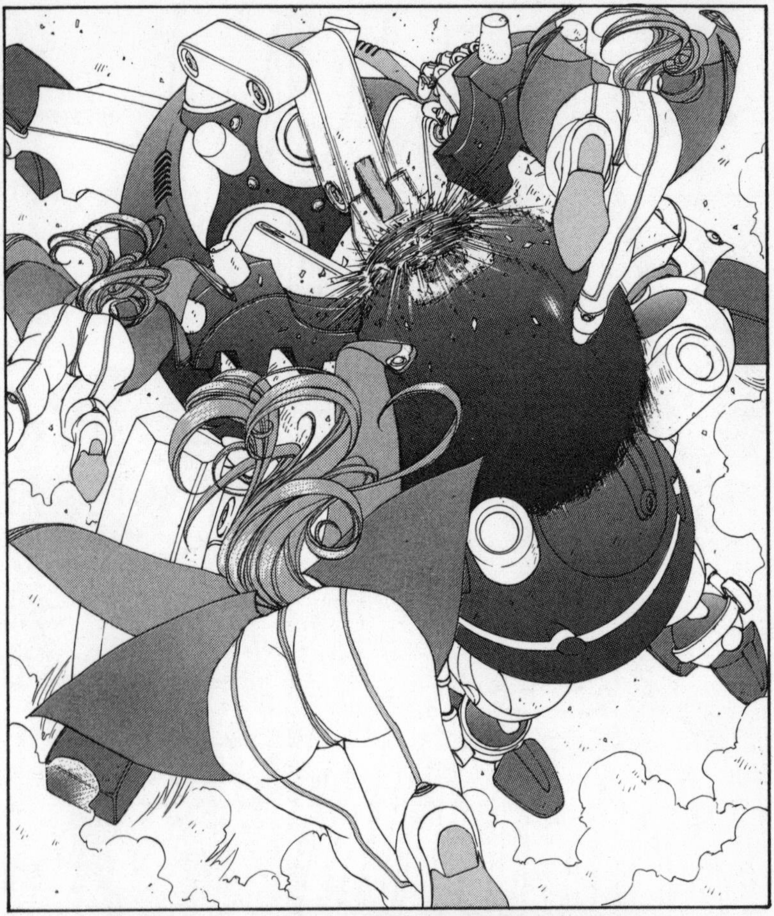
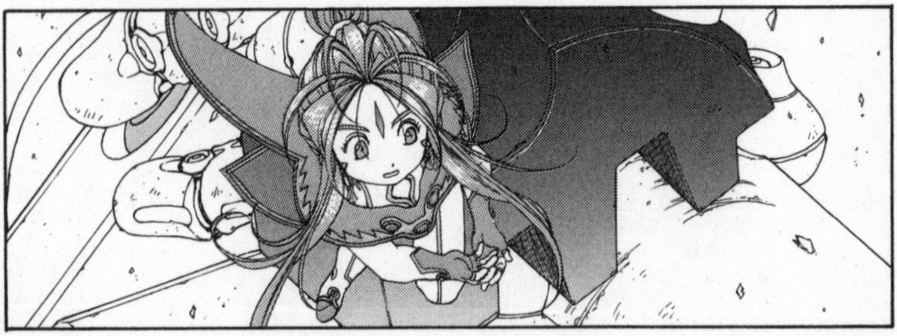

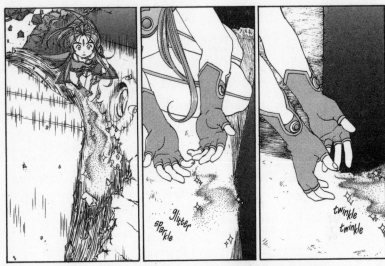

glitter
sparkle

twinkle
twinkle

NOW!!

URD!!

NOW,
NORMALLY,
THIS
WOULD
BLOW
AWAY THE
WHOLE
ROOM...

*HERE
I
COME!!*

113

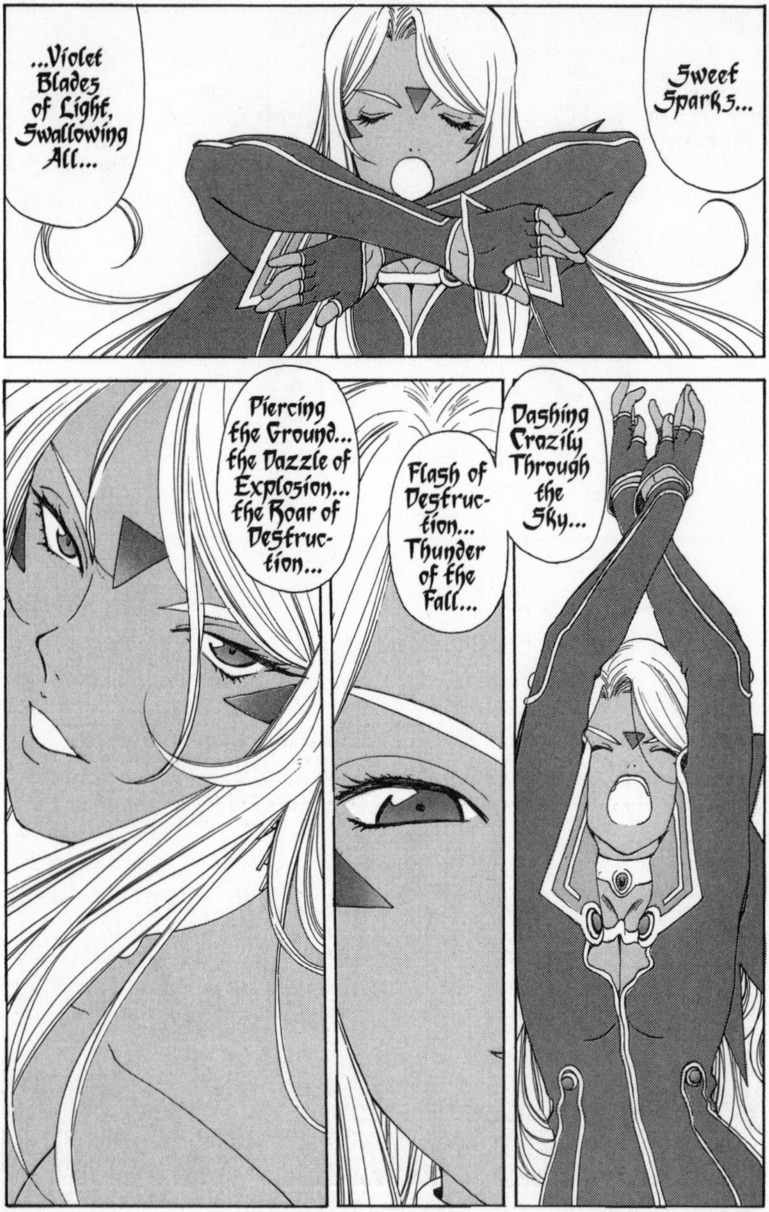
Sweet Sparks...
...Violet Blades of Light, Swallowing All...
Dashing Crazily Through the Sky...
Flash of Destruction... Thunder of the Fall...
Piercing the Ground... the Dazzle of Explosion... the Roar of Destruction...

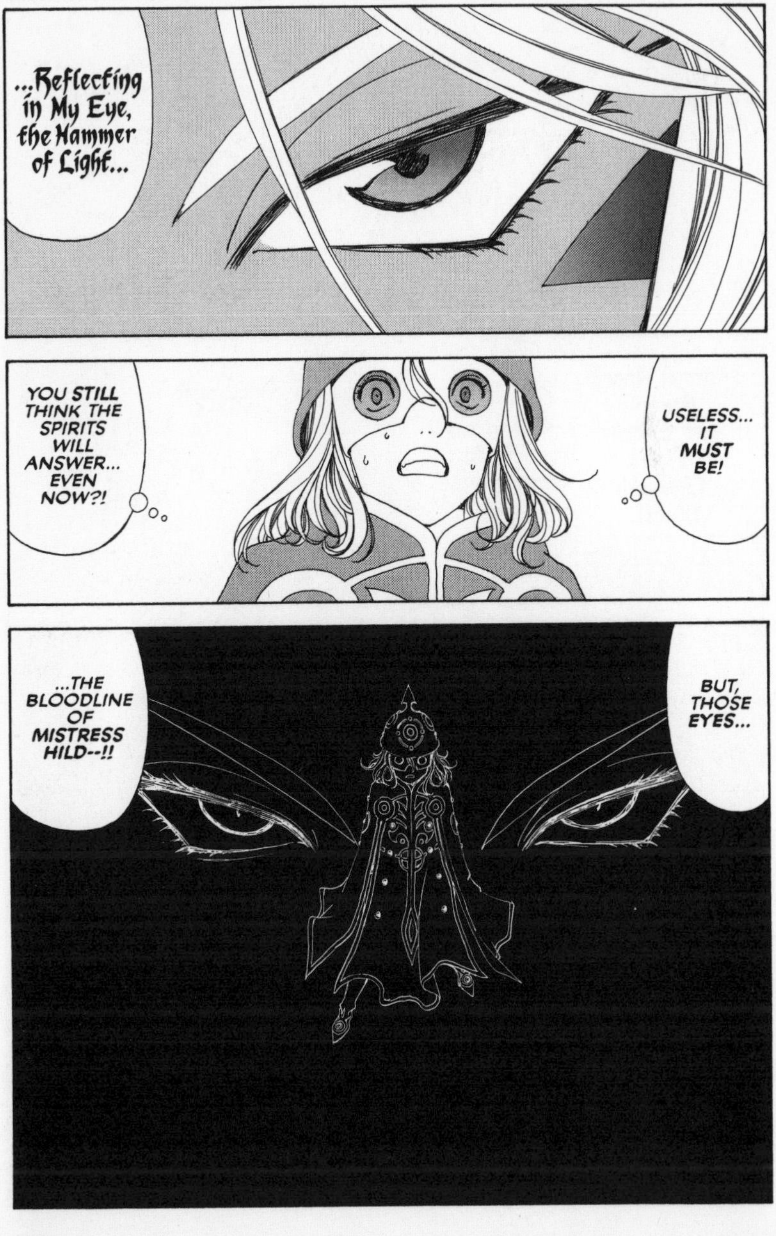
...Reflecting in My Eye, the Hammer of Light...
USELESS... IT MUST BE!
YOU STILL THINK THE SPIRITS WILL ANSWER... EVEN NOW?!
BUT, THOSE EYES...
...THE BLOODLINE OF MISTRESS HILD--!!

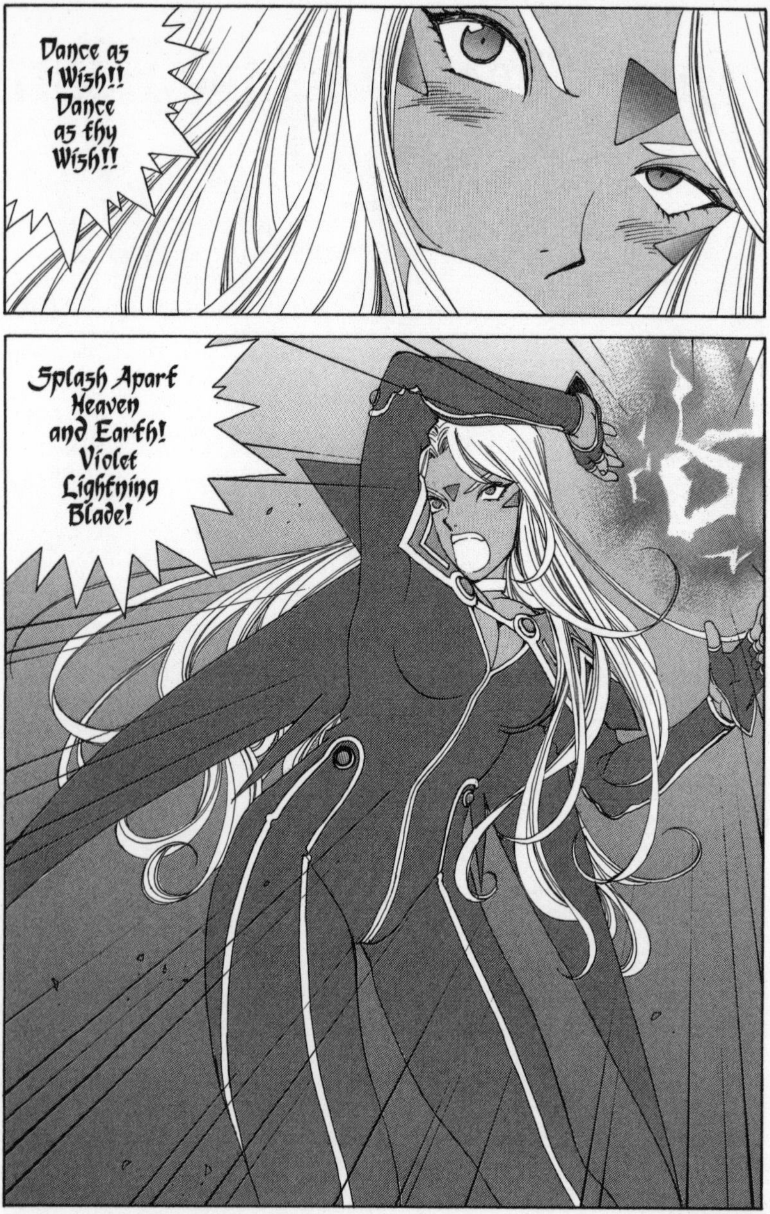
Dance as I Wish!! Dance as thy Wish!!
Splash Apart Heaven and Earth! Violet Lightning Blade!

CHAPTER 267

Burst Free, Machine Heart!

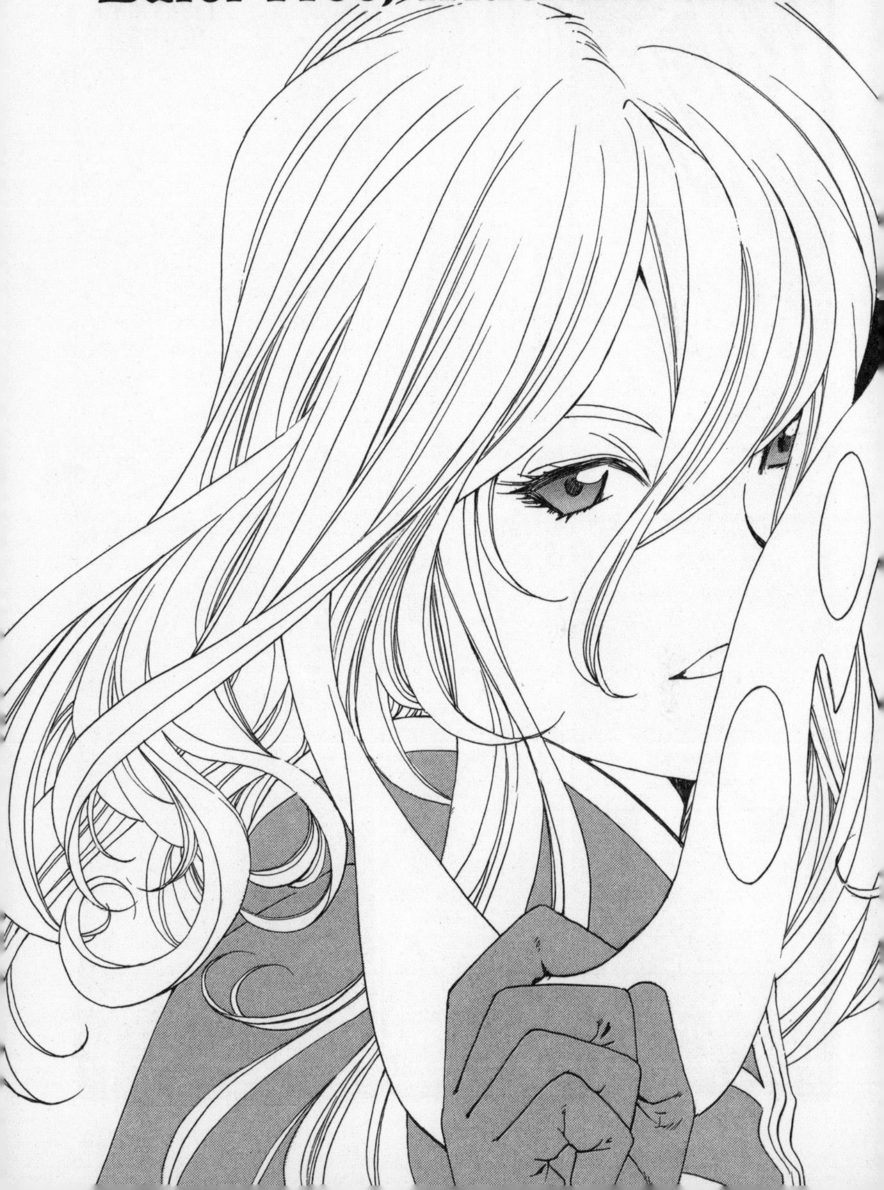

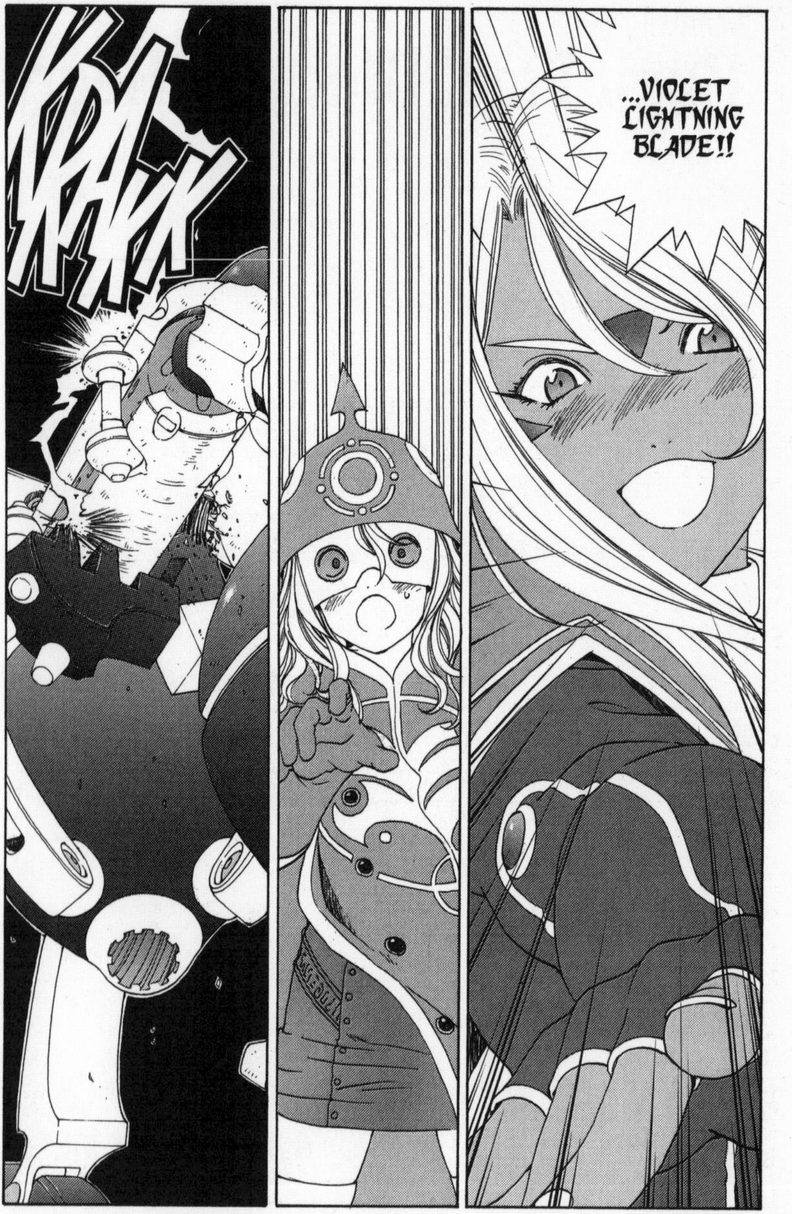
...VIOLET LIGHTNING BLADE!!
KRA KRAKK

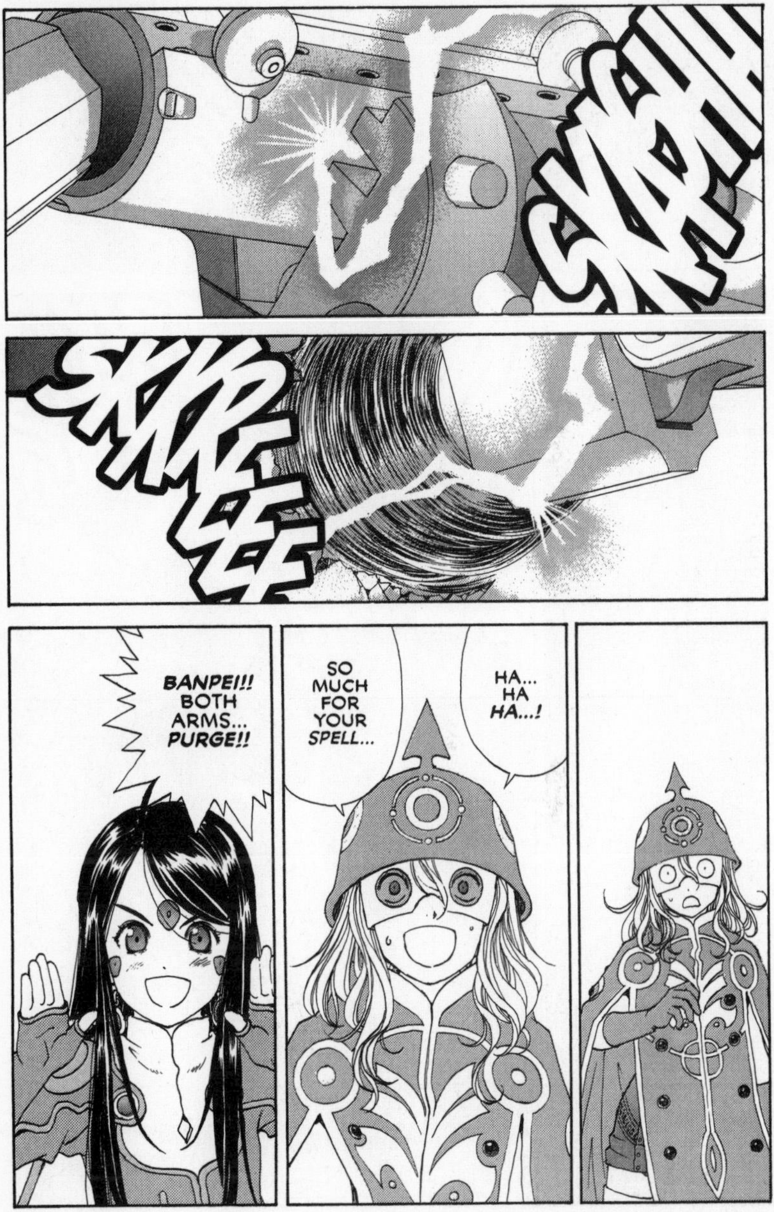
HA... HA *HA*...!
SO MUCH FOR YOUR *SPELL*...
BANPEI!! BOTH ARMS... *PURGE!!*

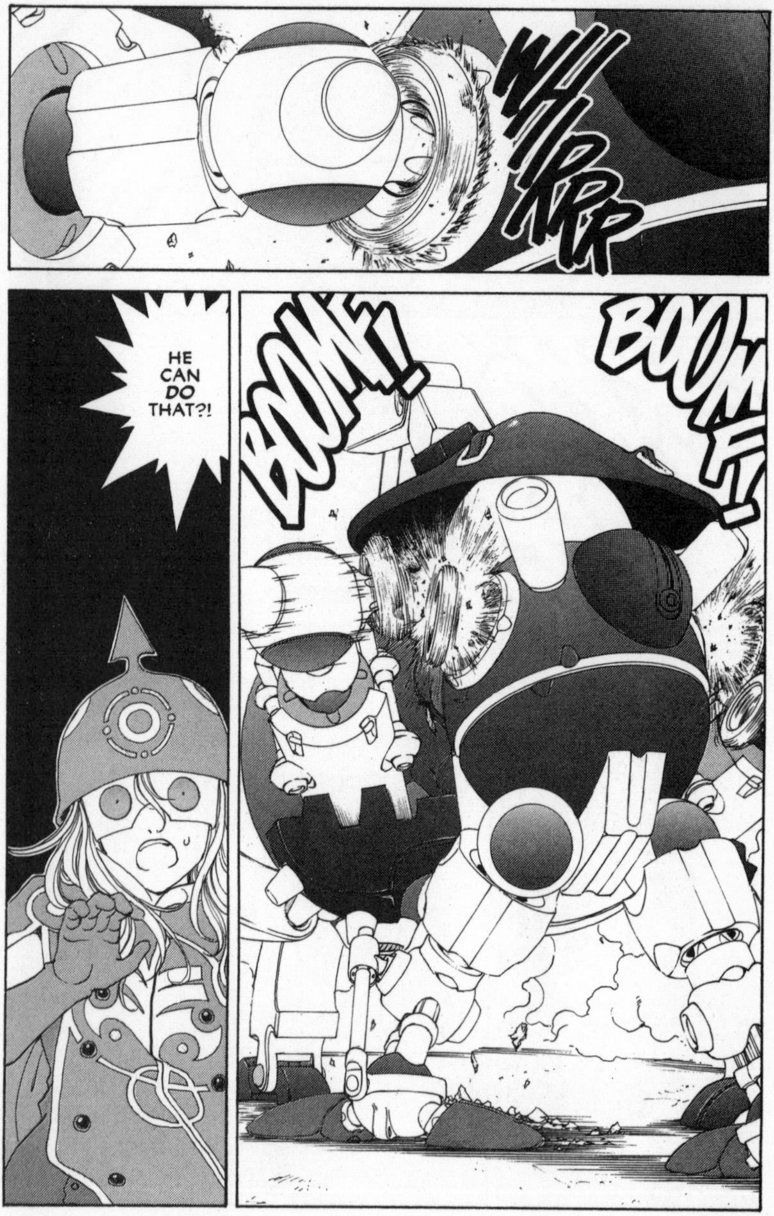
WHIRRR
BOOMF!
BOOM!
HE CAN *DO* THAT?!

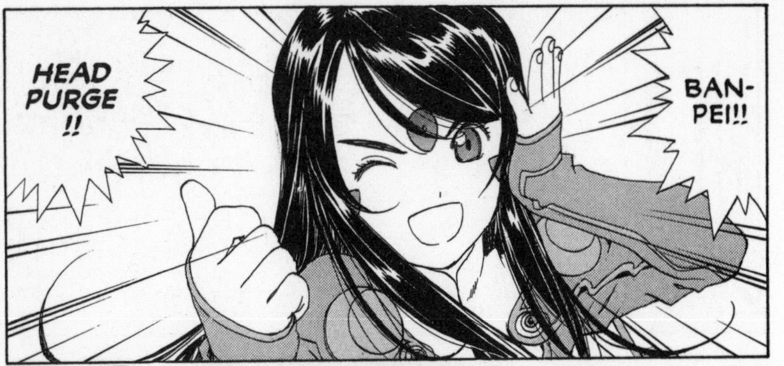
BAN-PEI!!
HEAD PURGE !!

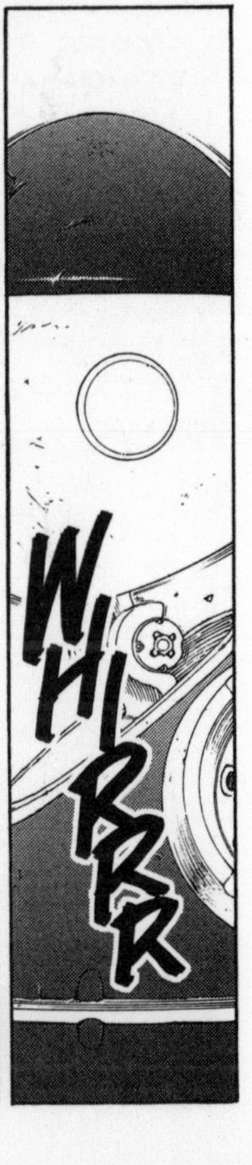
WHIRRR

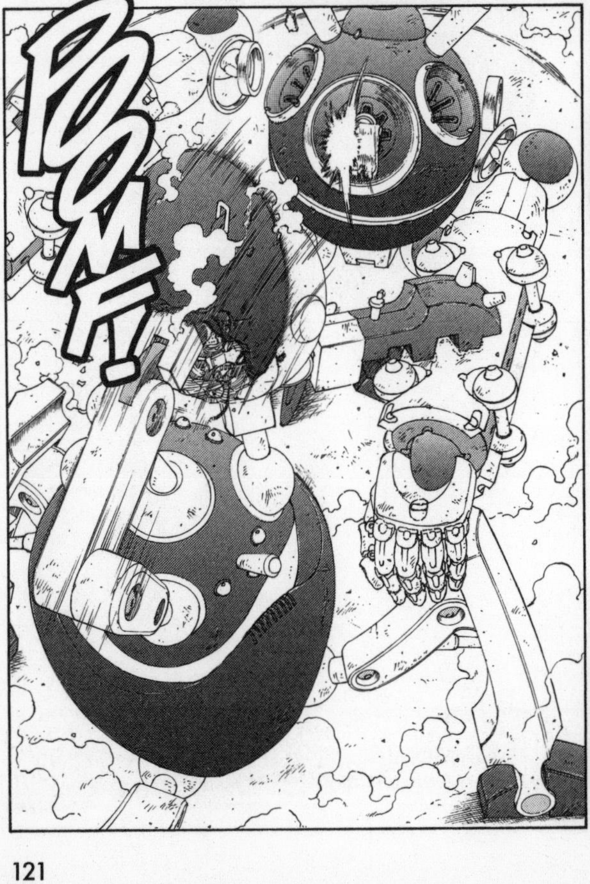
POOMF!

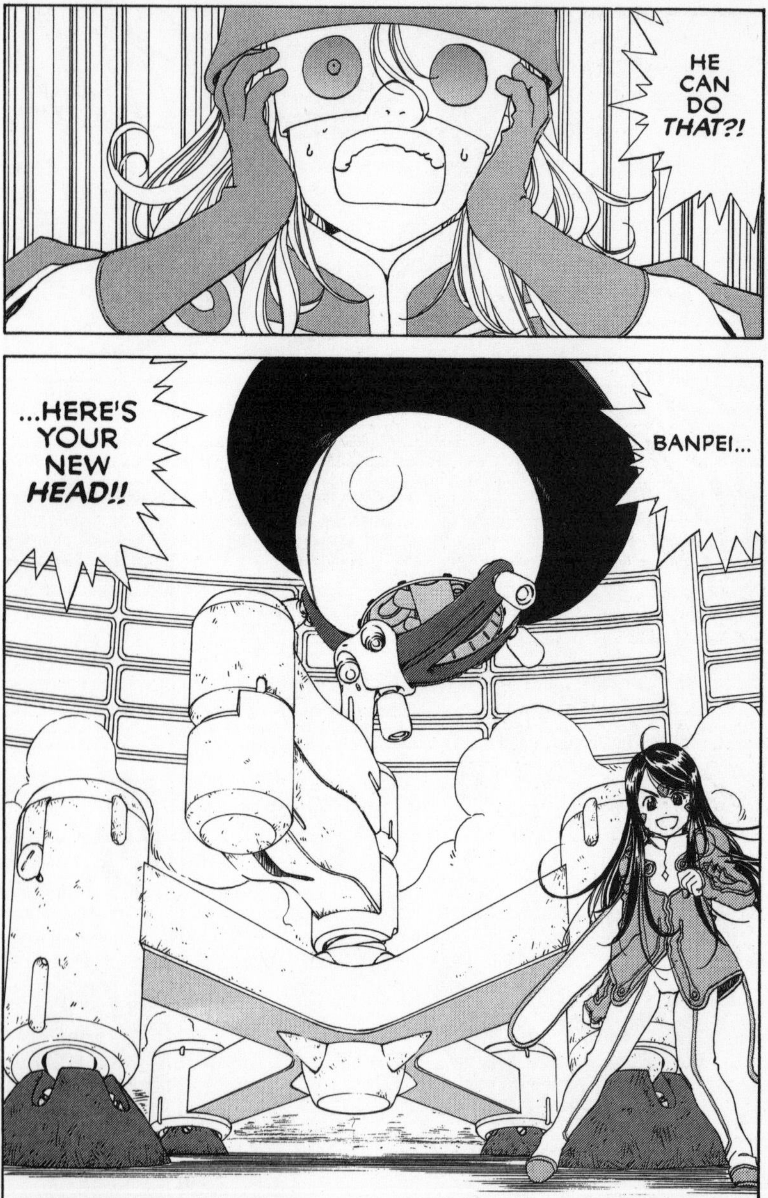
HE CAN DO THAT?!
BANPEI...
...HERE'S YOUR NEW HEAD!!

WHOOOOM

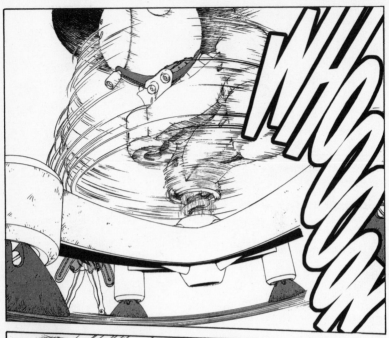

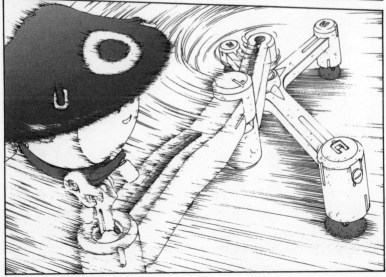

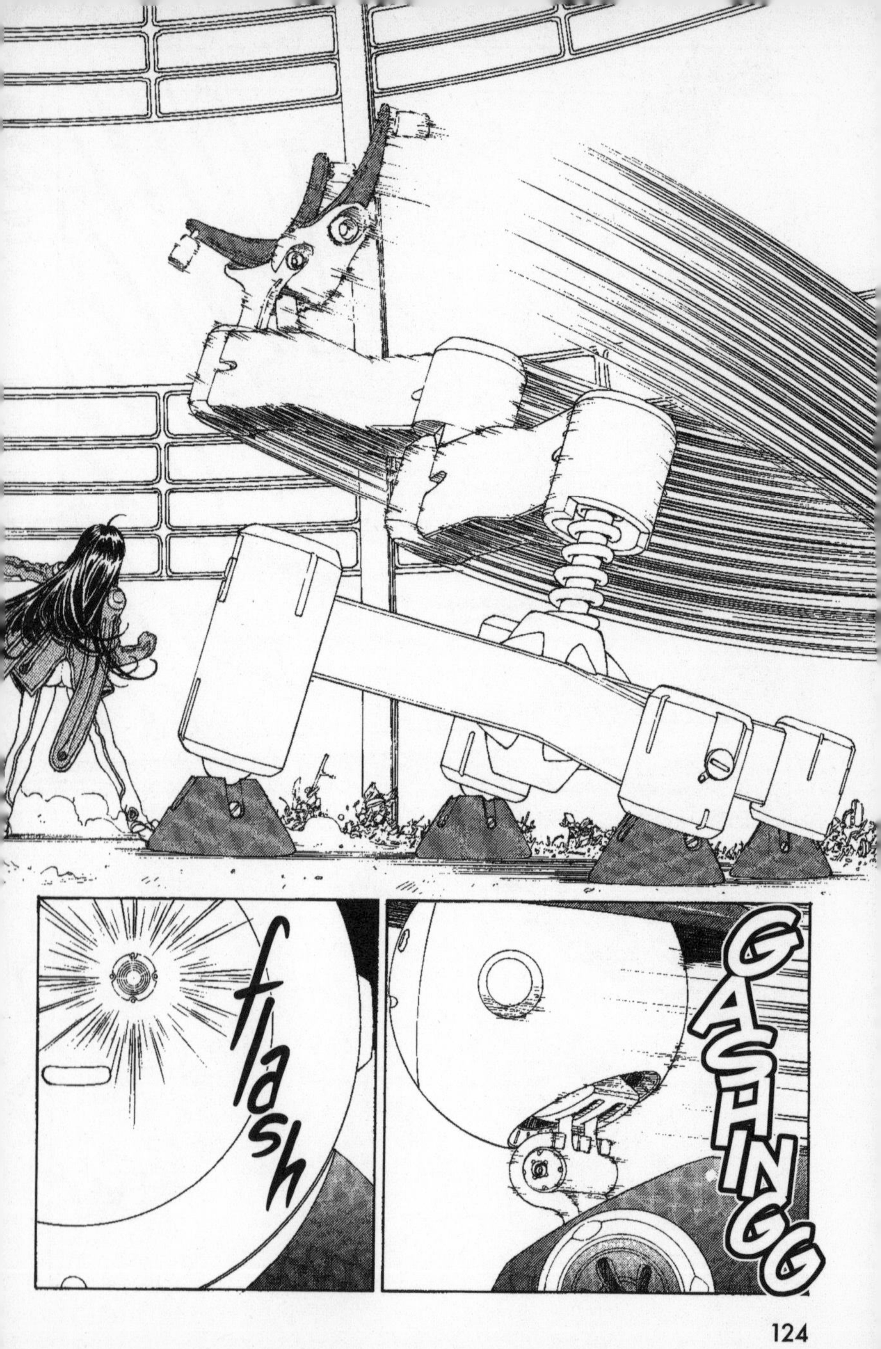
GASHINGG
flash

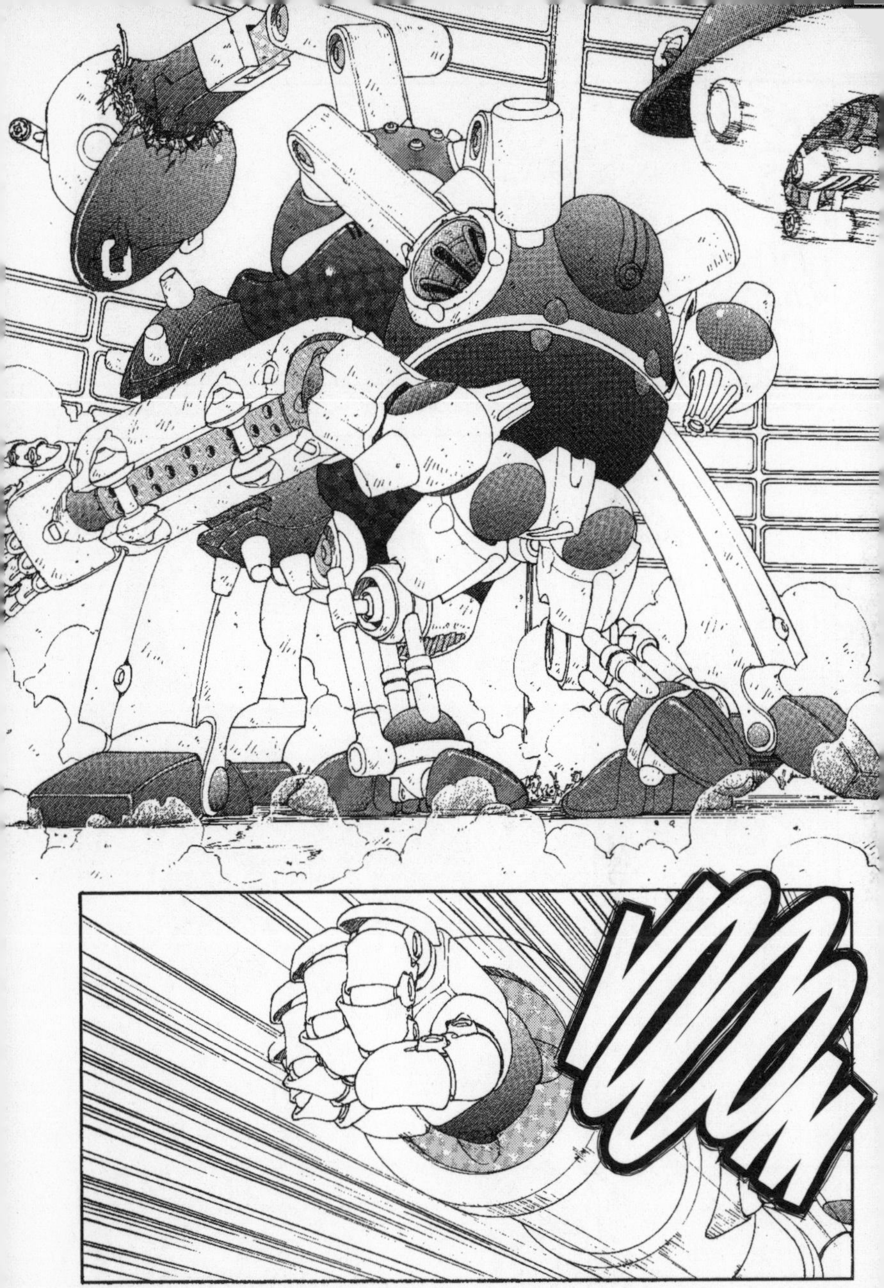
VOOM

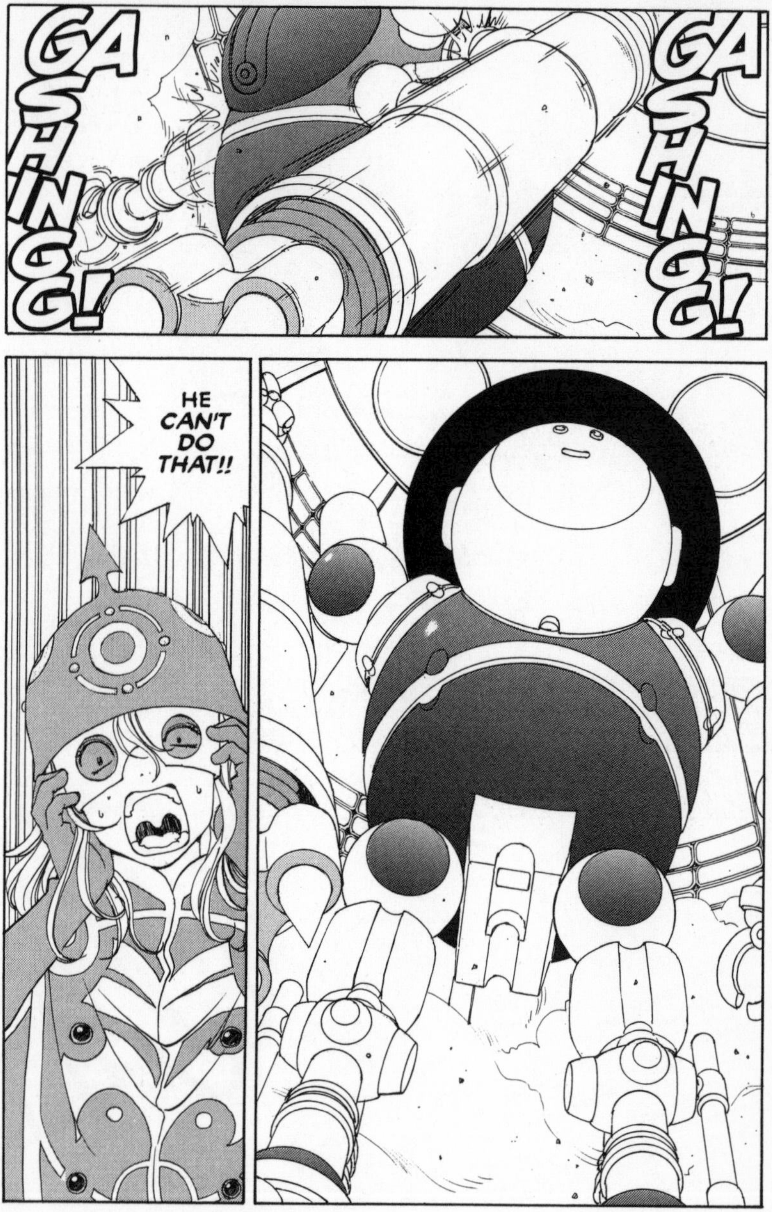
GASHING!
GASHING!
HE CAN'T DO THAT!!

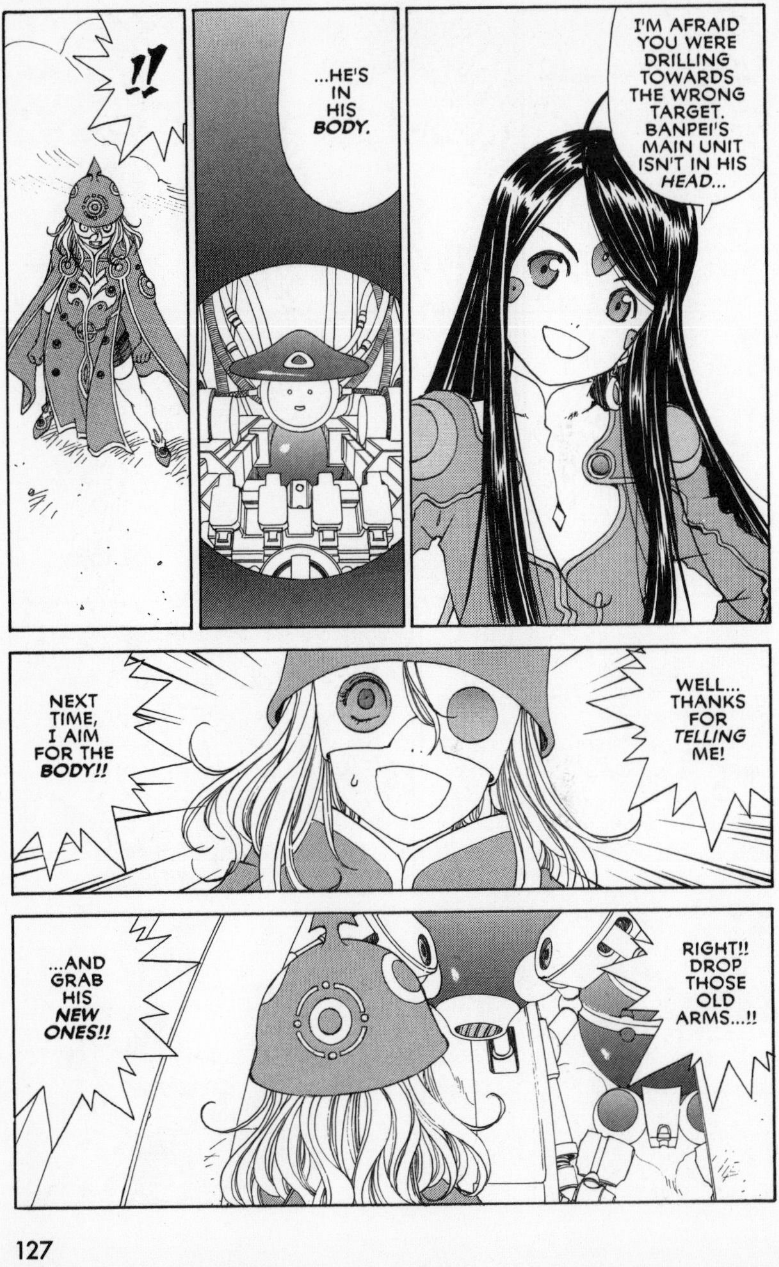
I'M AFRAID YOU WERE DRILLING TOWARDS THE WRONG TARGET. BANPEI'S MAIN UNIT ISN'T IN HIS *HEAD*...
...HE'S IN HIS *BODY.*
!!
WELL... THANKS FOR *TELLING* ME!
NEXT TIME, I AIM FOR THE *BODY!!*
RIGHT!! DROP THOSE OLD ARMS...!!
...AND GRAB HIS *NEW ONES!!*

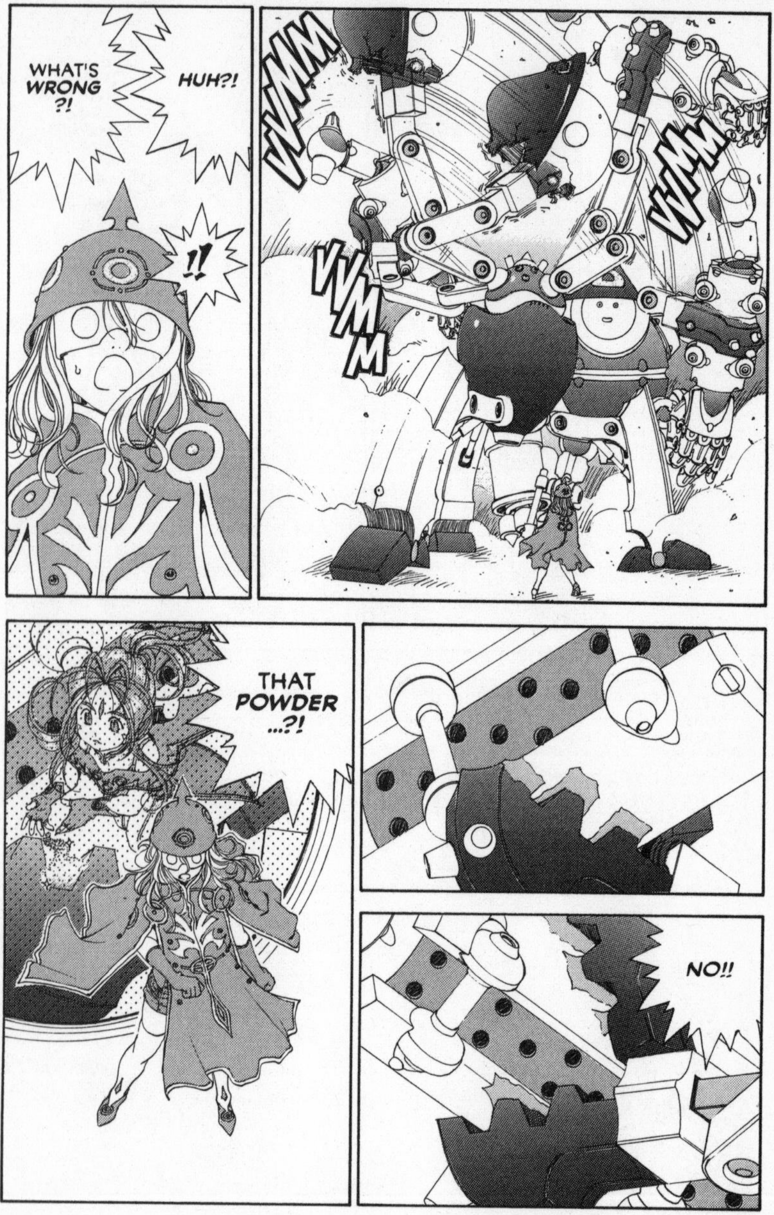
VVMM
VVMM
VVMM
HUH?!
WHAT'S WRONG ?!
!!
NO!!
THAT POWDER ...?!

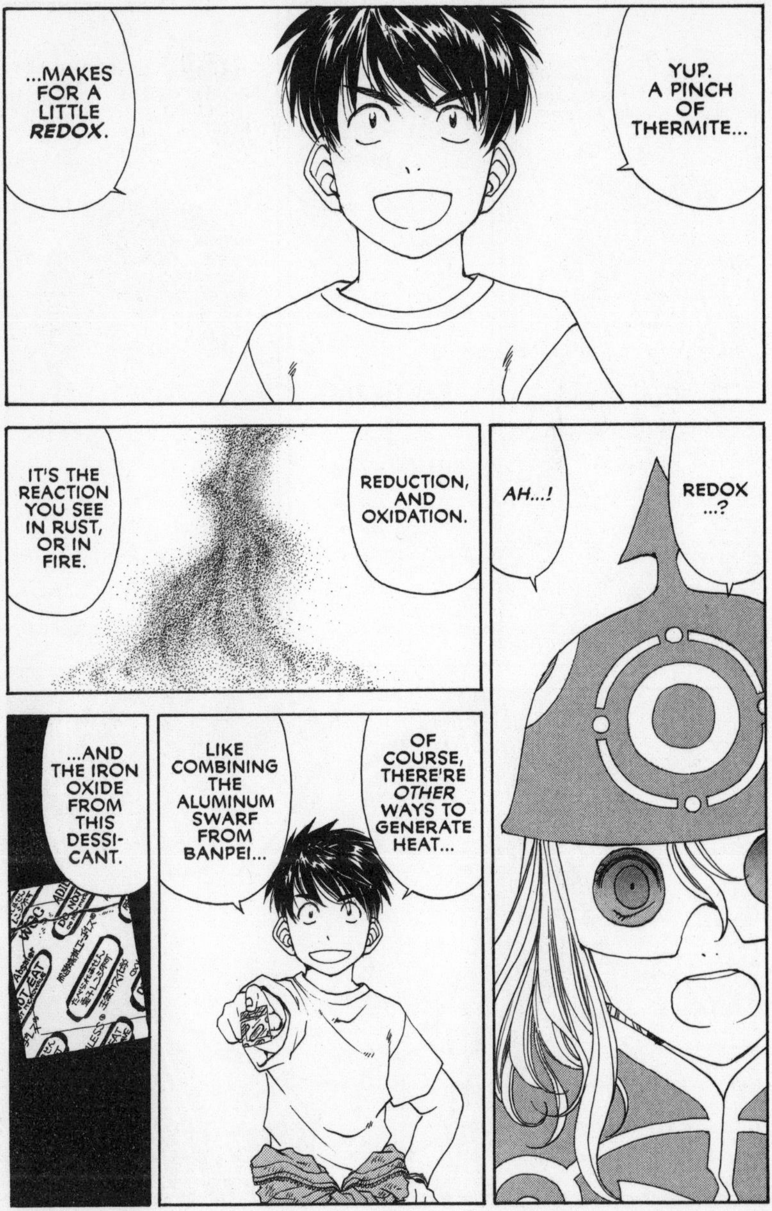
YUP. A PINCH OF THERMITE...
...MAKES FOR A LITTLE *REDOX*.
REDOX ...?
AH...!
REDUCTION, AND OXIDATION.
IT'S THE REACTION YOU SEE IN RUST, OR IN FIRE.
OF COURSE, THERE'RE *OTHER* WAYS TO GENERATE HEAT...
LIKE COMBINING THE ALUMINUM SWARF FROM BANPEI...
...AND THE IRON OXIDE FROM THIS DESSI-CANT.

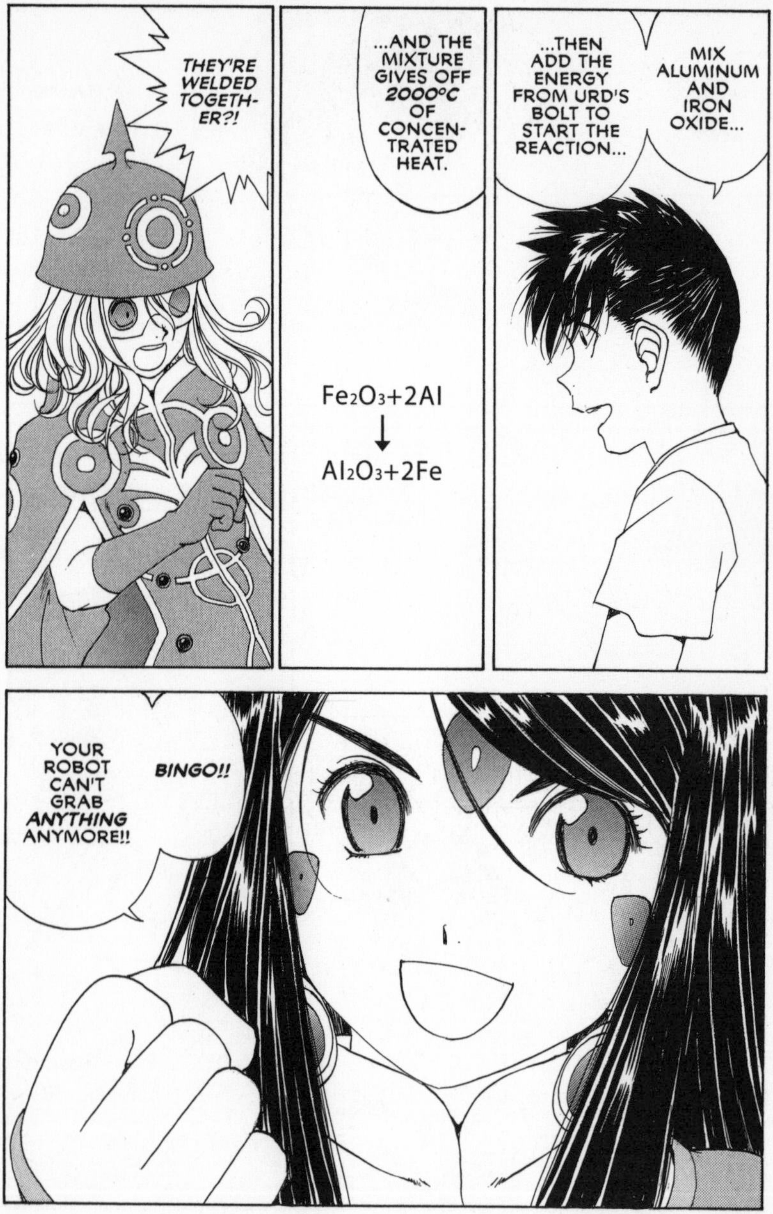
MIX ALUMINUM AND IRON OXIDE...
...THEN ADD THE ENERGY FROM URD'S BOLT TO START THE REACTION...
...AND THE MIXTURE GIVES OFF *2000°C* OF CONCENTRATED HEAT.
$Fe_2O_3+2Al \rightarrow Al_2O_3+2Fe$
THEY'RE WELDED TOGETHER?!
BINGO!!
YOUR ROBOT CAN'T GRAB *ANYTHING* ANYMORE!!

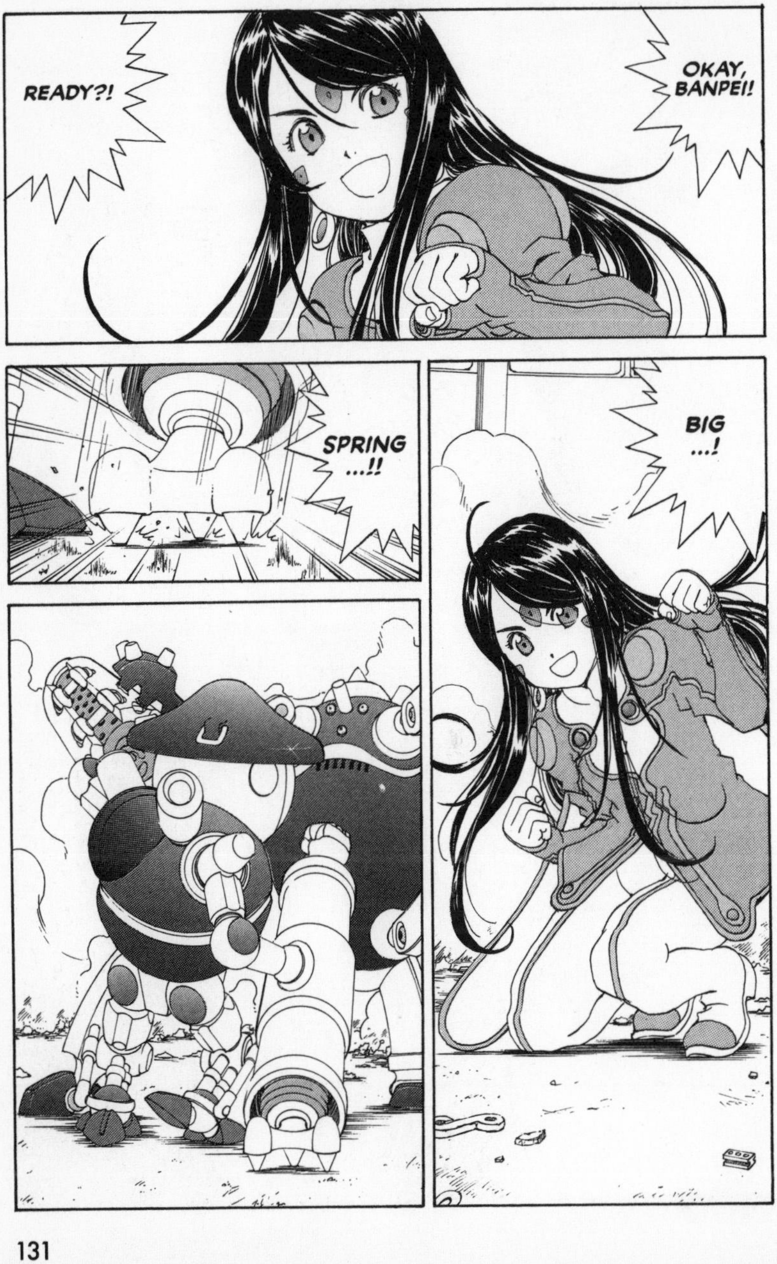
OKAY, BANPEI!!
READY?!
BIG ...!
SPRING ...!!

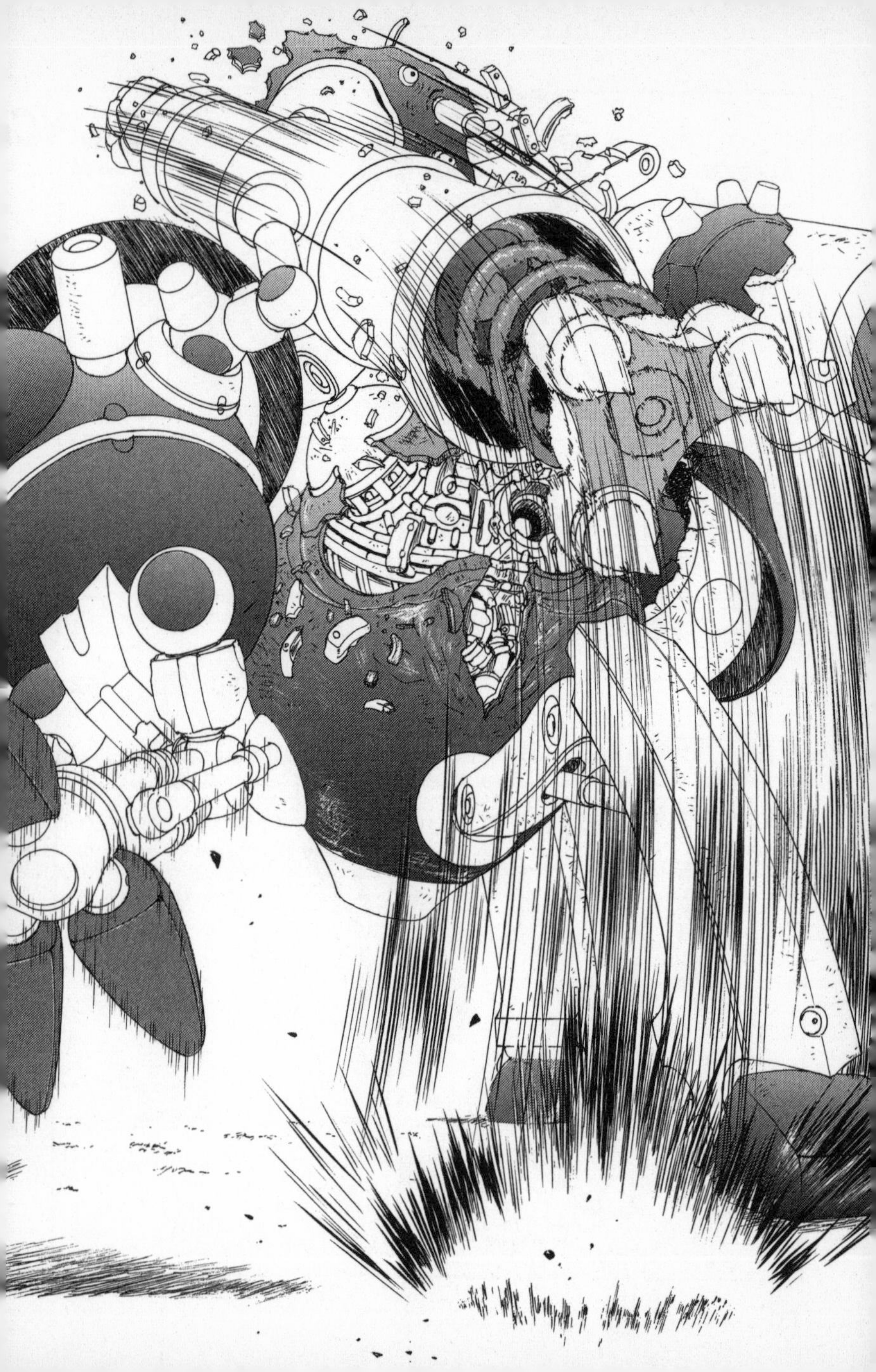

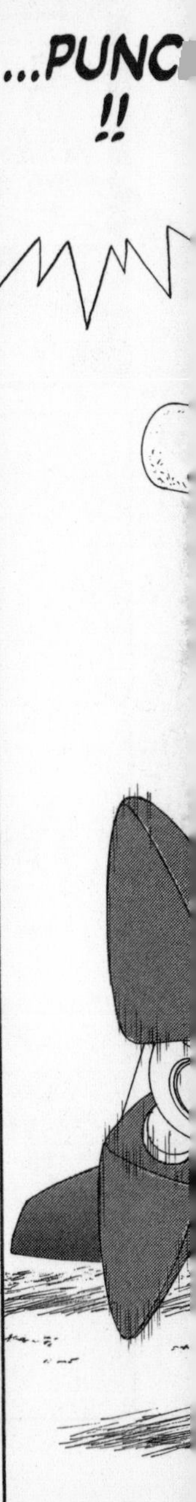
...PUNC
!!

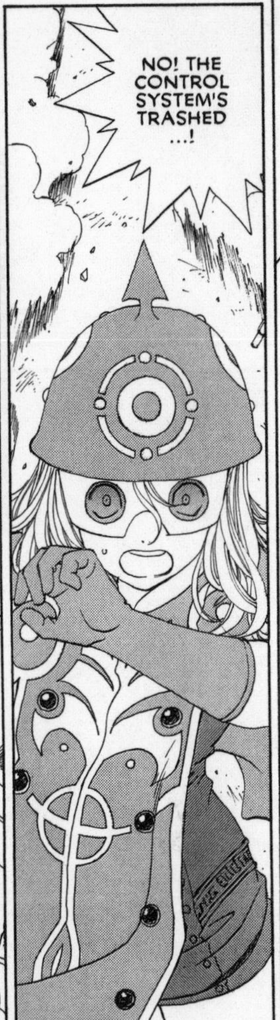
NO! THE CONTROL SYSTEM'S TRASHED ...!

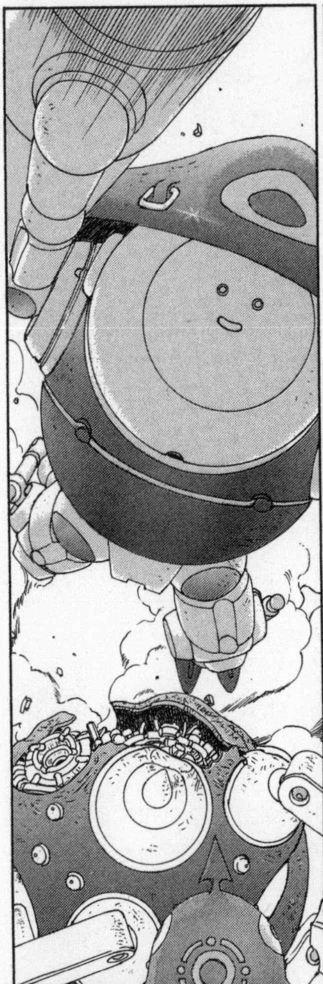

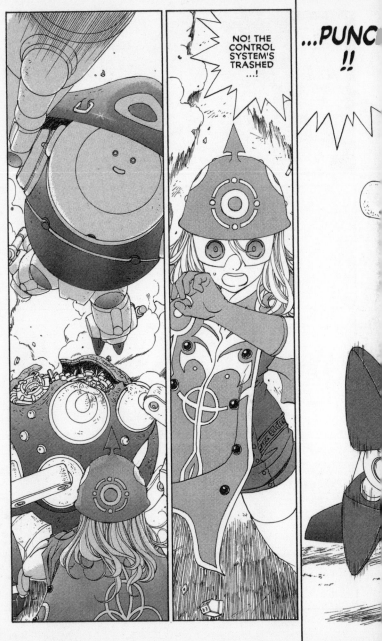

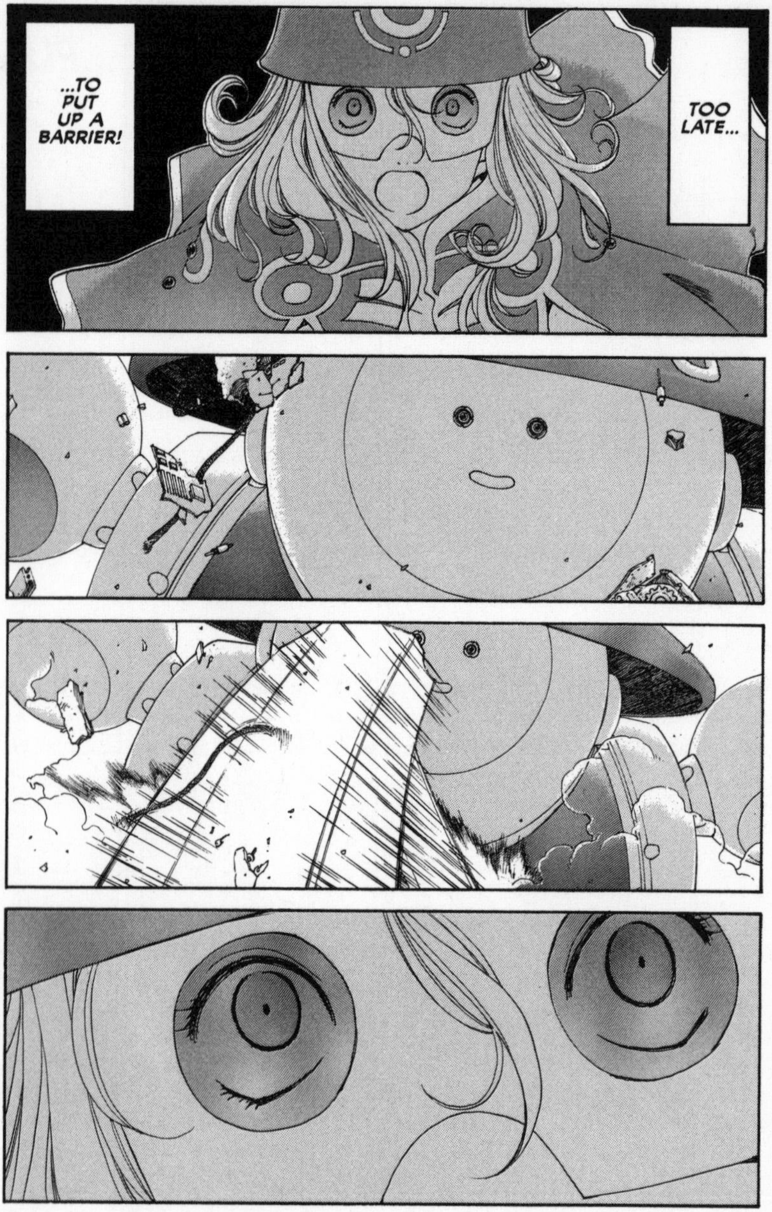
TOO LATE...
...TO PUT UP A BARRIER!

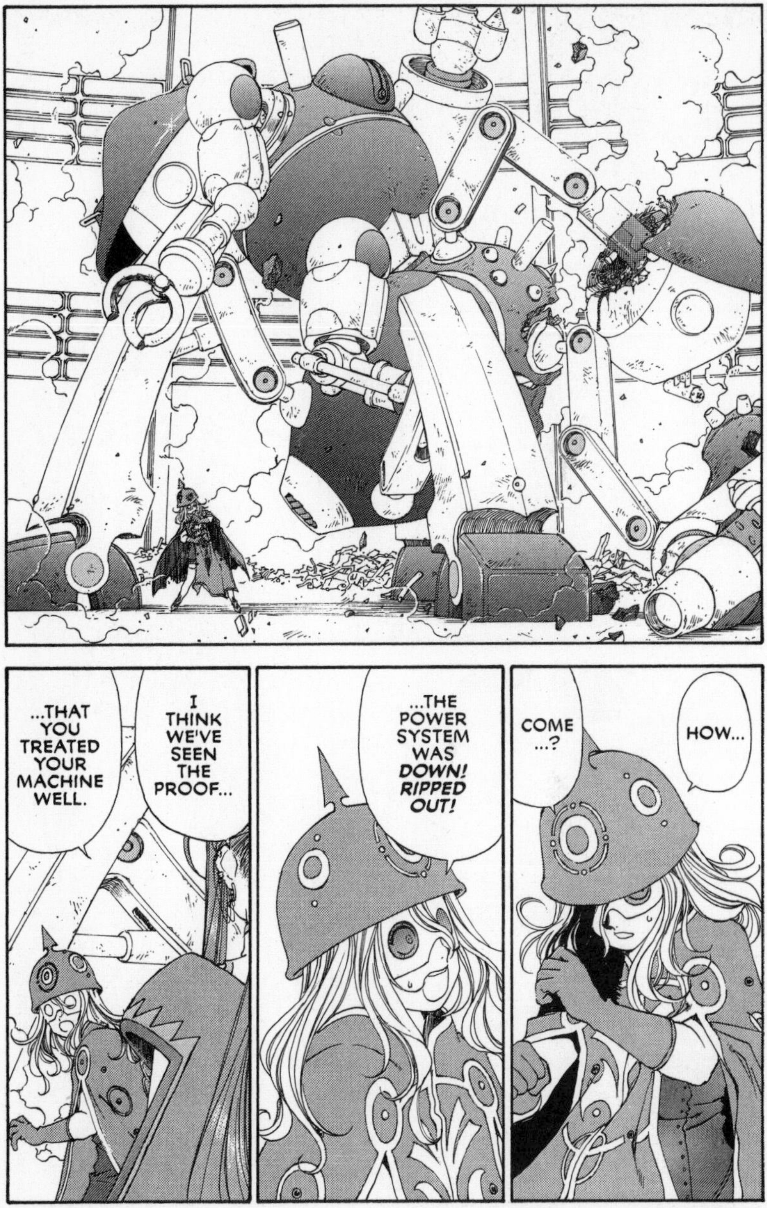
HOW...
COME ...?
...THE POWER SYSTEM WAS *DOWN! RIPPED OUT!*
I THINK WE'VE SEEN THE PROOF...
...THAT YOU TREATED YOUR MACHINE WELL.

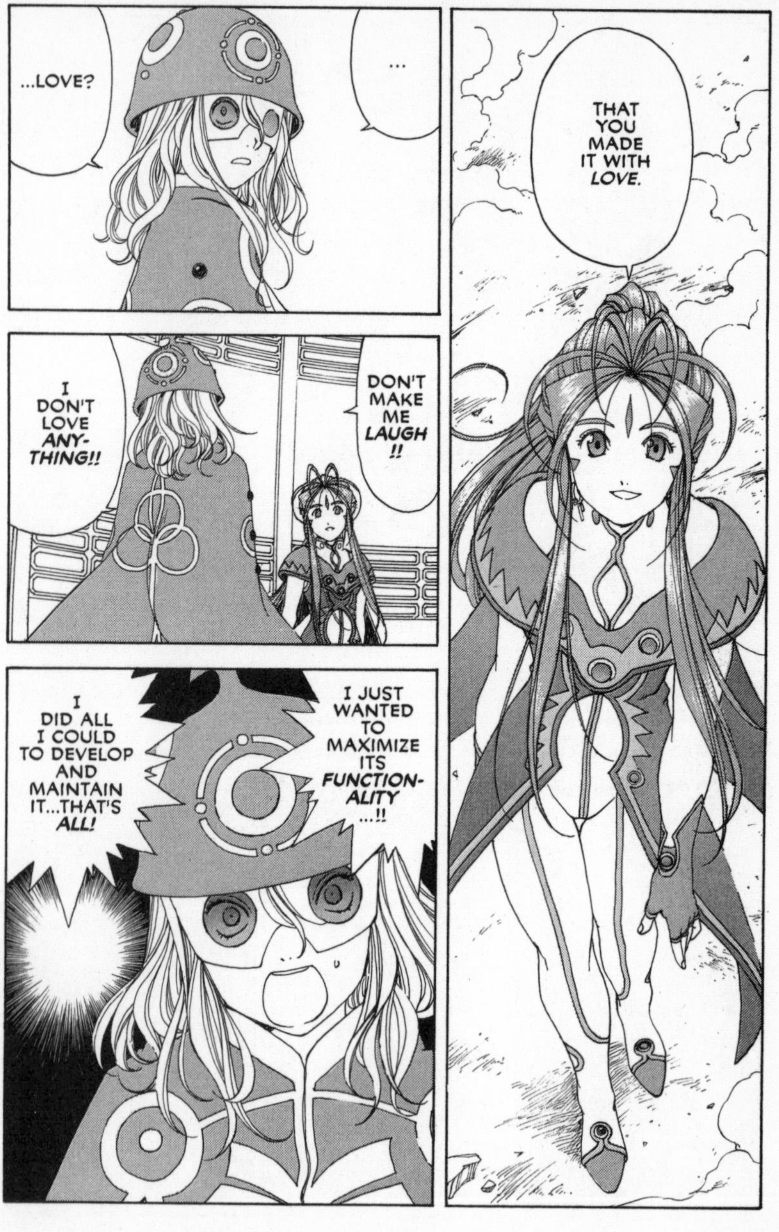
THAT YOU MADE IT WITH *LOVE.*
...
...LOVE?
DON'T MAKE ME *LAUGH!!*
I DON'T LOVE *ANYTHING!!*
I JUST WANTED TO MAXIMIZE ITS *FUNCTION-ALITY*...!!
I DID ALL I COULD TO DEVELOP AND MAINTAIN IT...THAT'S *ALL!*

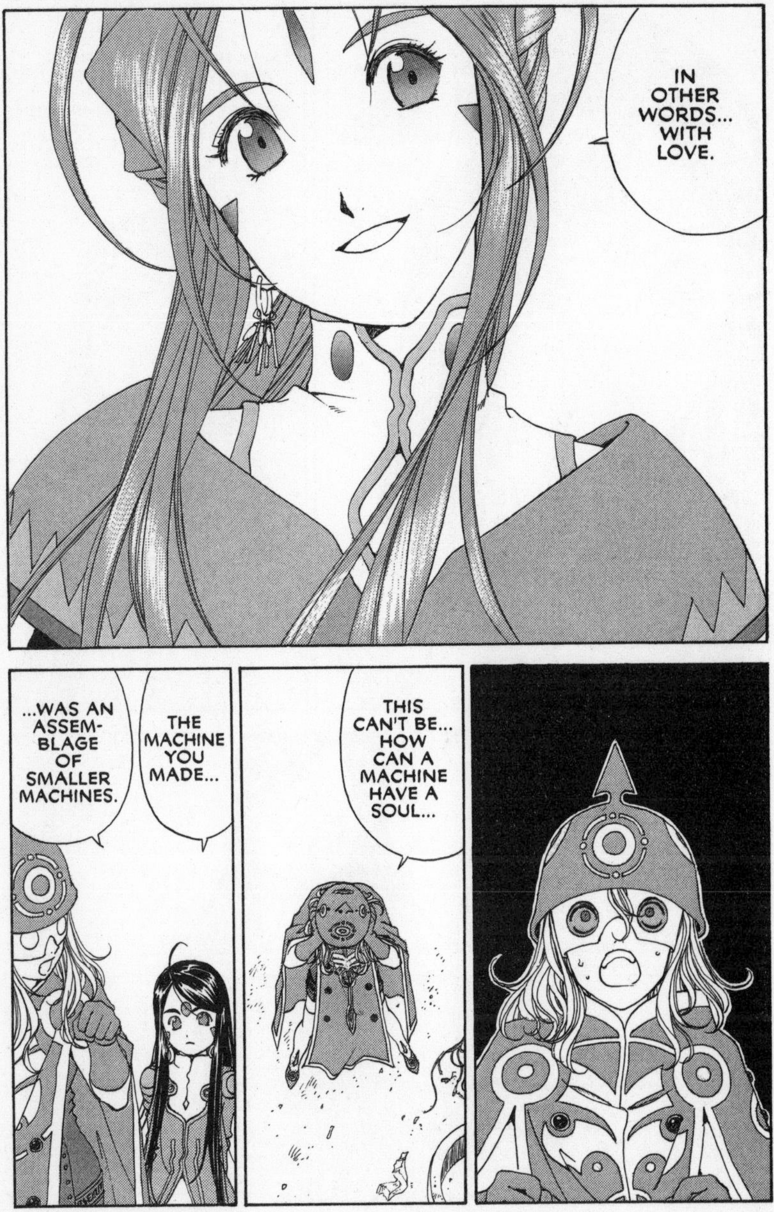
IN OTHER WORDS... WITH LOVE.
THIS CAN'T BE... HOW CAN A MACHINE HAVE A SOUL...
THE MACHINE YOU MADE...
...WAS AN ASSEMBLAGE OF SMALLER MACHINES.

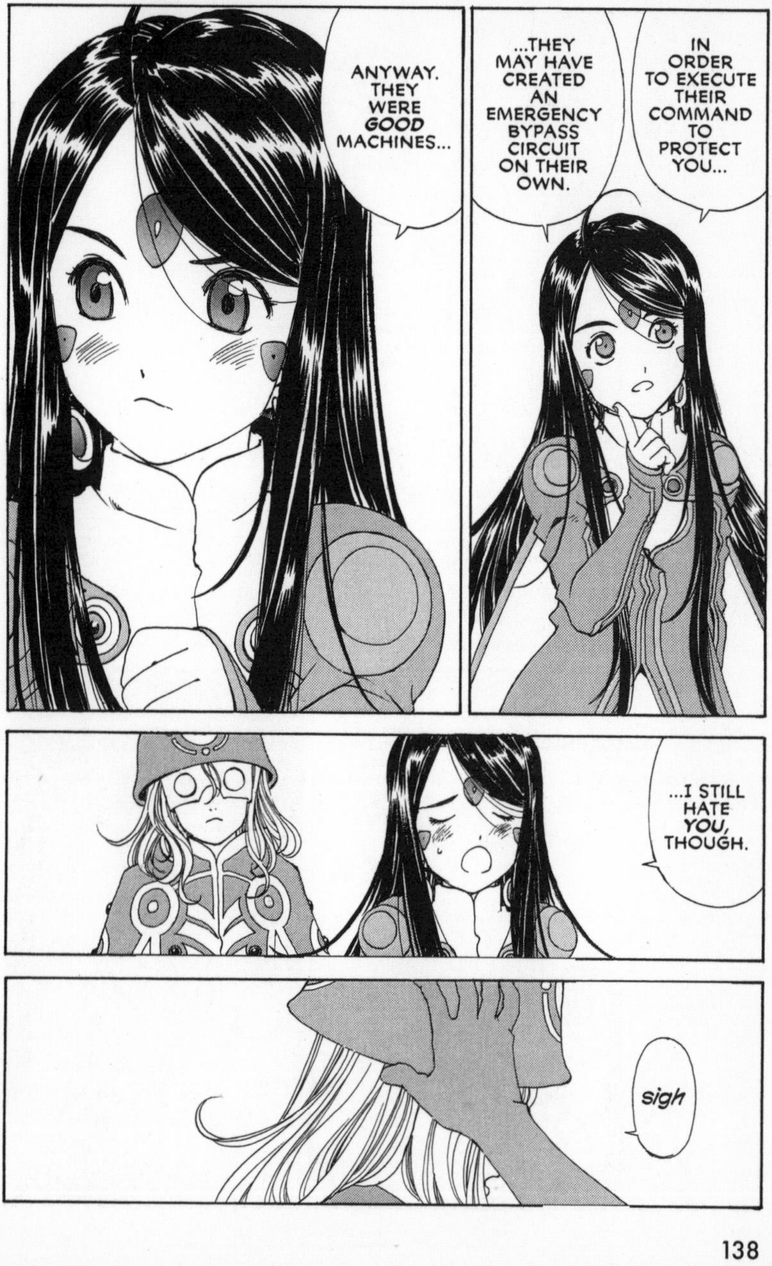
IN ORDER TO EXECUTE THEIR COMMAND TO PROTECT YOU...
...THEY MAY HAVE CREATED AN EMERGENCY BYPASS CIRCUIT ON THEIR OWN.
ANYWAY. THEY WERE *GOOD* MACHINES...
...I STILL HATE *YOU,* THOUGH.
sigh

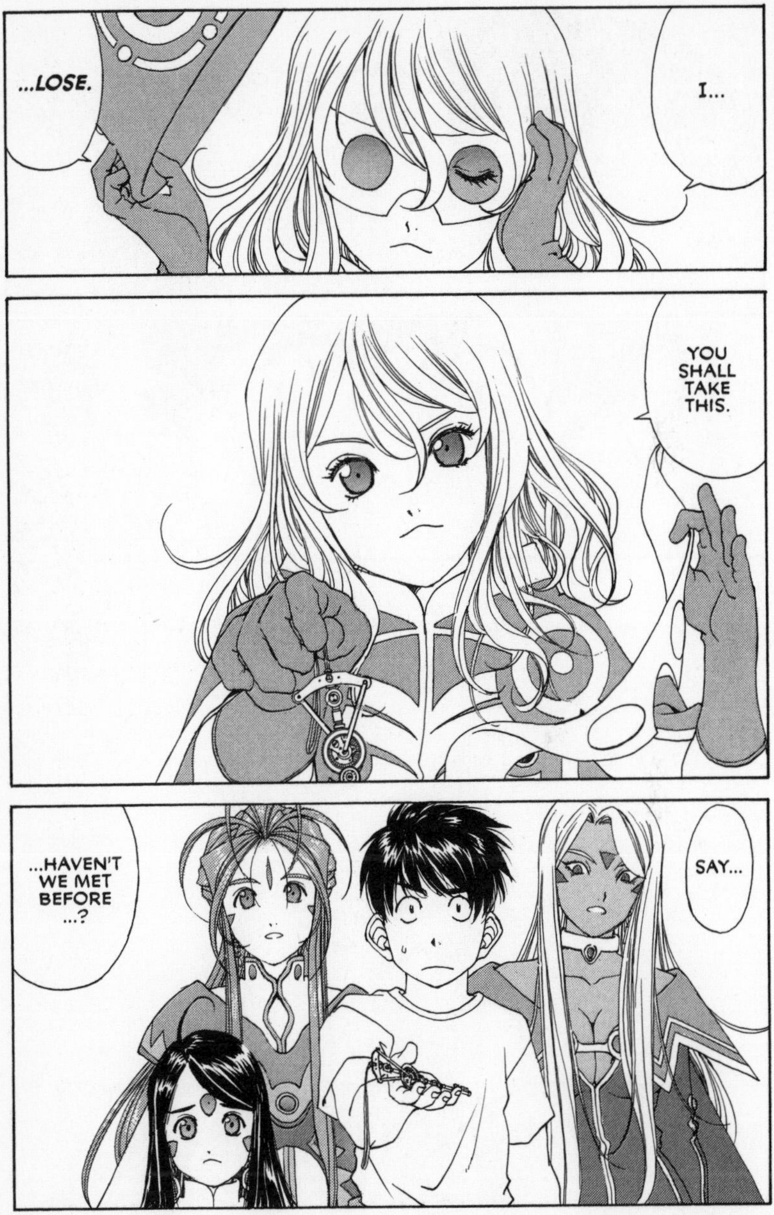
I...
...LOSE.
YOU SHALL TAKE THIS.
SAY...
...HAVEN'T WE MET BEFORE ...?

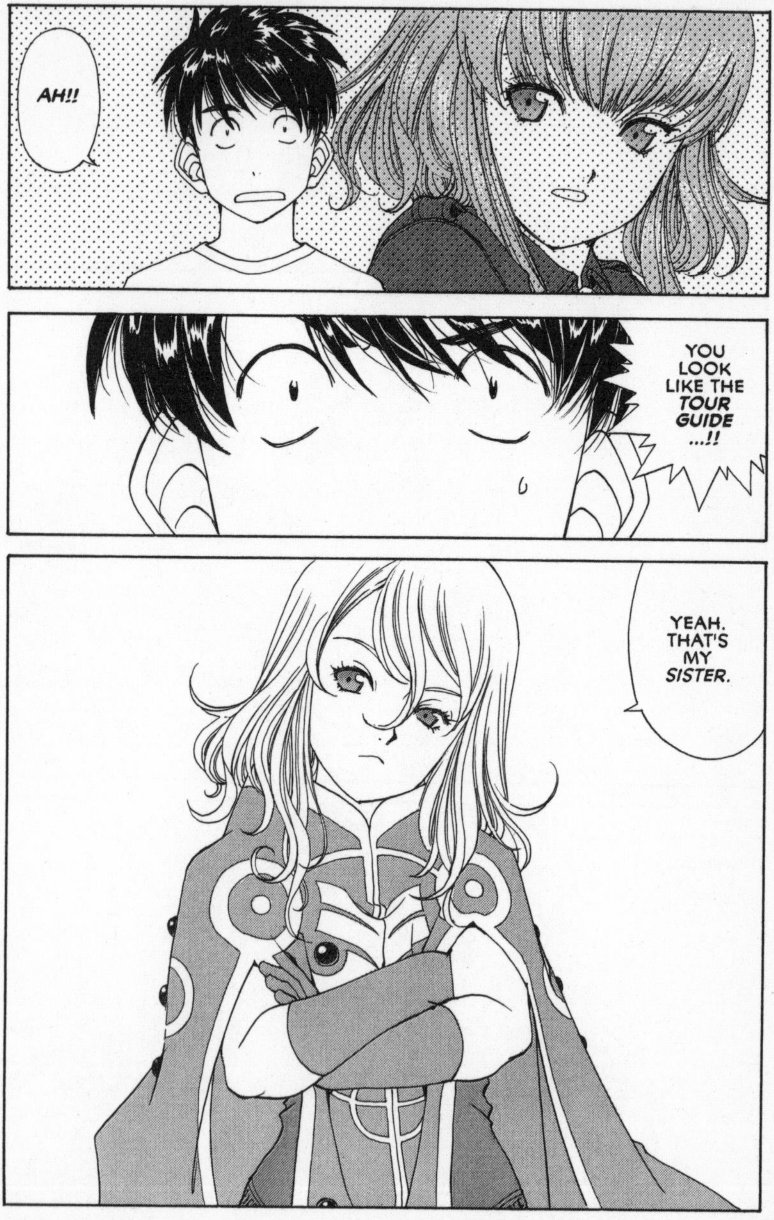
AH!!
YOU LOOK LIKE THE TOUR GUIDE ...!!
YEAH. THAT'S MY SISTER.

CHAPTER 268

A Test of Resolve

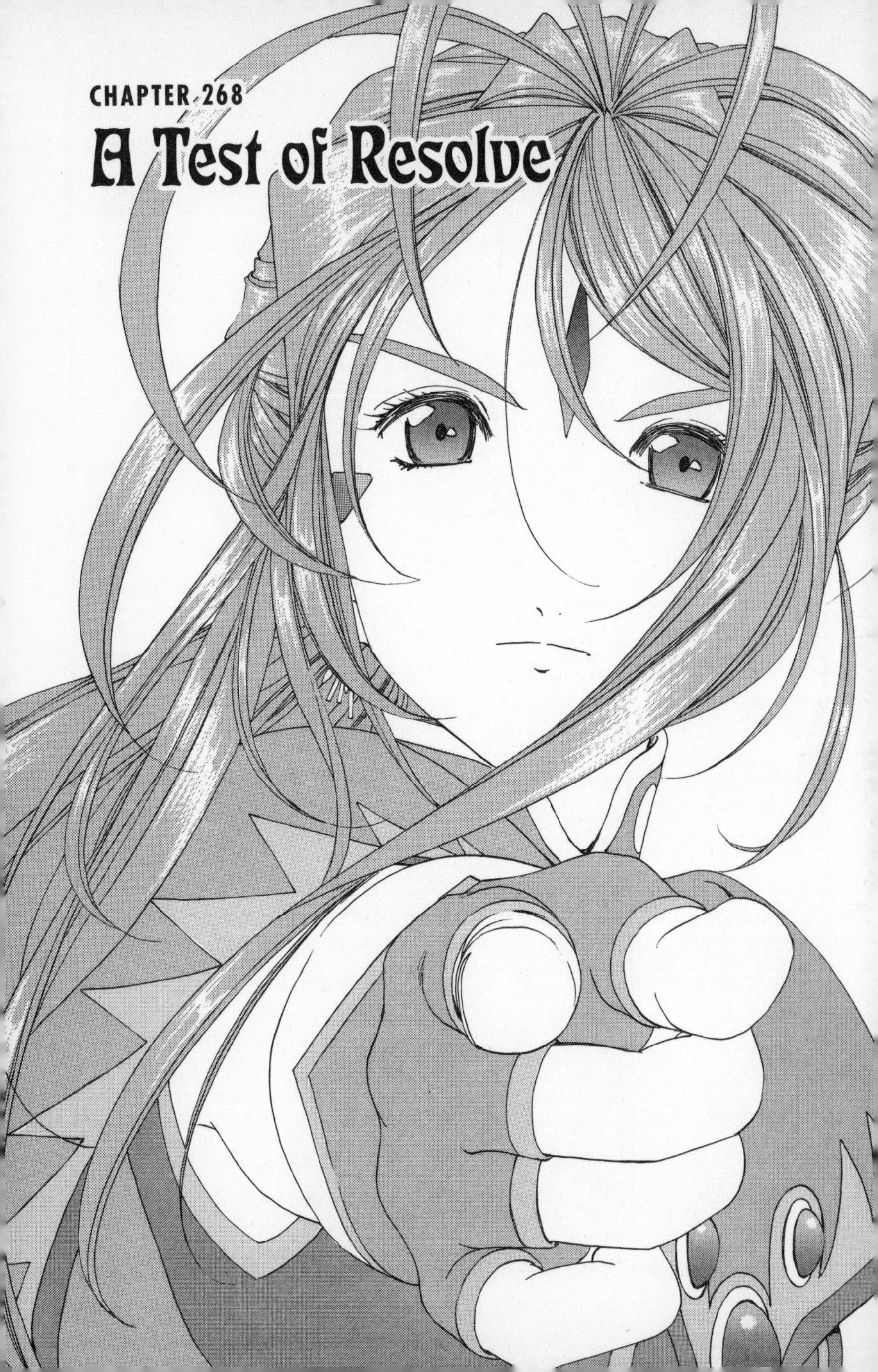

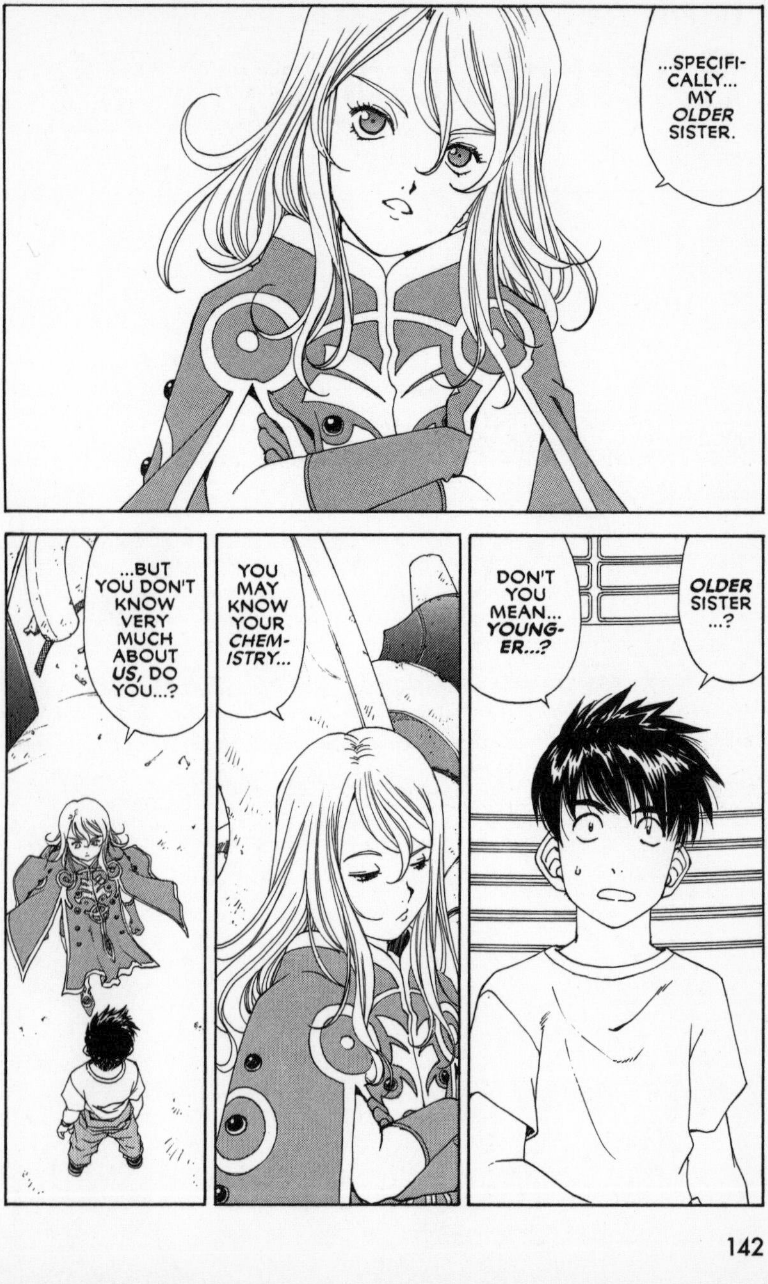
...SPECIFICALLY... MY OLDER SISTER.
OLDER SISTER ...?
DON'T YOU MEAN... YOUNGER...?
YOU MAY KNOW YOUR CHEMISTRY...
...BUT YOU DON'T KNOW VERY MUCH ABOUT US, DO YOU...?

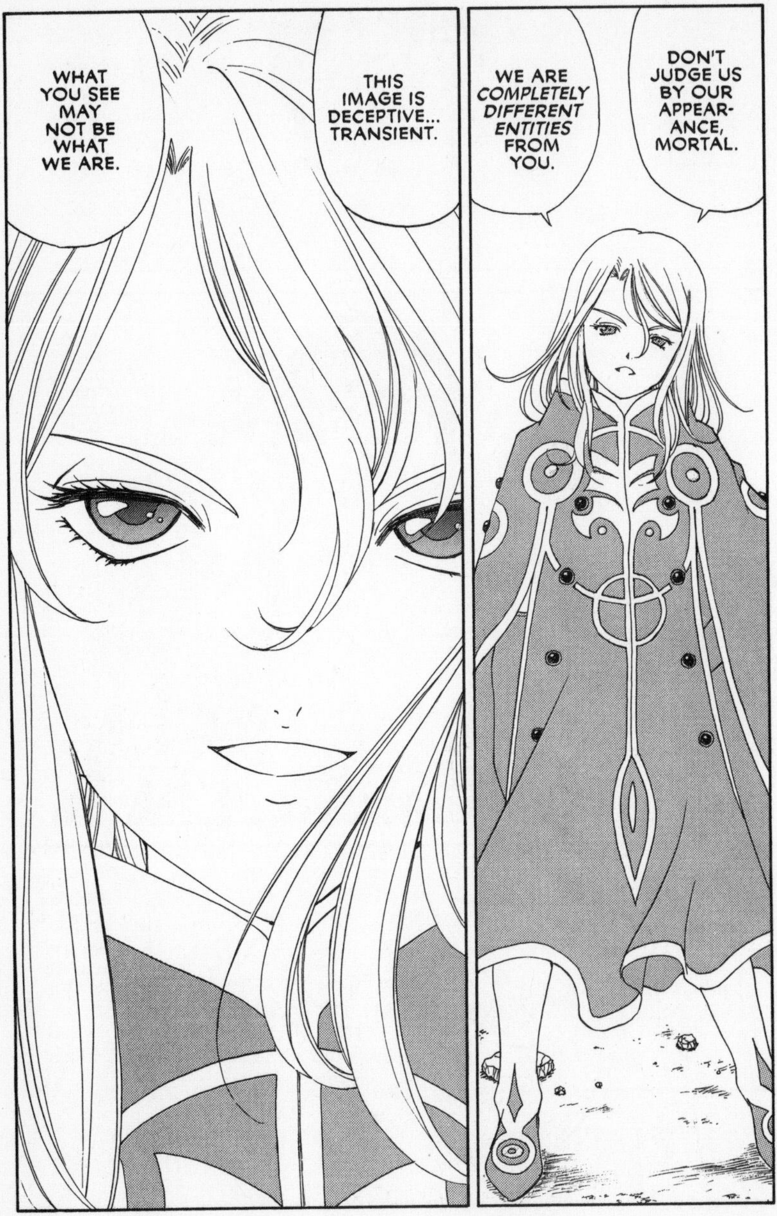
DON'T JUDGE US BY OUR APPEAR-ANCE, MORTAL.
WE ARE *COMPLETELY DIFFERENT ENTITIES* FROM YOU.
THIS IMAGE IS DECEPTIVE... TRANSIENT.
WHAT YOU SEE MAY NOT BE WHAT WE ARE.

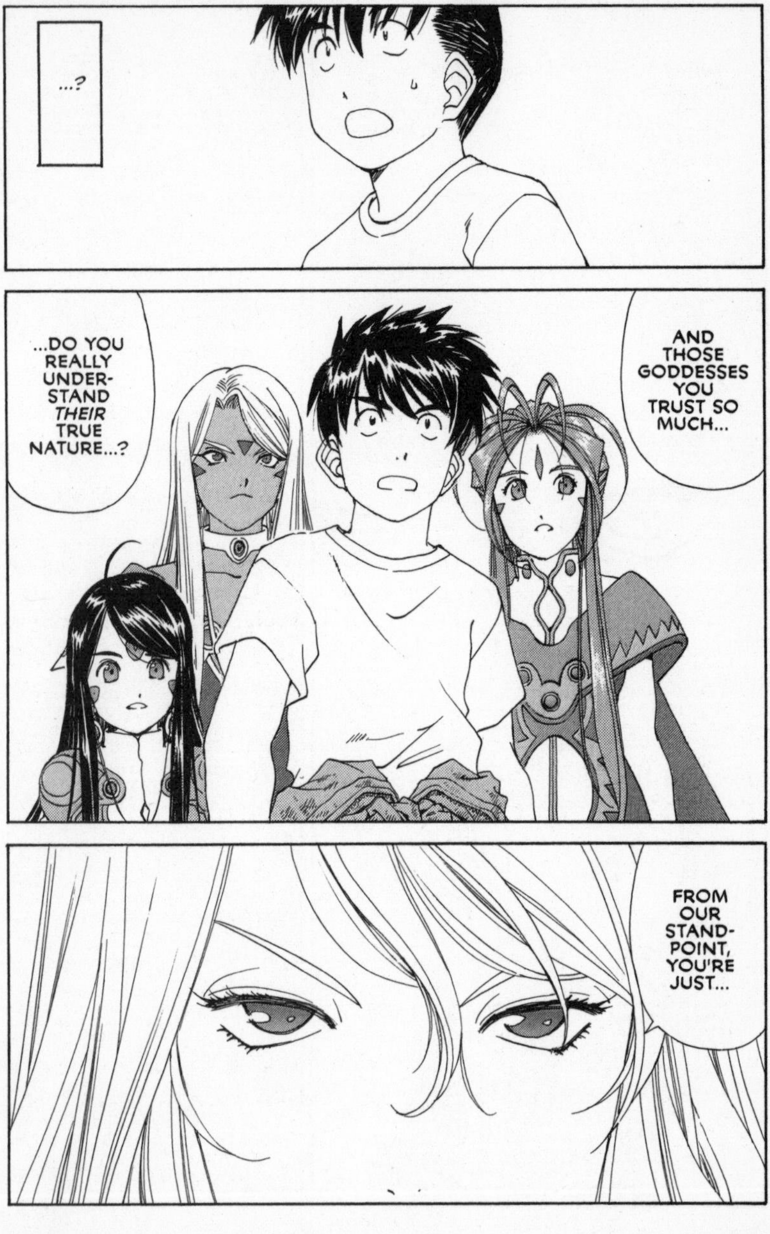
...?
AND THOSE GODDESSES YOU TRUST SO MUCH...
...DO YOU REALLY UNDER-STAND *THEIR* TRUE NATURE...?
FROM OUR STAND-POINT, YOU'RE JUST...

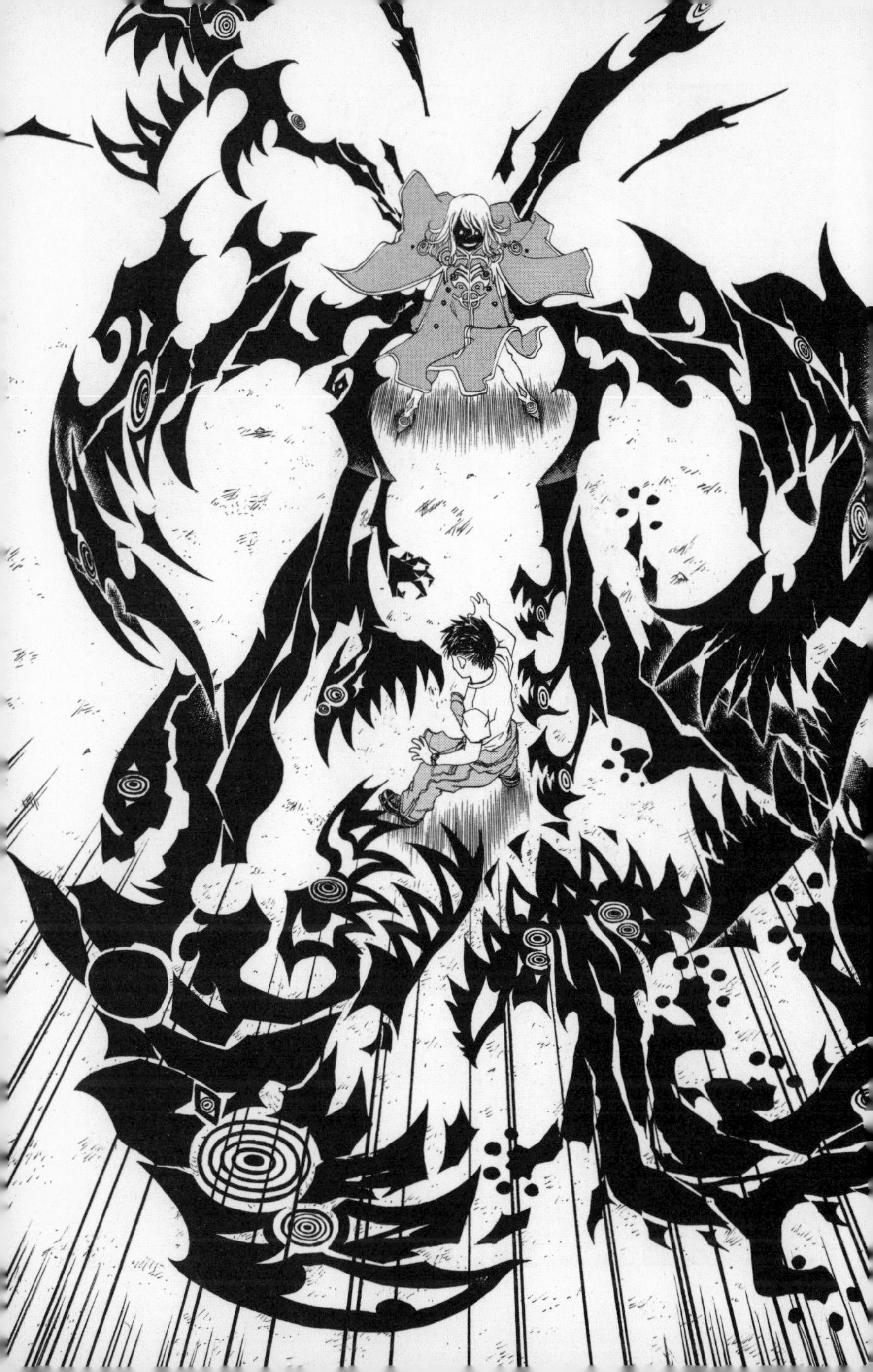

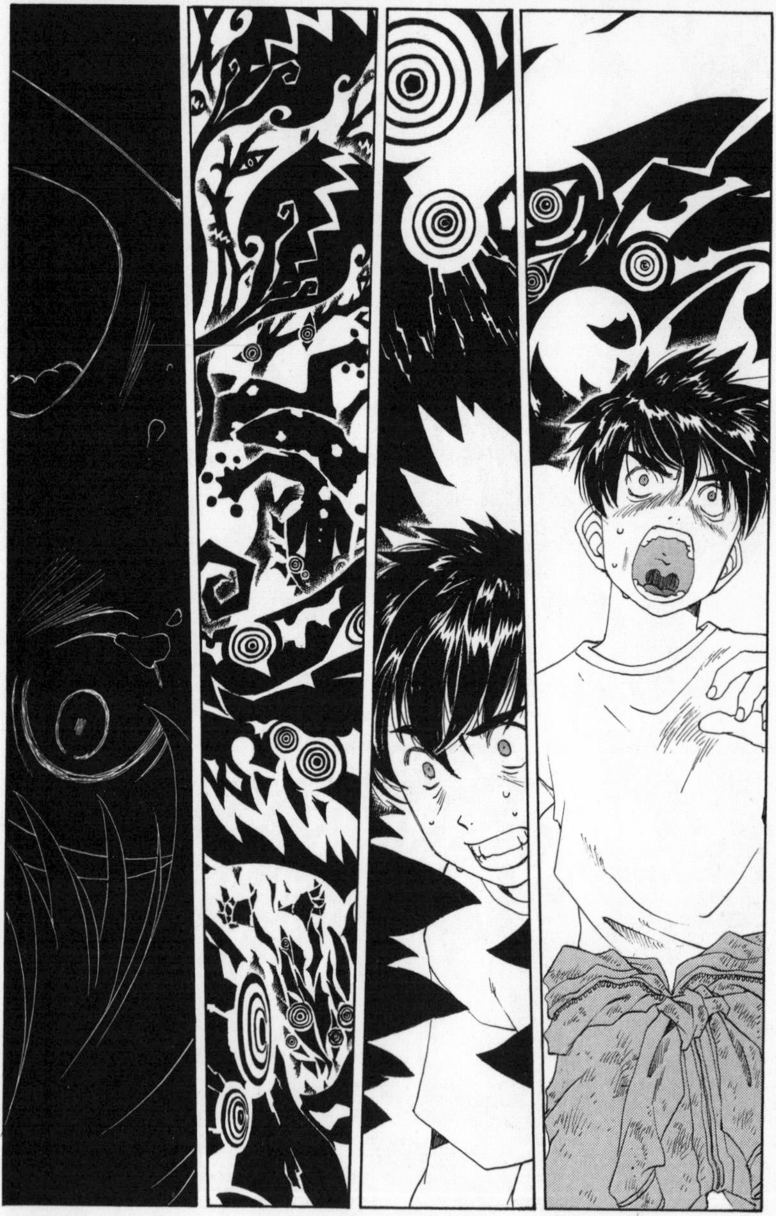

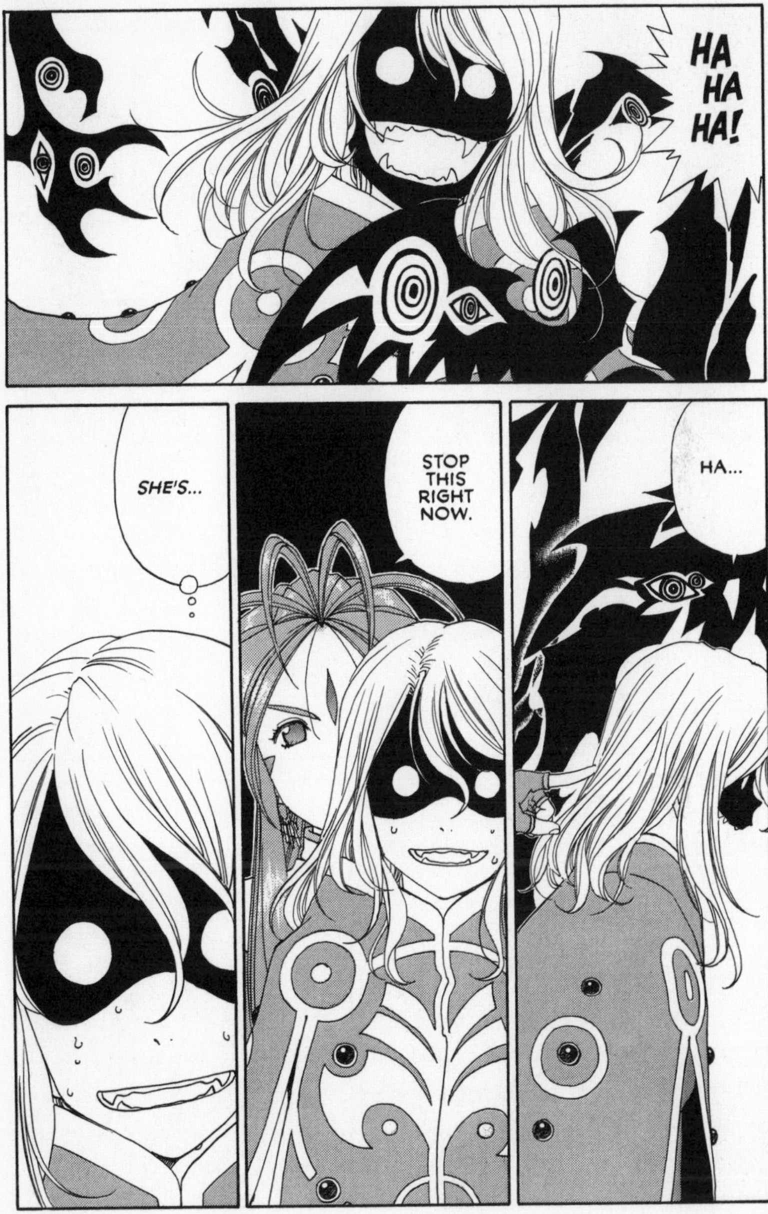
HA HA HA!
HA...
STOP THIS RIGHT NOW.
SHE'S...

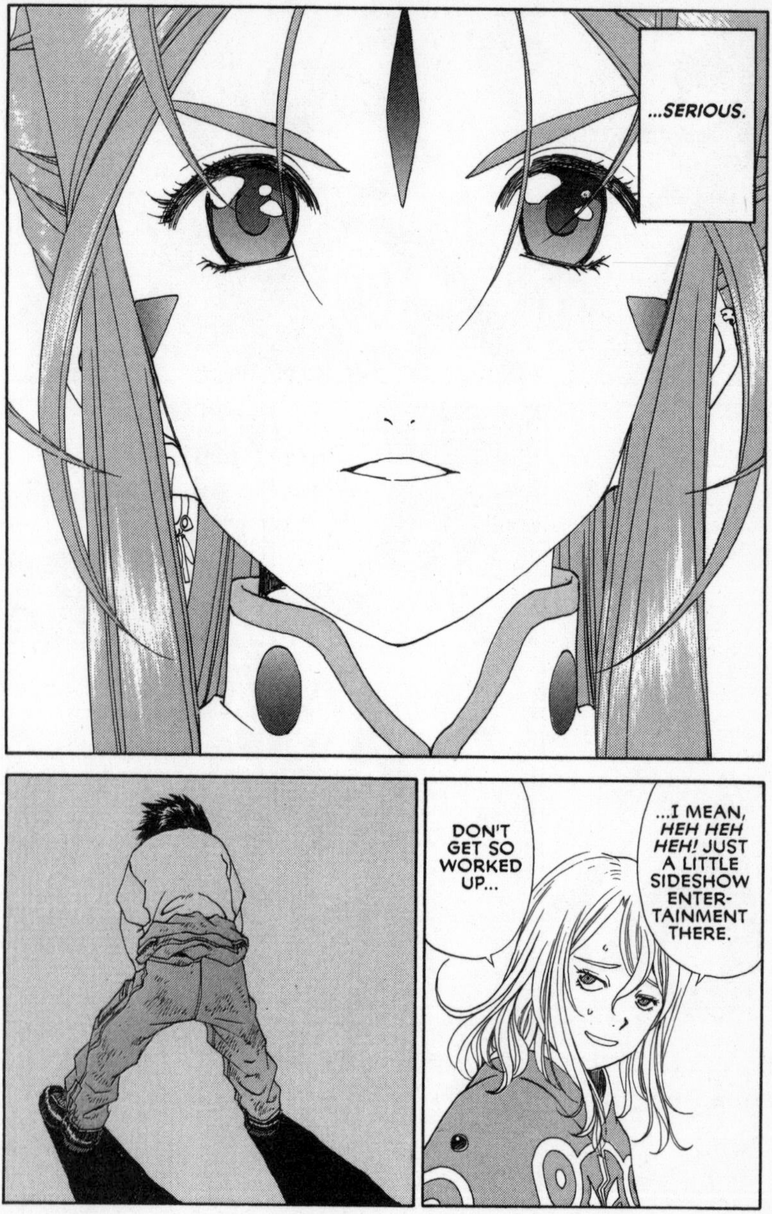
...SERIOUS.
...I MEAN, *HEH HEH HEH!* JUST A LITTLE SIDESHOW ENTER-TAINMENT THERE.
DON'T GET SO WORKED UP...

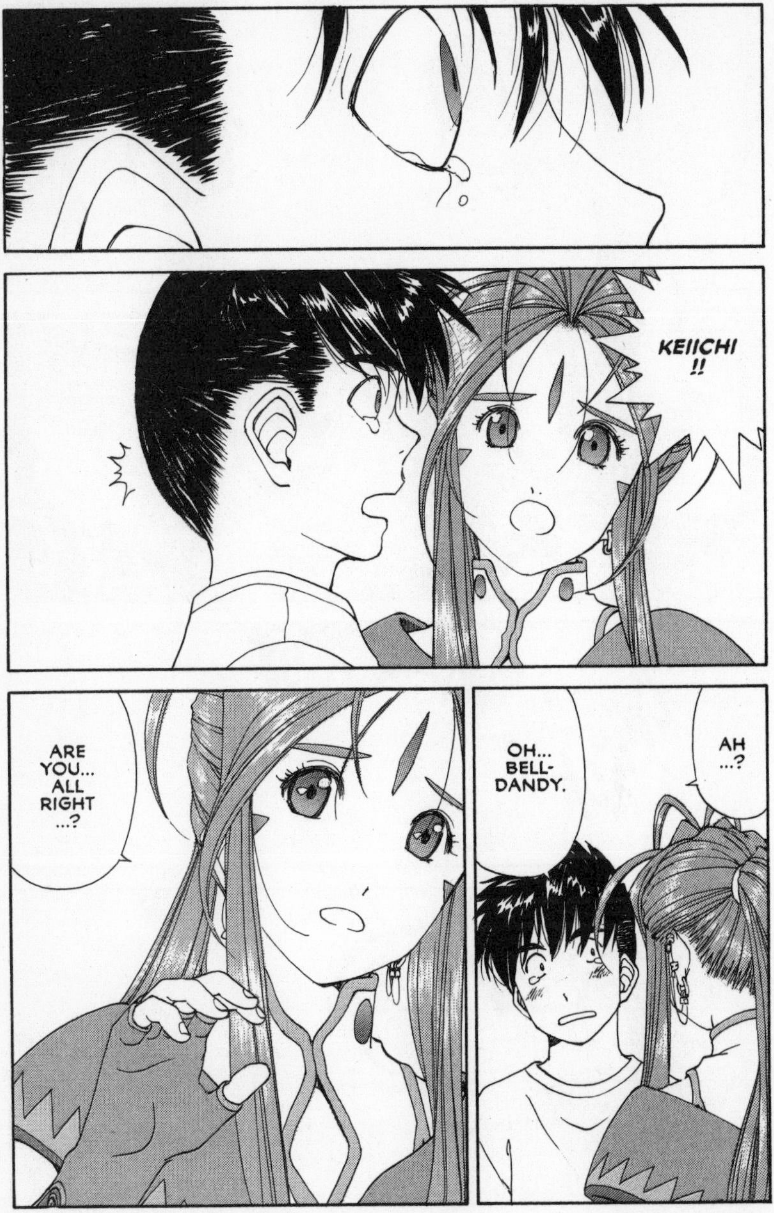
KEIICHI !!
AH ...?
OH... BELL-DANDY.
ARE YOU... ALL RIGHT ...?

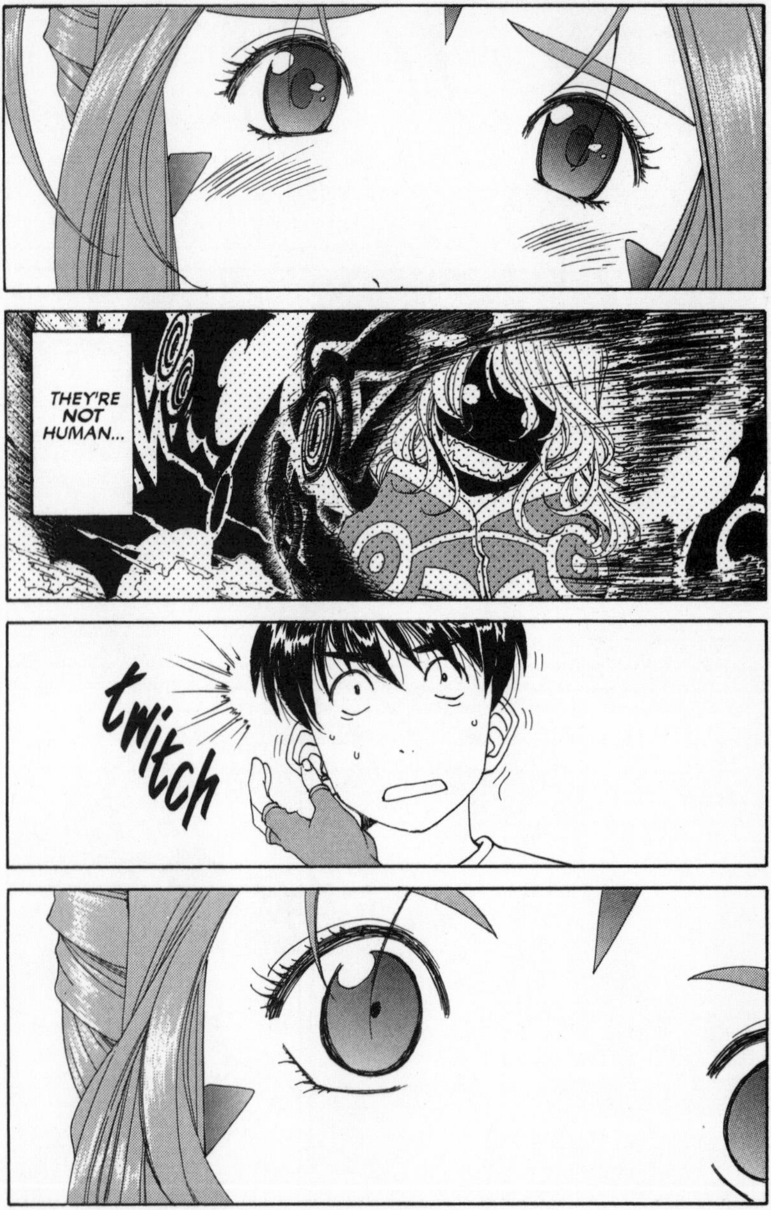
THEY'RE NOT HUMAN...
twitch

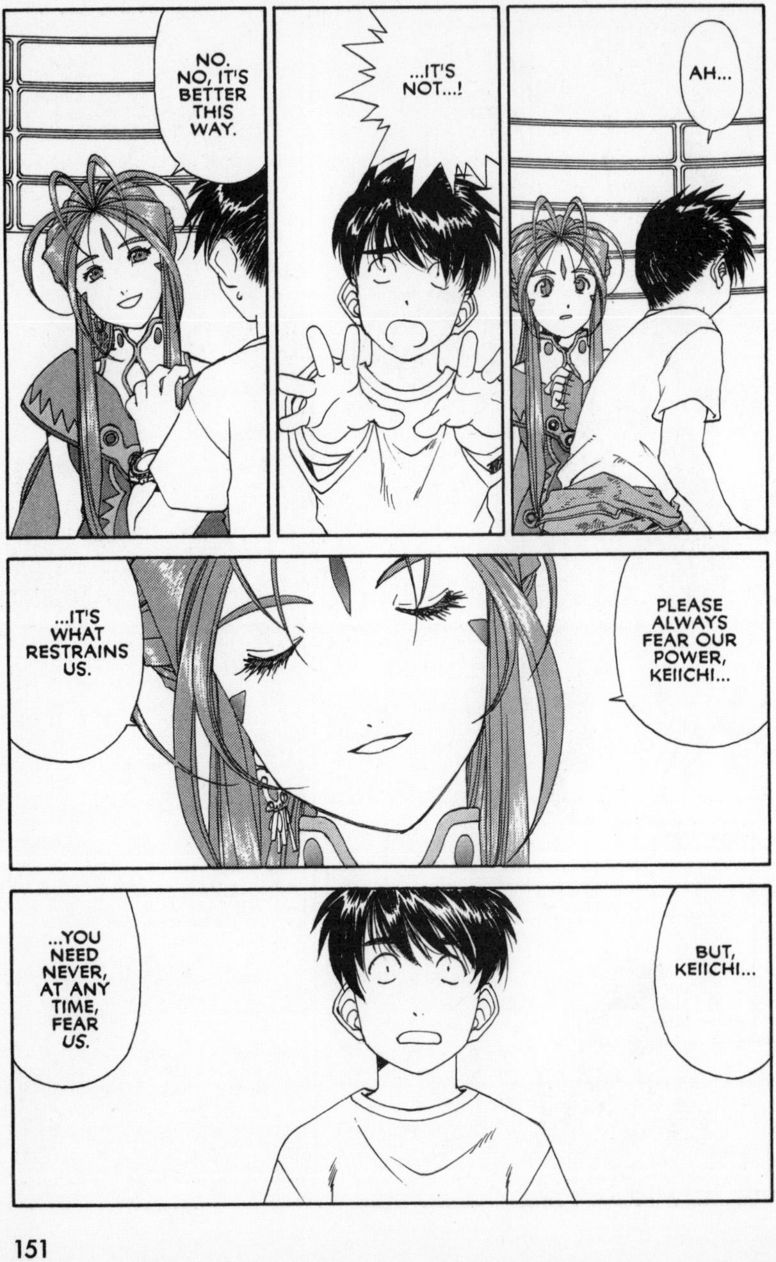
AH...
...IT'S NOT...!
NO. NO, IT'S BETTER THIS WAY.
PLEASE ALWAYS FEAR OUR POWER, KEIICHI...
...IT'S WHAT RESTRAINS US.
BUT, KEIICHI...
...YOU NEED NEVER, AT ANY TIME, FEAR *US*.

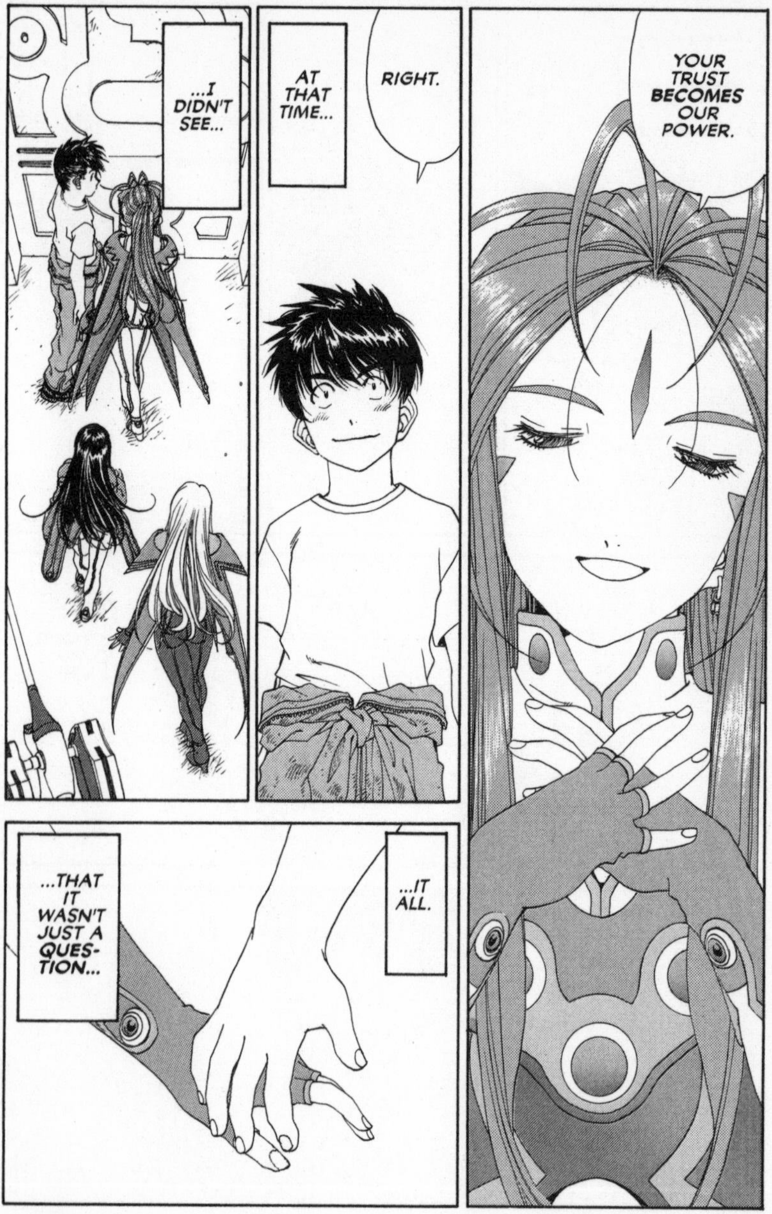
YOUR TRUST BECOMES OUR POWER.
RIGHT.
AT THAT TIME...
...I DIDN'T SEE...
...IT ALL.
...THAT IT WASN'T JUST A QUES-TION...

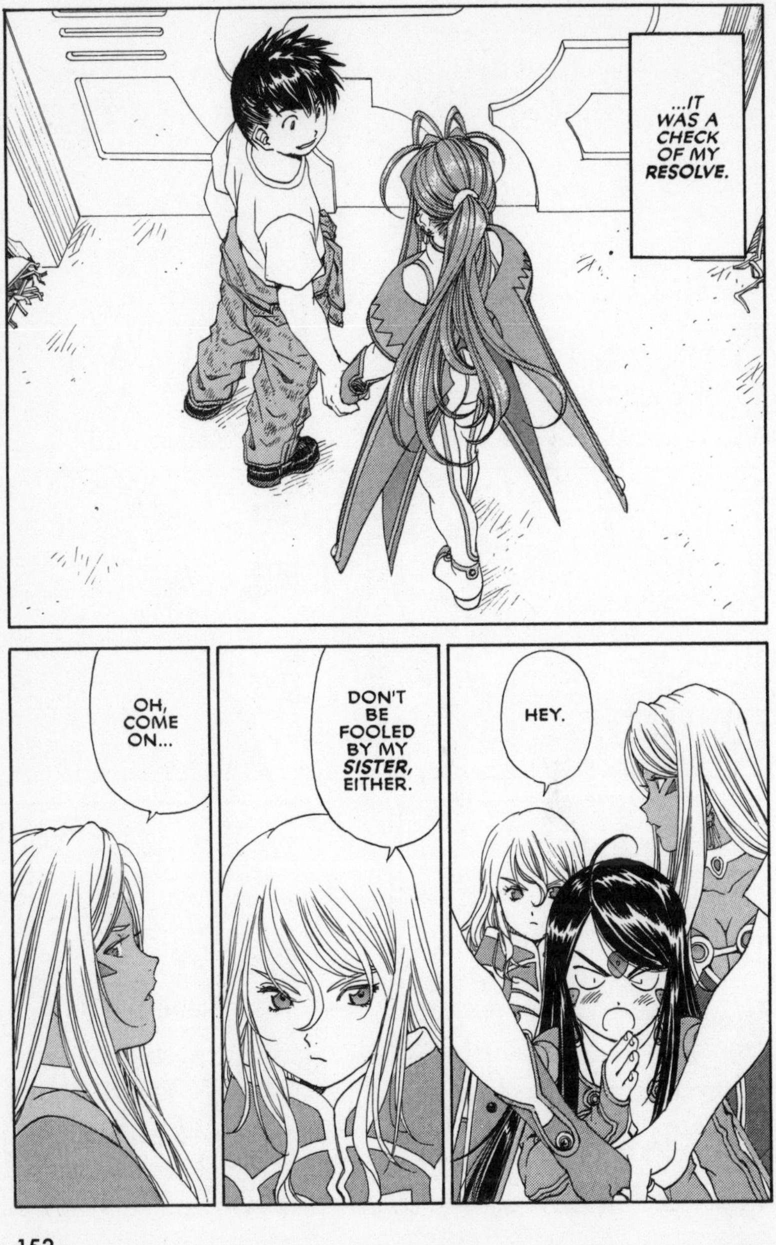
...IT WAS A CHECK OF MY RESOLVE.
HEY.
DON'T BE FOOLED BY MY SISTER, EITHER.
OH, COME ON...

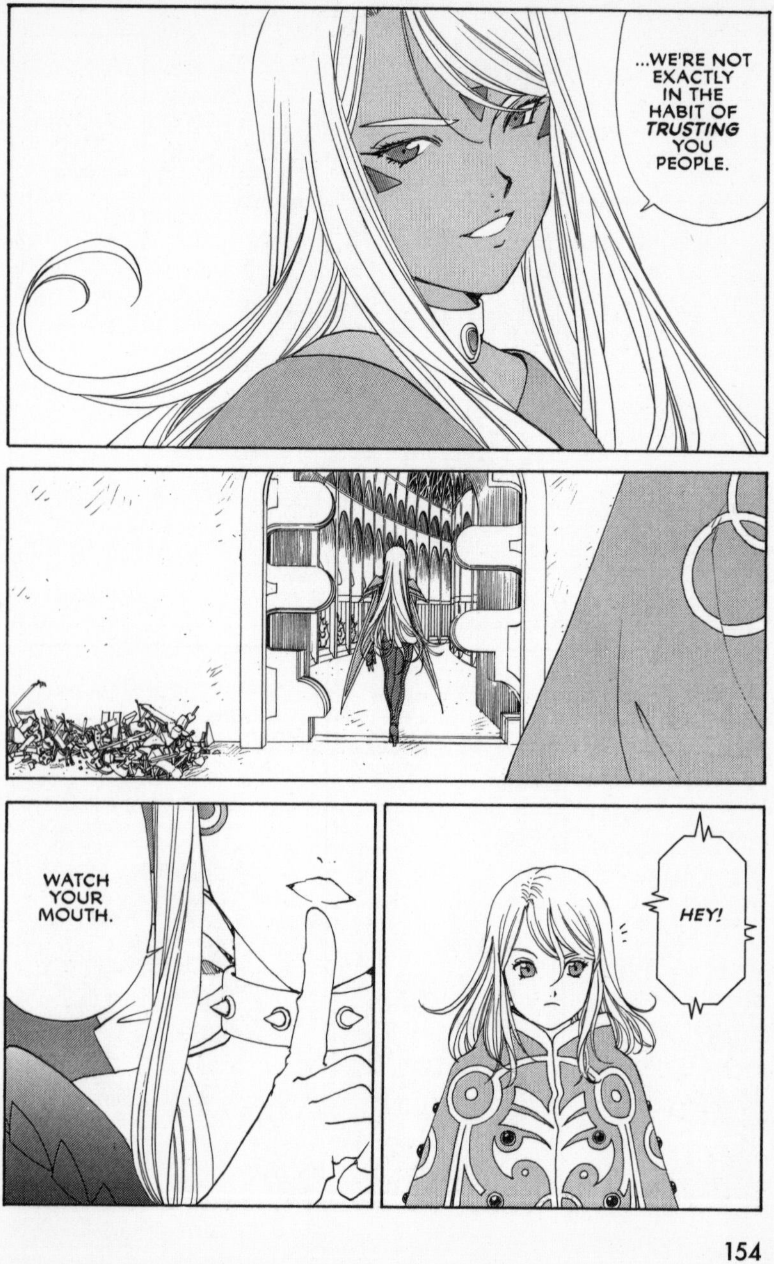
...WE'RE NOT EXACTLY IN THE HABIT OF *TRUSTING* YOU PEOPLE.
HEY!
WATCH YOUR MOUTH.

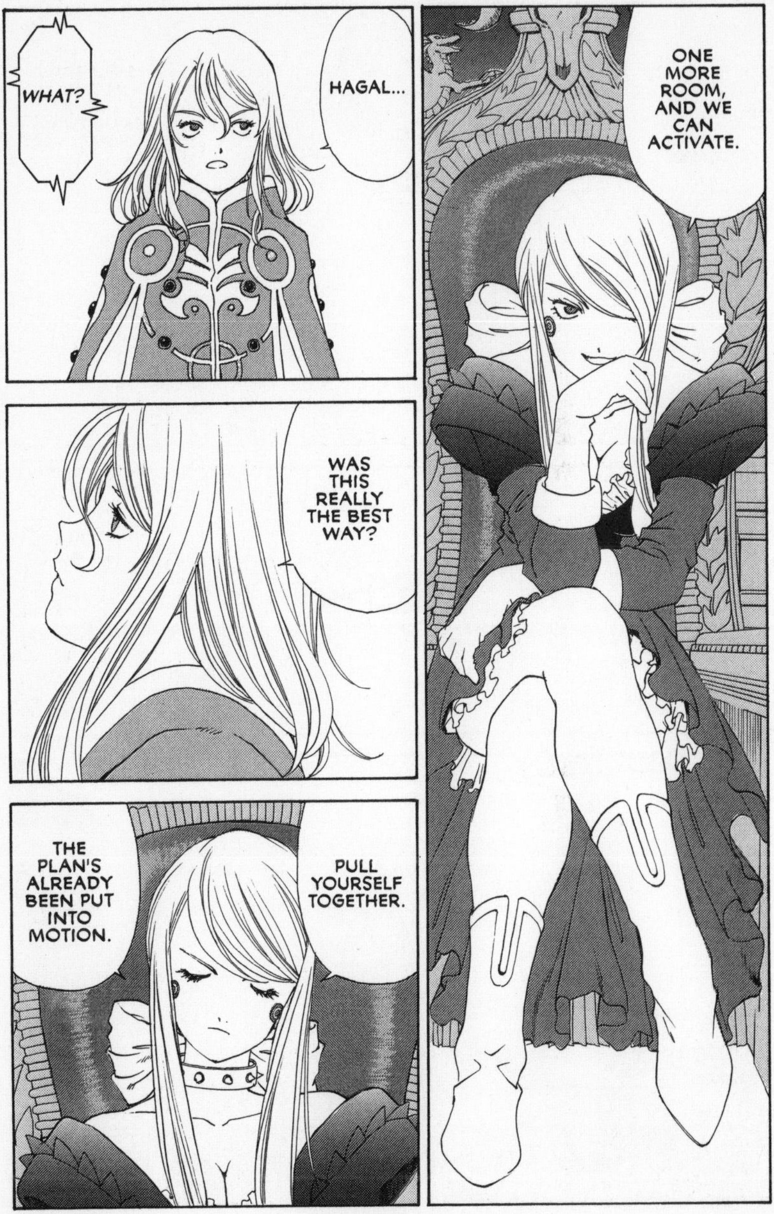
ONE MORE ROOM, AND WE CAN ACTIVATE.
HAGAL...
WHAT?
WAS THIS REALLY THE BEST WAY?
PULL YOURSELF TOGETHER.
THE PLAN'S ALREADY BEEN PUT INTO MOTION.

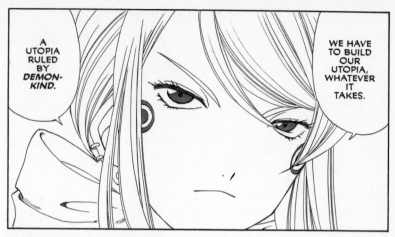

WE HAVE TO BUILD OUR UTOPIA, WHATEVER IT TAKES.
A UTOPIA RULED BY *DEMON-KIND.*
AFTER ALL...
...ISN'T THAT THE FINAL THING WE CAN DO FOR HER?
YES, MA'AM.

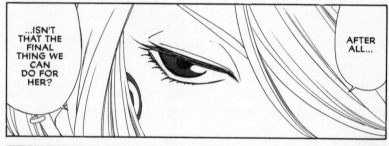

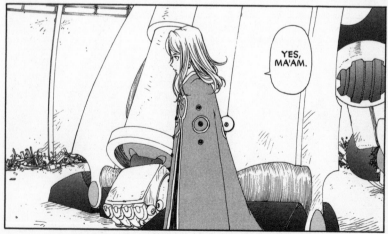

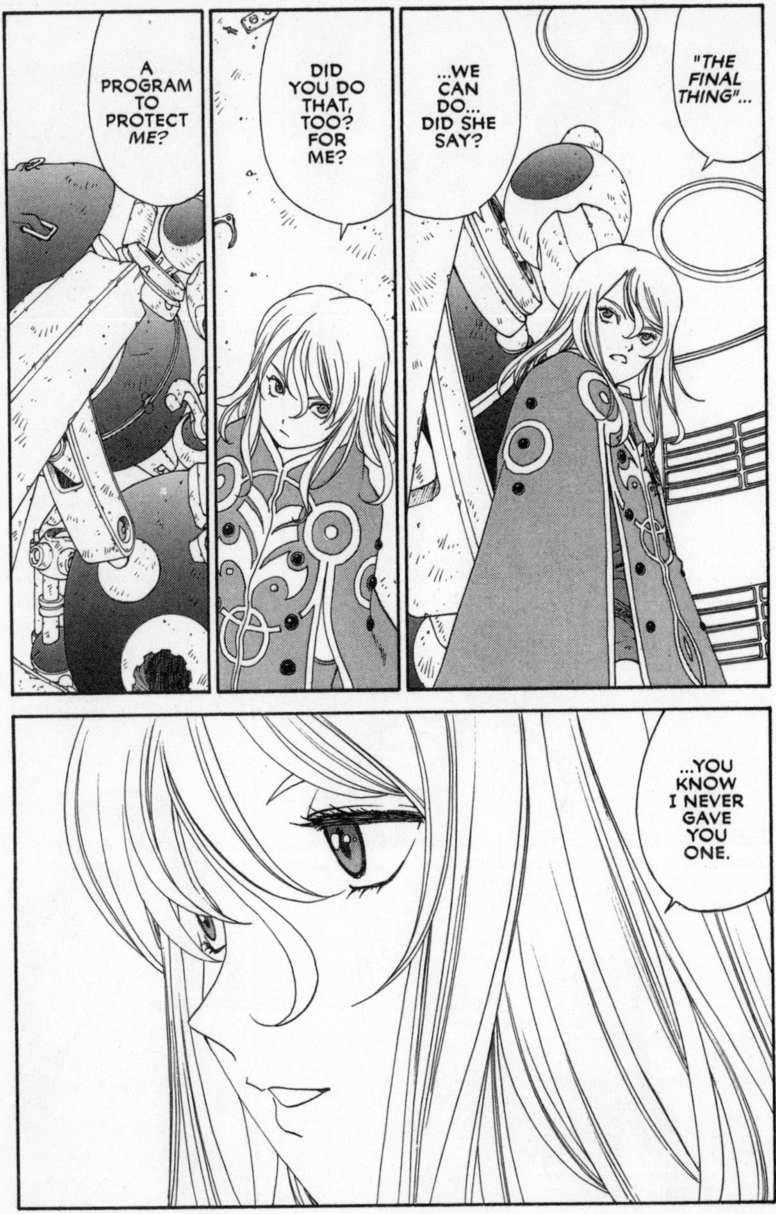
"THE FINAL THING"...
...WE CAN DO... DID SHE SAY?
DID YOU DO THAT, TOO? FOR ME?
A PROGRAM TO PROTECT *ME?*
...YOU KNOW I NEVER GAVE YOU ONE.

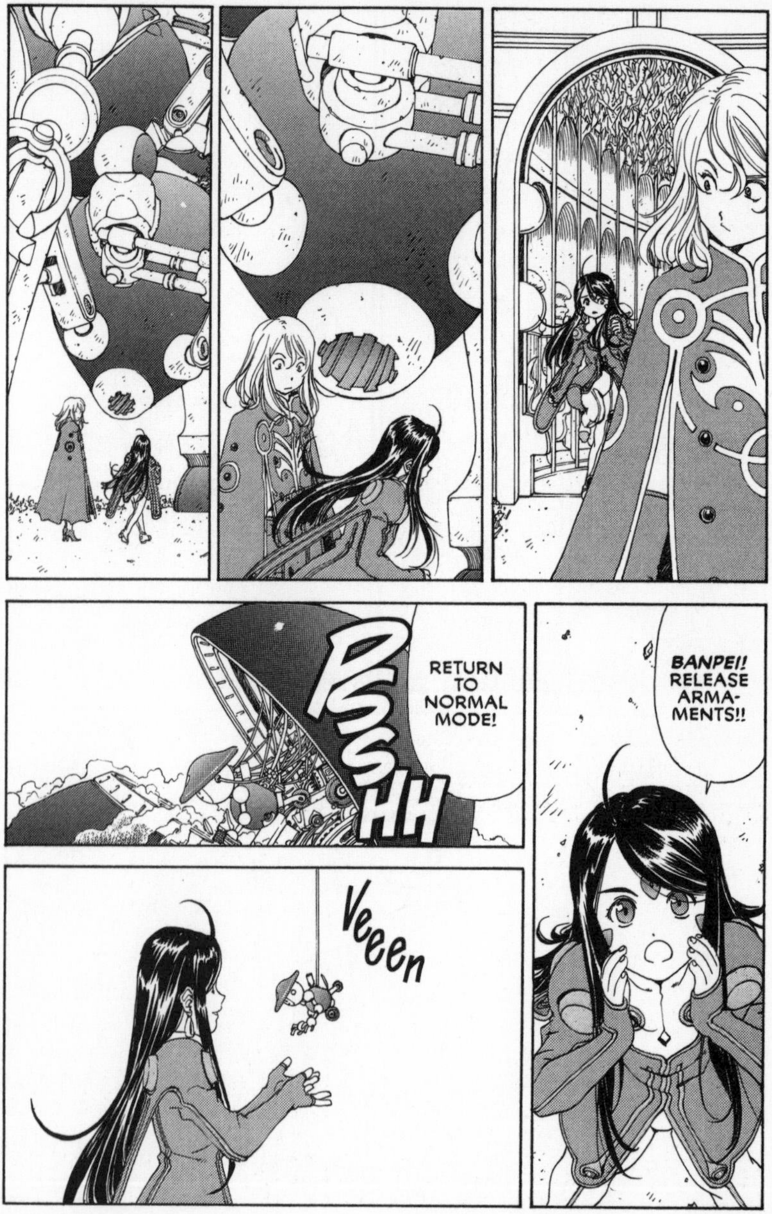
BANPEI! RELEASE ARMA-MENTS!!
RETURN TO NORMAL MODE!
PSSHH
Veeeen

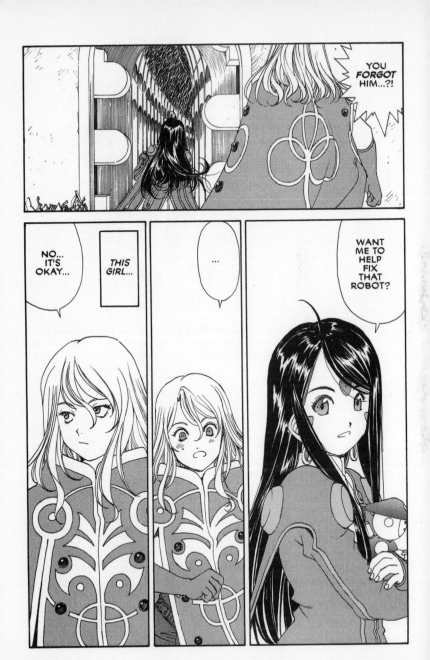

YOU *FORGOT* HIM...?!

NO... IT'S OKAY...

THIS GIRL...

...

WANT ME TO HELP FIX THAT ROBOT?

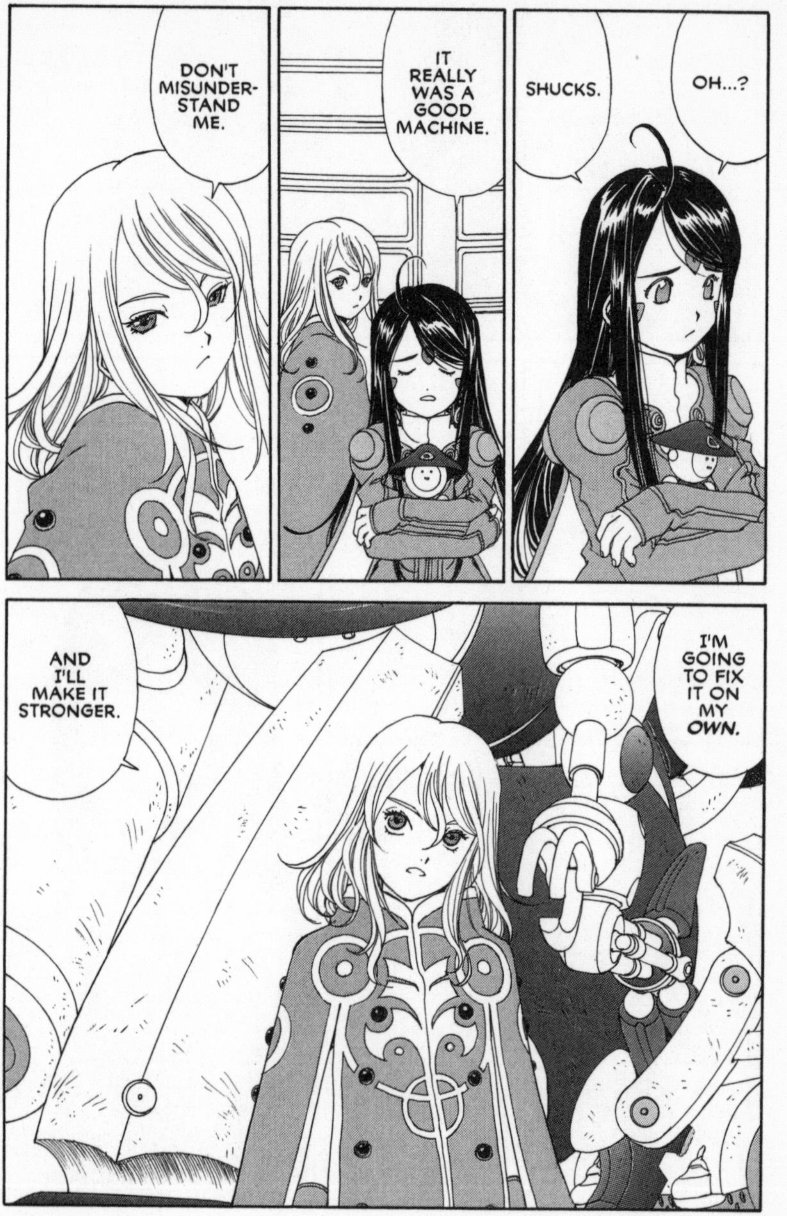
OH...?
SHUCKS.
IT REALLY WAS A GOOD MACHINE.
DON'T MISUNDER-STAND ME.
I'M GOING TO FIX IT ON MY *OWN.*
AND I'LL MAKE IT STRONGER.

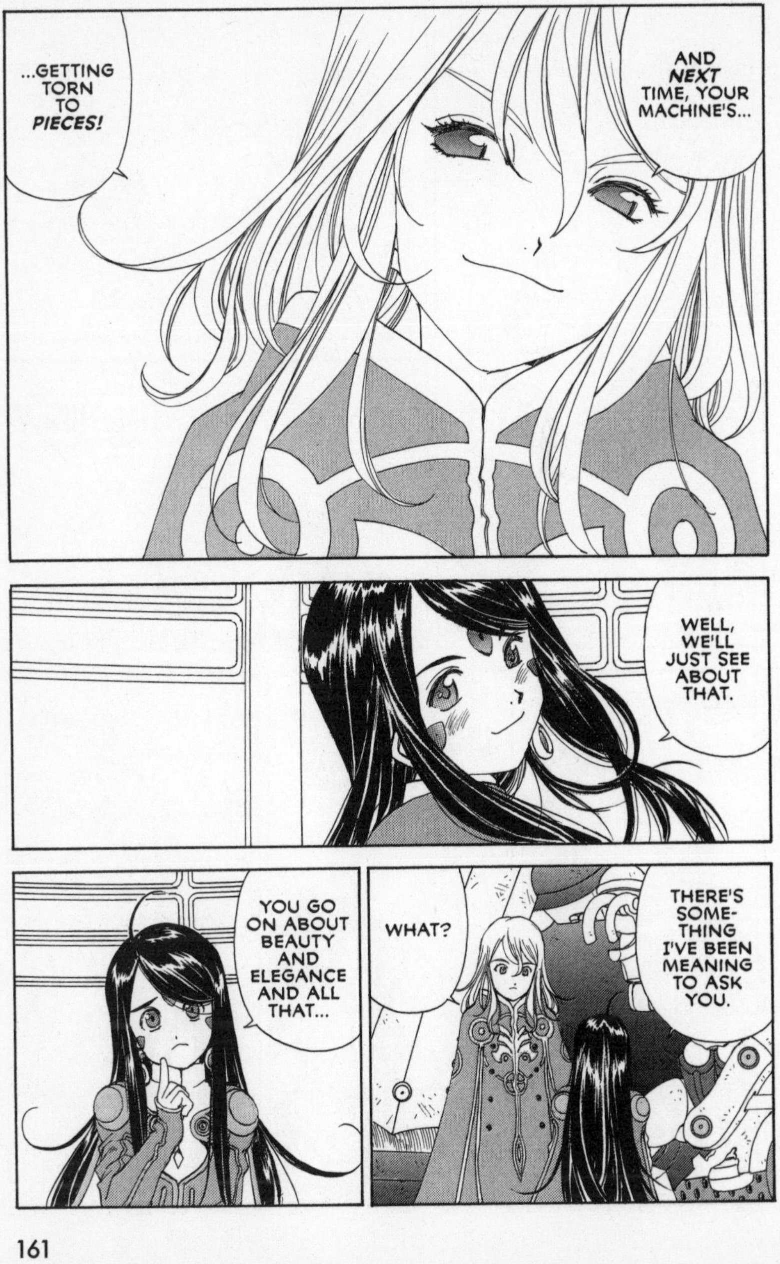
AND *NEXT* TIME, YOUR MACHINE'S...
...GETTING TORN TO *PIECES!*
WELL, WE'LL JUST SEE ABOUT THAT.
THERE'S SOME-THING I'VE BEEN MEANING TO ASK YOU.
WHAT?
YOU GO ON ABOUT BEAUTY AND ELEGANCE AND ALL THAT...

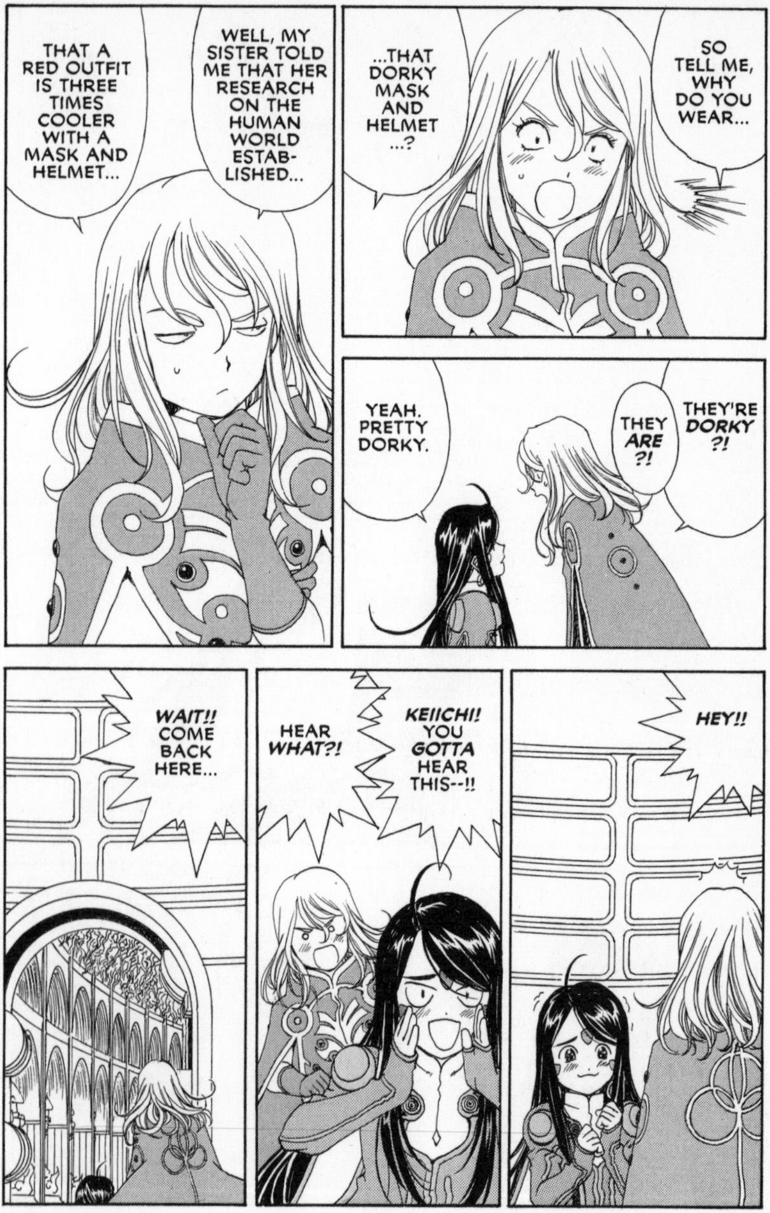
SO TELL ME, WHY DO YOU WEAR...
...THAT DORKY MASK AND HELMET ...?
THEY'RE *DORKY* ?!
THEY *ARE* ?!
YEAH. PRETTY DORKY.
WELL, MY SISTER TOLD ME THAT HER RESEARCH ON THE HUMAN WORLD ESTAB-LISHED...
THAT A RED OUTFIT IS THREE TIMES COOLER WITH A MASK AND HELMET...
HEY!!
KEIICHI! YOU *GOTTA* HEAR THIS--!!
HEAR *WHAT?!*
WAIT!! COME BACK HERE...

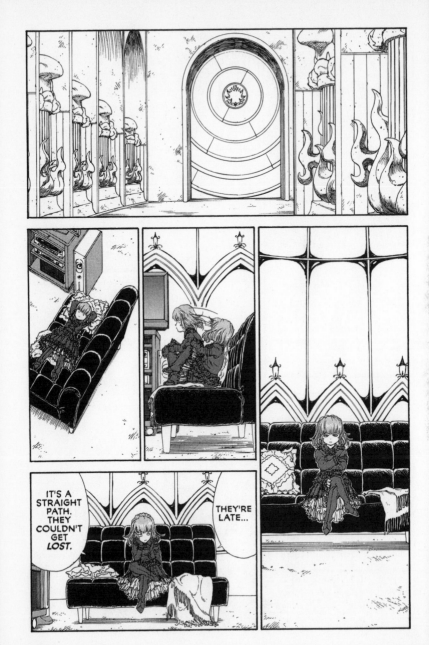

IT'S A STRAIGHT PATH. THEY COULDN'T GET *LOST*.

THEY'RE LATE...

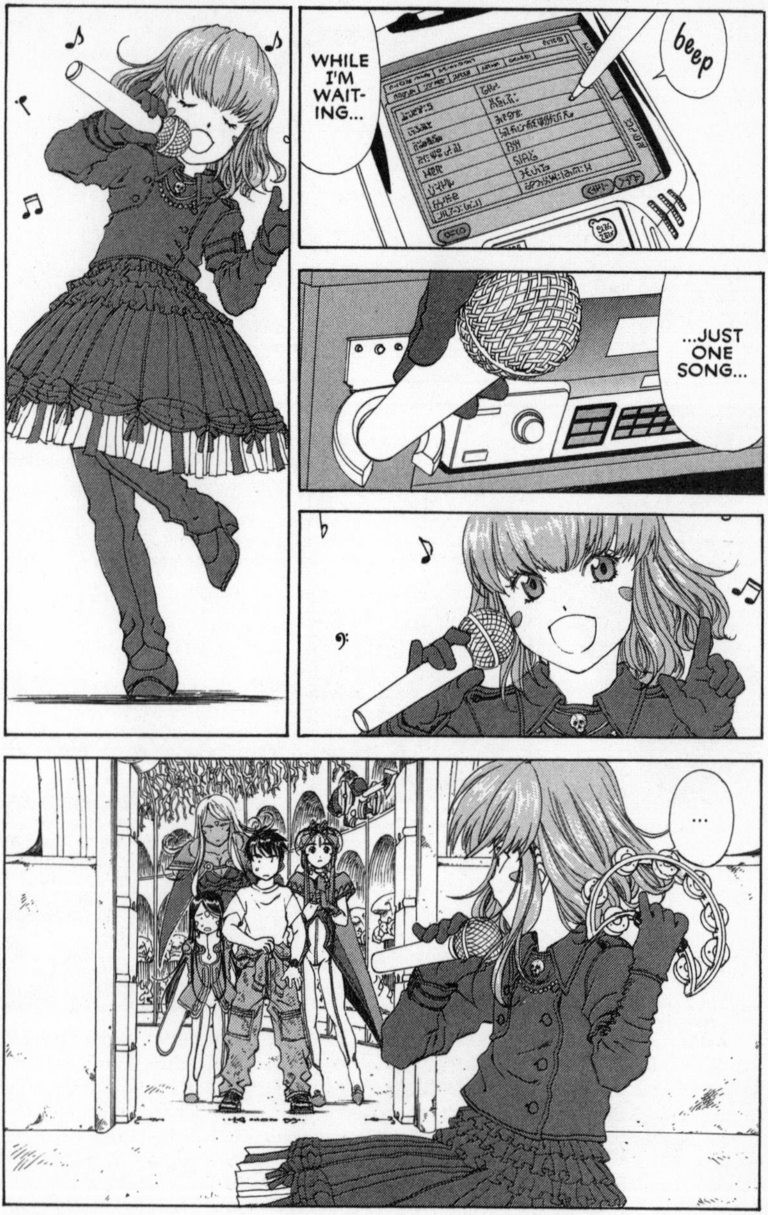
beep
WHILE I'M WAITING...
...JUST ONE SONG...
...

EDITOR
Carl Gustav Horn

DESIGNER
Kat Larson

PUBLISHER
Mike Richardson

English-language version
produced by Dark Horse Comics

OH MY GODDESS! Vol. 42
© 2012 Kosuke Fujishima. All rights reserved. First published in Japan
in 2011 by Kodansha, Ltd., Tokyo. Publication rights for this English edition
arranged through Kodansha, Ltd. All rights reserved. No portion of this
publication may be reproduced or transmitted, in any form or by any means,
without the express written permission of the copyright holders. Names, characters, places, and incidents featured in this publication either are the product
of the author's imagination or are used fictitiously. Any resemblance to ac-
tual persons (living or dead), events, institutions, or locales, without satiric
intent, is coincidental. Dark Horse Manga™ is a trademark of Dark
Horse Comics, Inc. All rights reserved.

Published by Dark Horse Manga
A division of Dark Horse Comics, Inc.
10956 SE Main Street
Milwaukie, OR 97222
DarkHorse.com

To find a comics shop in your area,
call the Comic Shop Locator Service
toll-free at 1-888-266-4226

First edition: August 2012
ISBN 978-1-59582-892-7

1 3 5 7 9 10 8 6 4 2

Printed at Lake Book Manufacturing, Inc.,
Melrose Park, IL, USA

letters to the
ENCHANTRESS

10956 SE Main Street, Milwaukie, Oregon 97222
OMG@DarkHorse.com • DarkHorse.com

NOTE: Full addresses and e-mail addresses will not be printed, unless you ask! All fan artwork, letters, and e-mails submitted become the property of Dark Horse Comics.

Welcome back! As you see, having completed our reissue of all the "old" volumes of *Oh My Goddess!* (volumes 1–20), we are continuing with the "new" (volumes 21 and up) at the same pace the new volumes were released before—every four months. Let's get into volume 42's Enchantress with a somewhat unusual series of letters—letters to and from a Japanese fan of *Oh My Goddess!* What's so unusual about that, you ask? He's a Japanese fan of the *English* version of *Oh My Goddess!*

Dear Mr. Horn,

Hello from Japan! My name is Syuntaro Yamaguchi, a Japanese high-school student. I was born in Hokkaido (just like Keiichi!).

I love *Oh My Goddess!* so much. So, I have all the *OMG!* Japanese manga editions so far. Half a year ago, I found that it was released in US and translated into English. I thought, "Really? I want to buy!" So, I bought vols. 31 to 38.

The translation is very splendid! I couldn't use English. But I can use it now after reading English *OMG!* (A bit, really . . .) I want to thank you for all your hard work. Thank you. ^_^

I'll collect the rest of the *OMG!* manga English edition next time!

My thoughts are with you from Japan.

Sincerely,
Syuntaro Yamaguchi
(via e-mail)

Well, needless to say, I was very surprised and pleased to receive Yamaguchi-san's letter. But maybe I shouldn't have been too surprised. In the US you can find imported manga in Japanese in bookstores like Kinokuniya. But the Kinokuniya bookstores in Japan (and some other bookstores in Japan, too) have a section of English import books, including manga. In fact, when I visited the main Kinokuniya store in Shinjuku in 2010, I saw a bookcase with six or seven shelves of English-language manga.

One thing I was curious about was that Yamaguchi-san is a high-school student, so he was born after *Oh My Goddess!* started in Japan (back in 1988!). Since people in

Japan (naturally ^_^) have the most access to new manga and have so many choices as to what to read, how did Yamaguchi-san discover *Oh My Goddess!* . . . ? What did he think about the older volumes (since Fujishima-sensei's character style has changed several times over the years)? I e-mailed Yamaguchi-san, and here is his reply:

Horn-sama!

Thank you for your reply! I'm very happy. ^_^

You're right that the recent *chara* [Japanese for "character"—*ed.*] art style is different from the volumes of the 1980s and 1990s. But I love the old style too! I think Mr. Fujishima's artwork is always great!!

There are a variety of people who are *OMG!* fans in Japan. Some started with the manga, others with the anime OAVs, movie, or TV series. So, it isn't mostly fans from 1980s.

In my case, I knew *OMG!* from my favorite magazine two years ago. Its name is *MacFan*, and it is a popular Macintosh magazine in Japan. *MacFan* produces the "Macne" series of virtual singers, just like the Vocaloids (Hatsune Miku, etc.). One of these singers, called "Macne Coco," is my favorite, and her voice is sampled from Kikuko Inoue, Belldandy's voice actress in the Japanese *OMG!* anime. So that's how I got into *Oh My Goddess!*

By the way, how about your country? How many people are *OMG!* fans in the US? How did they know about *OMG!* . . . ?

I am looking forward to your reply.
Thank you,
Syuntaro Yamaguchi

I don't often get called *sama* (actually, the cotranslator of *Oh My Goddess!*, Dana Lewis, calls me that, but honestly, I should be calling her that). Well, what Yamaguchi-san says makes a lot of sense. Since 1988 in Japan, new fans have often discovered *Oh My Goddess!* through indirect routes—most importantly, of course, the anime. *OMG!* anime was released in Japan in 1993–94 (the original OAVs), 1998–99 (the *Adventures of the Mini-Goddesses* TV series), 2000 (the movie), 2005–06 (the TV series), 2007 (the OAVs *Fighting Wings*), and 2011 (the OAVs *Itsumo futari de*). So any time a new *OMG!* anime comes out, it's a chance for people to get into the manga, too—and I'm sure that's one reason to keep making the anime.

But of course, Yamaguchi-san's way of discovering *Oh My Goddess!* through software is even more modern. ^_^ Well, of course, if you wanted to get someone to sing for your program, it would be Belldandy—she's the expert!

I told Yamaguchi-san that the best way to understand the diversity of *Oh My Goddess!* fans in the English-speaking world was to read everybody's letters from previous volumes of *OMG!* As you know, you all come from different backgrounds and have your own stories to tell about why you love *OMG!* I also mentioned that the Mac was important from the very beginning to US anime and manga fans. Back in the 1980s, I used a Mac in my high-school journalism class, where of course I wrote about anime for the student newspaper. ^_^ The first US anime fanzine with interior color, *ANIMAG*, was made on a Mac. Everybody at Viz Media and Dark Horse Comics uses Macs, too. Yamaguchi-san wrote back:

I didn't know *OMG!* was so popular in North America.

Manga and anime is very popular in Japan. But in fact, I didn't read manga before I knew of *OMG!* When I first read *Oh My Goddess!* I was surprised at how beautiful its story and artwork is. It touched my heart and changed my life. I really think *OMG!* is a wonderful story!

And I didn't know anime and manga fans in the US were fans of the Mac. Japanese fans aren't always Mac users. It's more popular here instead among animators, musicians, artists, scientists, etc.

I bought a MacBook Pro two years ago (and I'm writing you on this Mac now!). It's because I want to develop iPhone and iPad apps. So, I'm studying iOS programming. I want to develop apps someday!

As you know, Macne series is Mac-version Vocaloid (in fact, it is called "Macloid" in US and other countries). Let me introduce you to the characters. You can go to macne.net/character:

On the far left is Macne Coco Black,

and standing next to her is Macne Coco White. Both *chara* sample the voice of Kikuko Inoue. Going toward the right, the other characters are Macne Petit, Macne Nana, Macne Papa, and Whisper Angel Sasayaki-san. Petit, Nana, and Sasayaki-san are all sampled from the voice of Haruna Ikezawa [she plays Momoka Nishizawa in *Sgt. Frog*—ed.]. Papa is sampled from the voice of Jooji Nakata [Alucard in *Hellsing* (!)—ed.].

Your fan,
Syuntaro Yamaguchi

I was somewhat surprised again to hear that Yamaguchi didn't read manga before he discovered *Oh My Goddess!* But of course, not everyone in Japan reads manga. When we consider the difference between American comic books, where twenty to thirty thousand copies is considered very good sales (despite the fact *The Avengers* is the biggest movie in America! ^_^"), and Japanese manga, where a top magazine like *Shonen Jump* can still sell two to three million copies, it may seem like manga readership is universal in Japan, when the truth is, it's much more common but not universal. After all, if there are three million people in Japan who buy *Shonen Jump* every week, that means there are 124 million who don't. Still, I would be very happy to see three million more American comics fans. 8D

Not that we don't appreciate the fans we have! And here's another of them:

I remember waiting patiently back in 2003 for *OMG!* to be rereleased in the original right-left reading format. At the time it was the new industry standard and I thought it best to wait. I had to wait a few years, but it was worth it.

As well as reading the new re-released volumes for the first time, I started collecting volumes 21+ without reading them. I don't know how many dedicated fans there are out there that did the same, but somehow I overcame the temptation to read ahead. Back then I had worked out that the catch-up would hit in 2012. It seemed like a long way off, but nevertheless here we are! As I sit here typing this e-mail, I see my collection now spans all 40 volumes! I also notice something special, and that's how the colored spines from volumes 18-20 start blending in with the white spines that start from volume 21! It's a nice touch! :D

You guys at Dark Horse should pat yourselves on the back for the dedication, time, and love gone into not only producing the current releases but also the rereleases. Well done!

I thought I would also take this opportunity to ask why the volumes start to become very short after volume 20? I can't help noticing how thin volumes 33 and 40 are! Would this be on account of extra work Fujishima had on his plate during these times? Or was Kodansha (the Japanese publisher) restricting the number of allocated pages per chapter? I know I'm going to miss my volumes being as hefty as volumes 15–20! T_T

Keep up the good work!

Lan
(via e-mail)

Thank you, Lan! That blending of the spines between volumes 18–20 and 21 was the idea of Cary Grazzini, our director of print and development, working from Kat Larson's earlier cover designs. I made sure to let him know you noticed it!

I don't know for sure about the drop in page count in the second half of the series. My general impression is that Fujishima rarely misses doing a new chapter each month for *Afternoon* magazine, so it may be not so much that he's doing less, but that Kodansha wanted to put out the books at a faster pace, which means that each individual book has fewer chapters. Maybe it's part of a strategy to better hold reader interest in a series that, after all, has been running in Japan now for over twenty-three years (although as you see from Yamaguchi-san's letters above, it seems new people discover the series there, too)!

We'll see you again next time with *Oh My Goddess!* Volume 43—and as always, we'd like to see your letters here as well!

—CGH

P.S. I'm sure Yamaguchi-san knows this ^_^, but the joke on 162.3 is a refernce to Char, "The Red Comet" from Mobile Suit Gundam.

Kosuke Fujishima's

Oh My Goddess!

Winner of the 2009 Kodansha Award!
Discover the romance classic that's America's
longest-running manga series!

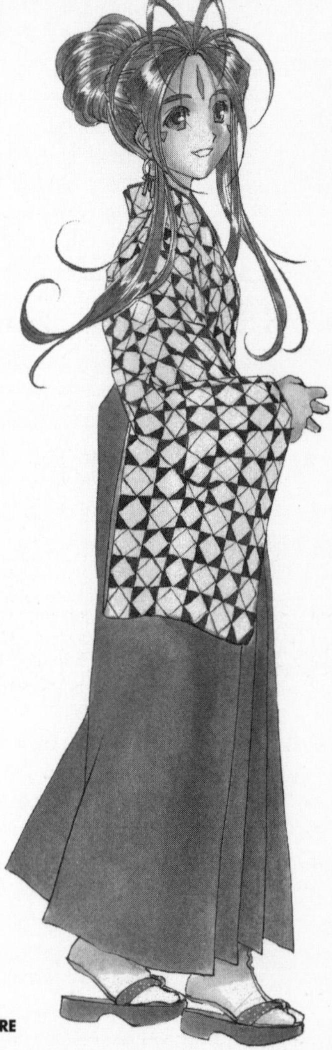

me 1
978-1-59307-387-9 | $10.99

me 2
978-1-59307-457-9 | $10.99

me 3
978-1-59307-539-2 | $10.99

me 4
978-1-59307-623-8 | $10.99

me 5
978-1-59307-708-2 | $10.99

me 6
978-1-59307-772-3 | $10.99

me 7
978-1-59307-850-8 | $10.99

me 8
978-1-59307-889-8 | $10.99

me 22
978-1-59307-400-5 | $10.99

me 23
978-1-59307-463-0 | $10.99

me 24
978-1-59307-545-3 | $10.99

me 25
978-1-59307-644-3 | $10.99

me 26
978-1-59307-715-0 | $10.99

me 27
978-1-59307-788-4 | $10.99

me 28
978-1-59307-857-7 | $10.99

Volume 29
ISBN 978-1-59307-912-3 | $10.99

Volume 30
ISBN 978-1-59307-979-6 | $10.99

Volume 31
ISBN 978-1-59582-233-8 | $10.99

Volume 32
ISBN 978-1-59582-303-8 | $10.99

Volume 33
ISBN 978-1-59582-376-2 | $10.99

Volume 34
ISBN 978-1-59582-448-6 | $10.99

Volume 35
ISBN 978-1-59582-509-4 | $10.99

Volume 36
ISBN 978-1-59582-581-0 | $10.99

Volume 37
ISBN 978-1-59582-660-2 | $10.99

Volume 38
ISBN 978-1-59582-711-1 | $10.99

Volume 39
ISBN 978-1-59582-795-1 | $10.99

Volume 40
ISBN 978-1-59582-870-5 | $10.99

Volume 41
ISBN 978-1-59582-891-0 | $12.99

Volume 42
ISBN 978-1-59582-892-7 | $12.99

AVAILABLE AT YOUR LOCAL COMICS SHOP OR BOOKSTORE
To find a comics shop in your area, call 1-888-266-4226
For more information or to order direct: • On the web: DarkHorse.com
• E-mail: mailorder@darkhorse.com • Phone: 1-800-862-0052 Mon.–Fri. 9 AM to 5 PM Pacific Time.

AN ALL-NEW NOVEL BASED ON THE HIT MANGA AND ANIME!

OH MY GODDESS!
—FIRST END—

WRITTEN BY
YUMI TOHMA

WITH ILLUSTRATIONS BY
KOSUKE FUJISHIMA AND HIDENORI MATSUBARA

Keiichi Morisato was a typical college student—a failure with women, he was strug-
gling to get through his classes and in general living a pretty nondescript life. That is
until he dialed a wrong number and accidentally summoned the goddess Belldandy.
Not believing Belldandy was a goddess and that she could grant his every wish, Keiichi
wished for her to stay with him forever. As they say, be careful what you wish for! Now
bound to Earth and at Keiichi's side for life, the lives of this goddess and human will
never be the same again!

ISBN 978-1-59582-137-9 | $14.95

DARK HORSE BOOKS

darkhorse.com

AVAILABLE AT YOUR LOCAL COMICS SHOP OR BOOKSTORE
To find a comics shop in your area, call 1.888.266.4226. For more information or to order direct: •On the we
darkhorse.com •E-mail: mailorder@darkhorse.com •Phone: 1.800.862.0052 Mon.–Fri. 9 AM to 5 PM Pacific Time.

STORY BY GAINAX
ART BY HAJIME UEDA

OMNIBUS

FROM THE STUDIO THAT BROUGHT YOU *EVANGELION!*

The complete *FLCL* manga adaptation–now with bonus color illustrations and remastered story pages!

"This show will change your life."
—Adult Swim

ISBN 978-1-59582-868-2
$19.99

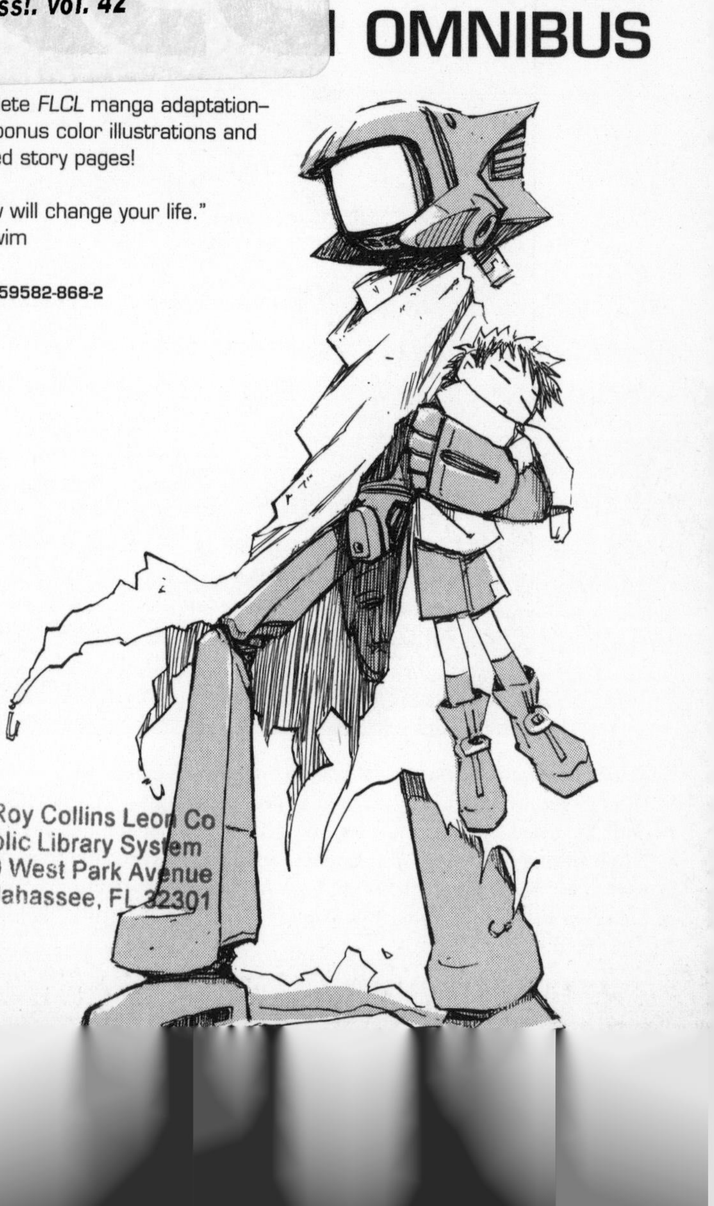

NEON GENESIS EVANGELION

Dark Horse Manga is proud to present two new original series based on the wildly popular *Neon Gen...*
Evangelion manga and anime! Continuing the rich story lines and complex characters, these new visio...
Neon Genesis Evangelion provide extra dimensions for understanding one of the greatest series ever m...

STORY AND ART
BY MINGMING

VOLUME 1
ISBN 978-1-59582-530-8 | $10.99

VOLUME 2
ISBN 978-1-59582-661-9 | $10.99

VOLUME 3
ISBN 978-1-59582-680-0 | $10.99

VOLUME 4
ISBN 978-1-59582-689-3 | $10.99

STORY AND ART
BY OSAMU TAKAHASHI

VOLUME 1
ISBN 978-1-59582-321-2 | $9.99

VOLUME 2
ISBN 978-1-59582-377-9 | $9.99

VOLUME 3
ISBN 978-1-59582-447-9 | $9.99

VOLUME 4
ISBN 978-1-59582-454-7 | $9.99

VOLUME 5
ISBN 978-1-59582-520-9 | $9.99

VOLUME 6
ISBN 978-1-59582-580-3 | $9.99

VOLUME 7
ISBN 978-1-59582-595-7 | $9.99

VOLUME 8
ISBN 978-1-59582-694-7 | $9.99

VOLUME 9
ISBN 978-1-59582-800-2 | $9.99

VOLUME 10
ISBN 978-1-59582-879-8 | $9.99

VOLUME 11
ISBN 978-1-59582-932-0 | $9.99

VOLUME 12
ISBN 978-1-61655-033-2 | $9.99

Each volume of *Neon Genesis Evangelion* features bonus color pages,
your *Evangelion* fan art and letters, and special reader giveaways!

BRIDE of the WATER GOD

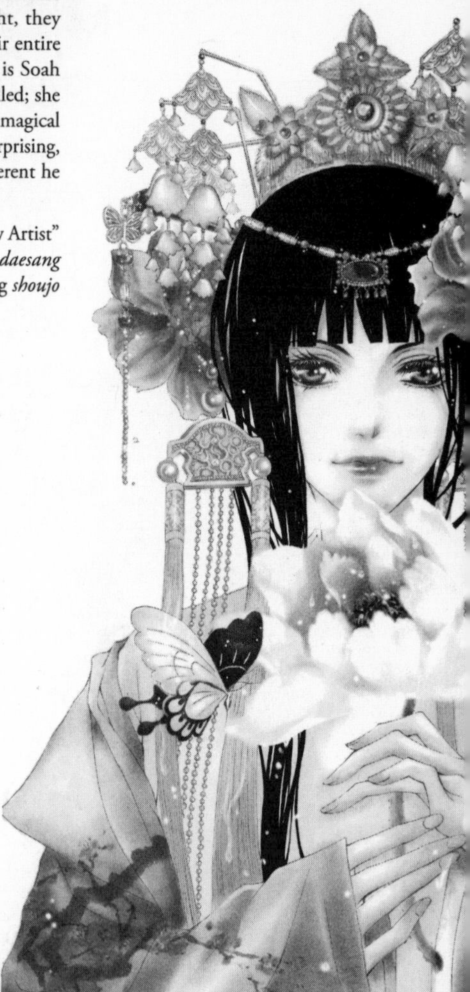

ıen Soah's impoverished, desperate village decides to sacrifice r to the Water God Habaek to end a long drought, they ieve that drowning one beautiful girl will save their entire mmunity and bring much-needed rain. Not only is Soah prised to be *rescued* by the Water God instead of killed; she ver imagined she'd be a welcomed guest in Habaek's magical gdom, where an exciting new life awaits her! Most surprising, wever, is the Water God himself, and how very different he rom the monster Soah imagined . . .

eated by Mi-Kyung Yun, who received the "Best New Artist" ard in 2004 from the esteemed *Dokja-manhwa-daesang* ganization, *Bride of the Water God* was the top-selling *shoujo* nhwa in Korea in 2006!

ume 1
N 978-1-59307-849-2

ume 2
N 978-1-59307-883-6

ume 3
N 978-1-59582-305-2

ume 4
N 978-1-59582-378-6

ume 5
N 978-1-59582-445-5

ume 6
N 978-1-59582-605-3

ume 7
N 978-1-59582-668-8

ume 8
N 978-1-59582-687-9

ume 9
N 978-1-59582-688-6

Volume 10
ISBN 978-1-59582-873-6

Volume 11
ISBN 978-1-59582-874-3

Volume 12
ISBN 978-1-59582-999-3

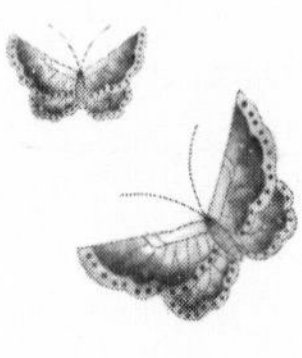

.99 each

views for BRIDE OF THE WATER GOD
other DARK HORSE MANHWA
es can be found at darkhorse.com!

AVAILABLE AT YOUR LOCAL COMICS SHOP OR BOOKSTORE! TO FIND A COMICS SHOP IN YOUR AREA, CALL 1-888-266-4226.

For more information or to order direct visit darkhorse.com or call 1-800-862-0052 Mon.–Fri. 9 AM to 5 PM Pacific Time. *Prices and availability subject to change without notice.

9.18

Cardcaptor Sakura

カードキャプターさくら

Story and Art by

CLAMP

Fourth grader Sakura Kinomoto has found a strange book in her father's library—a book made by the wizard Clow to store dangerous spirits sealed within a set of magical cards. But when Sakura opens it up, there is nothing left inside but Kero-chan, the book's cute little guardian beast . . . who informs Sakura that since the Clow cards seem to have escaped while he was asleep, it's now her job to capture them!

With remastered image files straight from CLAMP, Dark Horse is proud to present *Cardcaptor Sakura* in omnibus form! Each book collects three volumes of the original twelve-volume series, and features thirty bonus color pages!

OMNIBUS BOOK ONE
ISBN 978-1-59582-522-3 $19.99

OMNIBUS BOOK TWO
ISBN 978-1-59582-591-9 $19.99

DARK HORSE MANGA
DarkHorse.com

AVAILABLE AT YOUR LOCAL COMICS SHOP OR BOOKSTORE!

To find a comics shop in your area, call 1-888-266-4226

For more information or to order direct: • On the web: DarkHorse.com

E-mail: mailorder@darkhorse.com • Phone: 1-800-862-0052 Mon.–Fri. 9 AM to 5 PM Pacific Time

STOP! This is the back of the book!

This manga collection is translated into English, but arranged in right-to-left reading format to maintain the artwork's visual orientation as originally drawn and published in Japan. If you've never read comics this way before, take a look at the diagram below to give yourself an idea of how to go about it. Basically, you'll be starting in the upper right-hand corner, and will read each word balloon and panel moving right to left. It may take a little getting used to, but you should get the hang of it very quickly. Have fun! If this is the millionth manga you've read this way, never mind. ^_^

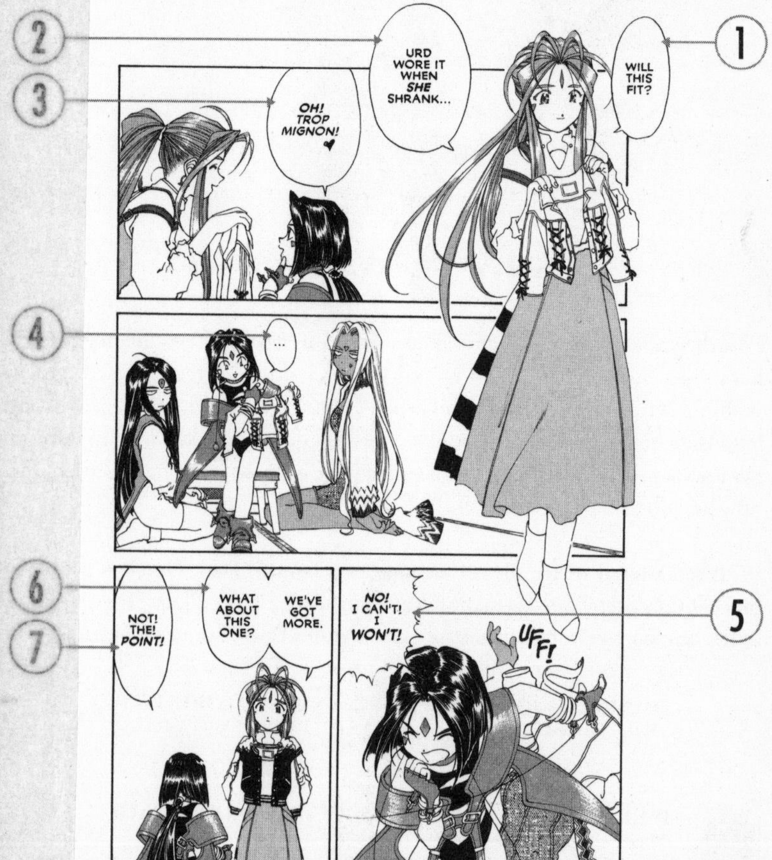
1
WILL THIS FIT?
2
URD WORE IT WHEN SHE SHRANK...
3
OH! TROP MIGNON!
4
...
5
NO! I CAN'T! I WON'T!
UFF!
6
WE'VE GOT MORE.
WHAT ABOUT THIS ONE?
7
NOT! THE! POINT!